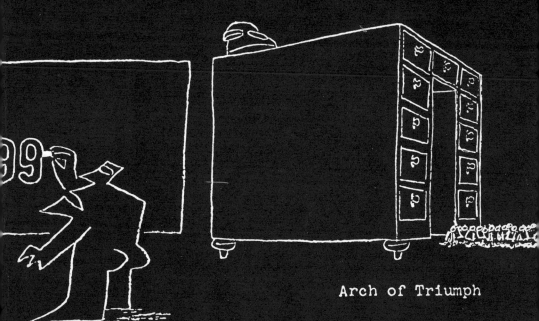

Arch of Triumph

The Judge
in a
Communist State

The Judge
in a
Communist State

A View From Within

By Otto Ulč

Ohio University Press

To Priscilla

Contents

Preface

The last weekend of June, 1959, was a significant one for me. Literally overnight, I changed from a judge in Czechoslovakia to a refugee in a home for unwed Protestant mothers in West Berlin. Pleased with the city, but not with a residence which was patently absurd in view of my sex and spiritual orientation, I left the shelter and eventually found my way to the United States. A certain oddity persisted. One who had been a law student during the reign of Stalin and a practitioner of law in the post-Stalinist period now became a retired judge at the age of twenty-nine. I was told that there were not many others, if any, around with a similar background.

Atypical and unverifiable experience sounds respectable only at cocktail parties. Hence, I rather hesitated to write about my past, despite my gradual involvement in the American academic life, the award of a Ph.D. in political science from an Ivy League school, and the decision of the New York State Supreme Court to accept me as a certified Yankee. It was mainly Professor Harold J. Berman of Harvard Law School who caused me to reconsider writing about my adventures within the Bolshevik judiciary. Encouraged, I promised to produce an account of several court cases over which I had presided or of which I had at least some first hand knowledge.

This book is proof that I have not lived up to my word. With the data on several hundred cases assembled, I became increasingly dissatisfied with the original project. The legal formulae appeared to be less significant than the actual individuals affected by the verdicts. When wrestling with an abstract assessment of some finding, an anecdotal episode seemed to me more relevant and more revealing than the esoteric jargon likely to be of interest only to the initiated. Forfeiting the opportunity to produce a scholarly treatise, I attempted to recreate the atmosphere of an environment undergoing a transformation from one social order to another—a transformation viewed through the eyes of the judge, who was both an observer and a participant. I wanted to show what the judge could and could not do, what he had to do and had to refrain from doing, and, in more general terms, how the administration of the law facilitated the political metamorphosis of a society. The narrative is meant to be informal and easy-going, with documentation kept to a minimum. The mosaic of concrete happenings substitutes for theoretical schemes and authoritative analyses. The book is also almost footnote-free.

I decided to trade a more scholarly approach for one which could affect a wider range of readers. Directing oneself to the general reader without falling into disrepute with the academic community is, of course, taking a risky ride on two horses of varying temperaments and velocities. An elementary elaboration is likely to be redundant for the expert but incomprehensible to the outsider who does not distinguish between Czechoslovakia and Yugoslavia, not to mention the bewildering dissimilarity between Transylvania and Pennsylvania. However, as long as both acquire a rudimentary appreciation of the quality of the enviroment I have dealt with, I shall not consider the book a complete failure.

Before defining the kind and scope of the narration I shall first point out what this book is not about. It is not a "confession." It is not that kind of political soap opera of a one-time idealist who, after his beliefs have been devoured by reality, has assuaged his guilt by denouncing both. I have never prayed at the altar of intolerance, class struggle, and historical inevitability. Accident of circumstances made me part of a system, and departing from Czechoslovakia was consistent with my values, rather than a sign of their break-down.

I do not paint a gigantic landscape of the entire scope of Bolshevik justice. The body of the text, save for some minor points, deals with one country only. In this respect the book is not comparative, though the overall picture is quite comparable to the developments in other People's Democracies during the same period. The role of law and of the judge vis-a-vis political desiderata in Eastern Europe was, at least in the formative years of the totalitarian age, anything but dissimilar.

Neither is this book structured to serve as a parallel text to the problems of law and its application in the United States. However, I do make some trans-Atlantic references for emphasis and clarity. I do not do this with the authority of an American lawyer, since I am not, but as an interested and somewhat informed American citizen.

The story is neither an indictment nor a glorification: it presents neither a Bolshevik Eden of equality and justice for all, nor a macabre spectacle of paranoid commissars trampling upon helpless subjects. The Communist system recognizes law, albeit of a rather peculiar kind. For the man-in-the-street, boredom is more oppressive than a prison term, the stupidity of local mini-Stalins more frustrating than the whims of a jailer. Despite all the odds, the supreme art of adjustment to the self-defeating absurdities of the system is within reach of the average citizen.

The Czech pursuit of conformity with the Soviet model still bore the imprint of national mentality. A hybrid was born—a petty bourgeois totalitarianism. Revolutionary in gesture and a Schweik in almost everything else, the average citizen claims class hatred where he really feels envy and translates Communist Nirvana into the coziness of an undisturbed privacy. He acts rather than lives his loyalty to the strange cause. He dislikes fanatics and fails to appreciate heroes.

The book covers the postwar period until the end of the fifties, when the Czech government, by heralding the achievement of socialism, terminated the transient period of People's Democracy, and I, coincidentally, just happened to terminate my employment with the government. Within this time-span the reader will be exposed to the operation of Czechoslovak laws and courts. In particular, he will share my experience at the court in Plzeň. The place, better known as Pilsen, is a relatively large city by local standards (population about 150,000) and is noted for the production of Škoda military hardware and equally successful beer.

xi

The last two and a half years (1957-1959) of my judicial career were spent in the neighboring small district town of Stříbro. Unlike the urban, industrial Plzeň, the Stříbro area was predominantly agricultural, and the court work well reflected the discomforts attendant upon decreed collectivization.

The early chapters deal with what the judge is and how he is made, and the reader will sit at the bench, will meet the people's assessors, and will learn about the kind of law to be administered. Later chapters explore the limits of permissible judicial behavior, the building of the right image, and the juggling for the benevolent toleration of Party officials. We will be introduced to the prosecutor and the counsel for defense.

After this section concerning the nature and techniques of judicial work, we proceed to the "adjudication proper," first in criminal and finally in civil law matters. The thoroughness with which the subject is covered in individual chapters is not necessarily commensurate with its importance, due to my not always sufficient firsthand knowledge and to my concern with keeping the book within publishable length. Yet, on the whole, I do not think that any fundamental aspect of Czechoslovak court work has been entirely neglected.

As indicated before, the stress of the narrative is not so much upon the law as upon its social and political impact on the citizenry. The names of places, litigants, defendants, judges, prosecutors, attorneys, Party officials, members of the secret police, etc., are real. The book abounds with quotations of reconstructed conversations and statements written and oral. In anticipation of criticism on this account, I must explain that the quotations are meant to add to the book's authenticity and are not offered as a claim to an infallible memory.

The rest of the Preface, save for the last paragraph, is addressed only to the reader lacking in fundamental knowledge about Czechoslovakia and may well be omitted by the cognizant.

The country was established an independent republic in 1918 as the result of World War I and the dismantling of the Hapsburg Empire. The founding father, T. G. Masaryk, became the President and retained the office for almost the entire period between the two World Wars. An essentially healthy state was handicapped by its nationality problem. The Czechs, as the largest national group, were looked upon with suspicion by their Eastern, less sophisticated, Slovak brethren and were exposed to the outright hostility of other minorities—notably the three million Germans of the Sudeten. The Sudeten question led to the Munich settlement of 1938, the liquidation of Czechoslovakia and its occupation by the Third Reich. The war years passed with relative tranquility, and the liberated country was counted among the allied victors, if only by default. The government-in-exile and President E. Beneš —the successor to T. G. Masaryk—returned from London to Prague. The Germans were expelled, collaborators with the Nazis punished, and the unrealistic dream of building a bridge between the West and the East got under way. The Communists were represented in the cabinet from the beginning. Along with other ministries, they controlled the police force; their opponents had to be satisfied with the command of the mailmen. In the 1946 free elections, the Communists, though not winning an absolute majority, emerged as the strongest party. The Soviet Red Army did not control the contest, as it had left Czechoslovakia by the end of 1945. The uneasy coalition, with the Communists at its head, lasted until February, 1948. This marked the end of the only successful democracy—according to Western standards—ever to fall within the Communist orbit.

In the spring of 1948 we began to sovietize: Jan Masaryk jumped—or was thrown—out of a window, Beneš abdicated and died, and the Communist leader Klement Gottwald became the head of the state. A thorough turnover of personnel followed, from the members of the cabinet to kindergarten teachers. Vacancies abounded for upstarts whose only qualification often was verbal loyalty to the Party.

The dogmatic adherence of the leadership to the Soviet model of restructuring the society was a mistake. Because Stalin was modernizing backward Russia through a crash program of industrialization, the highly industrialized Czechoslovakia had to follow the same path. Because the Soviets waged class struggle against the rich peasants—the kulaks—we had to do the same, even though we had no kulaks. Where they were missing, they were invented and then duly liquidated. We purged, nationalized, collectivized, and then, in March, 1953, Stalin died. His faithful disciple Gottwald followed the master within ten days. Gottwald's successor, Antonín Zápotocký, headed the state until 1957, and for the next ten years Antonín Novotný was in charge.

Following the coup of 1948, the socio-political structure of the state underwent a substantial change and the legal system along with it. A flood of new laws replaced almost all pre-Communist statutes. The country was reorganized into nineteen administrative units—regions (provinces)—that were further broken down into districts, altogether about three hundred in number. State administration, the judiciary, and Party organization were adjusted to this pattern.

De-Stalinization and restoration of "socialist legality" did not reach Czechoslovakia during the fifties. The judicial practices I am rather critical of in this book eventually became the target of identical or of almost equal criticism by official Czechoslovak sources. Notably between 1963 and 1965, the legal reviews *Právník*, *Právný obzor*, and *Socialistická zákonnost* condemned the interference in the work of courts by political organs, discriminatory adjudication, and other symptoms of "class justice." They also regretfully admitted that violation of socialist legality had not yet stopped. This manuscript was completed just before the beginning of the exciting challenge of 1968, experimenting with "Socialism with Human Face," an experiment only to be crushed by fraternal Soviet tanks. Before this had happened, the mass communications media, benefitting from the temporary suspension of censorship, revealed the sins and vices of totalitarianism in their depth. Stalinism of the fifties being my topic, however, the 1968 Czechoslovak surprises are not reflected here.

For good measure some cartoons from Czechoslovak periodicals appear on the endpapers to indicate that the soul-searching of the sixties was not devoid of a sense of humor.

Binghamton, New York   OTTO ULČ

The Judge
in a
Communist State

PART ONE. THE PARTICIPANTS AND THE ENVIRONMENT

1 THE FORTUNATE GENERATION OR HOW TO BECOME A JUDGE WITHOUT REALLY TRYING

In 1948, Charles University in Prague became six hundred years old. The anniversary coincided with the accession to power of the Communists, and some of the first acts of the government did not add to the festive mood. It was decreed that the house had to be cleared of infidels. Many students and teachers were expelled, and the school was assigned the task of producing a new intelligentsia that would, in all walks of professional life, be faithful to the tenets of the Marxist creed and would replace the adult and supposedly bourgeois-oriented generation. By the accident of my age I was caught up in the prevailing political wind. I was nineteen when I enrolled in 1949 at the law school in Prague. There I spent four years, graduating in the summer of 1953, only a few months after the death of Joseph Stalin, the Georgian father of us all.

The education we received was in the best Stalinist tradition. Success depended on the following considerations, in descending order of importance: first, performance in the Catechism (course in Marxist doctrine, political economy and the history of the Soviet state); second, participation in extracurricular activities ("functions" in a host of organizations, weekend manual labor, demonstrations, petitions); and finally, the study of law.

The curriculum represented the perfection of boredom. Sloganizing, clichés-mongering and empty repetitiveness demoted knowledge, in the true sense of the word, to something vaguely obscene. The Party-appointed pedagogues did not know otherwise, and the old professors who had been bypassed by the purge tried their best to emulate these upstarts. Only a few habits reminiscent of prewar academic life survived, notably the arrogance and inaccessibility of the teachers. During all the four years I spent at the law school I never went to see any of them during their office hours. They kept no office hours.

To combat the dullness of the lectures we invented a sort of numbers game. Each participant chose a word he expected the teacher to repeat most often during his one-hour performance. The favorite horses were "comrades," "world peace," "exploitation," "socialism," "communism," "capitalism," "class struggle," and "class enemy." One could easily become addicted to this exciting diversion. Once I wagered on "socialism." The lecturer used the word seventy-two times, but I still lost by two points to a classmate who had backed "comrades." Illegal betting, so to speak, went beyond the confines of the class room and was quite popular during such inconveniences as examinations. For example, I bet a sizable sum that at the final oral examination on the Civil Code of Procedure I would be able to refer, in all three questions, irrespective of the substance, to the "struggle of the toiling masses for world peace" and the professor would not dare to consider my comment irrelevant. I won.

About sixty per cent of our class managed to graduate, untouched by the purges. Of some one hundred and twenty graduates, everyone (including a widow who was well over forty) was a member of the Youth Organization — the Czechoslovak counterpart of the Soviet Komsomol. However, only about ten were card-carrying Communists. Whether believers, opportunists, or non-believers, it was, of course, imperative that all of us daily demonstrate active identification with the System. To obtain a reliable estimate of the feelings of a relatively large group is a difficult matter. With the assistance of a possibly clumsy parallel, let us picture the infidels as adulterous husbands and the Party as a consortium of worried, suspicious and occasionally betrayed wives. The adulterers, sensing a common brotherhood of sin, honored a conspiratorial pledge of silence. The wronged wives — our law school Bolsheviks — consumed by indiscriminate doubt, saw infidelity in all corners. This attitude made it truly hard to distinguish between guilt and innocence.

From the official viewpoint everything was in our favor, except our class origin. Surprising as it may seem, in the 1953 graduating class, hardly anyone was of proletarian or peasant background.

Fortunately, in view of our presumed political virginity and intellectual ignorance, the objectionable background became a matter of secondary concern. It would have been difficult to accuse us of harboring vestiges of bourgeois democratic thought. After all, we had been ten years old, at most, when Hitler had taken over the country. When and how could Masaryk have poisoned our minds? Similarly, we were barely likely to betray any longing for democratic processes, because when we had reached the voting age in 1948, there had been nothing left to vote about. Absence of knowledge became our strongest bargaining point. These privileges conferred upon us by accident of well-timed birth were not without drawbacks. In my case, for example, there was the bestowal of a judgeship I did not seek. My lack of enthusiasm was made irrelevant by the "Assignment Order" (umístěnka) issued by the Ministry of Justice, and I became a judge without really trying.

The post-February, 1948, regime inherited about fourteen hundred judges, almost none of whom satisfied the Communists' expectations. The reasoning of the Party is understandable: How on earth can we trust these justices who, in the last ten years, have pledged their loyalty to four different masters?[1.]

In my case loyalty was presumed, but in case of my older colleagues it had to be proved. A judge of prewar vintage who had a family to take care of and children he was anxious to enroll in the university, who was afraid of losing his apartment or pension, would do his best to prove to the masters of the day that he was worthy of their confidence. Some of the greatest injustices perpetrated in the name of Communism and of the "merciless class struggle" were, ironically, committed by these non-Communist or, to a considerable extent, anti-Communist judges. This is not to accuse the elders of being more immoral than the rest of us. A struggle of survival rather than a malevolent nature caused them to comply with Party pressures. If, however, the moral criterion is their subsequent judicial records rather than their motives, the older judges do not score well. For example, Judge M. came from a family of a rich farmer — a kulak. In order to expiate this sin he became the most dreaded jurist when trying the kulak defendants.

The effect of the judge's age and social background on his professional performance and the double standard of face-saving militancy in operation can be illustrated by the following case: A seventy-year-old watchmaker, the last one running his decrepit private business in the town of Klatovy, was indicted in 1958 for hoarding some mechanical parts or, as the Criminal Code stated, "speculation." In 1939, just before the occupation by the Germans, the defendant had hidden some of his materials by walling them up. In the course of years the aging "entrepreneur" allegedly forgot all about the cache, but a hostile relative (a son-in-law, if I am not mistaken) remembered and informed the police. The police dug out the utterly worthless rusty wheels and pins. The defendant pleaded guilty, in the sense of admitting to having withheld certain articles from the Germans, which fact, with years, had slipped from his memory. In the opinion of the court, an act that occurred in 1939 still qualified as a felony of speculation two decades later, even though the object of speculation had become worthless. The district judge in Klatovy, Jaromír Fikerle, sentenced the defendant to seven months imprisonment without probation. The watchmaker limited his appeal to a request of a re-classification of the penalty to a probationary one, in view of his previous clean record, his advanced age and serious illness. The case was reviewed by the Court of Appeals in Plzeň in January, 1959. The panel of five judges consisted of two of the old school — Komers (Chairman) and Sedláček — one young judge (myself, appointed *pro tempore* to this bench), and two "people's assessors," both workers in the Škoda factory. The proceedings were uneventful, and after the closing remarks of the prosecutor and the defense attorney, we retired for deliberation. Komers and Sedláček argued for the dismissal of the appeal, emphasizing our obligation to the "merciless struggle against the surviving remnants of the class enemies." The message I tried to get across to the people's assessors was less bellicose: "Comrades, our working class is, first of all, a generous one. Do we need a martyr? No, of course not. This old man is about to die. Why should he die in the prison hospital? Generosity of the victorious proletariat is what counts. Don't forget it." They did not forget, and in the voting there was a rare exception to the rule of unanimity. The two

Communist lay assessors, who had no inhibitions about leniency toward an "enemy," and I (who at this time thought I could afford the same opinion), overruled Komers and Sedláček, for whom concurrence would have been political suicide. All votes being equal, three votes (two from the working class and one from a member of the "new, progressive intelligentsia") against two votes cast by the reluctant militants Komers and Sedláček meant that the defendant was set free and could go home to die in peace.

In addition to the old and new university-trained lawyers, a third category of Communist judges was introduced. These were the ex-proletarians, the only group with power and real political importance. They had what we could not offer, namely, the right social background. These were the co-called PŠP people.

Immediately after the February, 1948, Communist takeover, it was agreed that the new regime could not delay the purges within the judiciary until the time when the law school could provide graduates of sufficient political desirability. Minister of Justice Alexej Čepička — the ill-fated son-in-law of President Klement Gottwald — set up a special "Law School of the Toiling People" (*Právnická škola pracujících*, known as PŠP. The school (at the time of writing, still in existence) was situated in the former castle of the Lobkowicz family at Hořín, near Mělnik, and functioned as a mill to convert carefully selected proletarians with no prior advanced education into "lawyers" in less than one year. The annual output of about one hundred graduates facilitated the implementation of the purge of a roughly equivalent number without lessening the numerical strength of the judiciary. The individuals of PŠP creation gradually took over all the posts of political significance. They dominated the Supreme Court and the Ministry of Justice. By the end of the fifties, eighteen out of nineteen Regional Prosecutors came from PŠP — the only exception was Dr. Vašek, head of the office in the province of Western Bohemia. In the case of the heads of the nineteen Regional Courts there was no exception. To become a judge, it takes a student with adequate undergraduate training at least four years at the "regular" law school plus two extra years as a trainee at the court ("Assistant Judge"). A PŠP graduate advances immediately to full judgeship if not to a higher position. A certain Číhal, for example, was simultaneously transformed within a less than a year from a manual laborer into a jurist, a Deputy Minister of Justice, and the chief of the military justice in the country with the rank of a colonel in the armed forces. Certainly no one would doubt Číhal's loyalty toward the Establishment. Where else could one find a regime so generous?

Číhal's speedy elevation saved him, at least, from the blunders and the embarrassments experienced by others who had to put on the judicial robes. To make up for their deficiency in formal education, the Ministry ordered each PŠP graduate, while functioning as a judge, to take correspondence courses with the law school in Prague (or Bratislava for those in Slovakia) in order to obtain a university law degree in no more than five years. This arrangement invites a comparison to a situation in which, let us say, the Ministry of Health would establish a crash program for "surgeons," send them to operate on people, and then direct them to get familiar with human anatomy via a remote TV course.

Both the political priority given to criminal law, and its less complex nature in comparison with civil law made it the obvious area for the PŠP masterminds. Thus, in the late fifties, a typical District court consisted of two judges — the PŠP man, who was the official head of the court and in charge of the punitive agenda, and the civil law judge, who was either of the old school or a new university graduate.

The threefold variety of permissible behavior became well established. In our offices a training program was going on called "Year of Party Schooling." Irrespective of political affiliation, every employee within the judiciary had to participate in the courses. On top of that, all the judges from the districts were required to gather periodically at the provincial court for an extra helping of this diet. In 1958, the Ministry of Justice ordered us to start a new and very militant line with respect to the "liquidation of the surviving vestiges of the class enemies." The statement was read by PŠP Miroslav Tlapák, deputy head of the provincial court. I asked to speak and said: "In my opinion the new directive does not make much sense. We are supposed to achieve socialism, the non-antagonistic society, by 1960. It is now the middle of 1958. Is there any real point in changing our policy at this late hour? Why should we suddenly become over-excited about the matters of class struggle when in a short time the whole struggle will be abolished, anyway?"

Tlapák, somewhat perplexed, responded: "This is a wrong approach, and you, Otto, try to be funny at any cost. This is not a laughing matter." In other words, Tlapák reprimanded me as a friend, without any thought of further punishment. If a judge of pre-Communist vintage had dared to say what I said, this might well have been the kiss of death. If a PŠP graduate had repeated my words he would have been praised for an inventive, though somewhat mistaken, approach to the problem.

The unequal presumption of loyalty to the cause deflated the importance of Party membership as a determinant of one's political standing. While the PŠP people were, by definition, organized Communists, the proportion of card-carrying members in my group was far lower than that among the prewar colleagues. When we attended the university all that was expected from us was an active participation in the youth organization. At the same time, however, the older judges were busy signing Party applications.

Our generation had the inestimable opportunity, denied our elders, of mastering Marxism-Leninism without a trace of a foreign accent. This is not meant solely in a figurative sense. This political philosophy, which ostensibly underpinned all our reasoning, was mainly a set of clichés and verbose slogans, perfectly memorized, which slipped so naturally from our lips. It is common knowledge that with increasing age the chance of learning a foreign language decreases significantly. The same applies to the liturgical style of Marxism-Leninism, inflated with the most improbable adjectives, each requiring its proper place and emphasis, which proved to be an unsurmountable obstacle for the older jurists. They tried so hard, and yet the result was a strange concoction of haphazard, ill-fitting, artificial-sounding pronunciamenta.

Lack of punctilio when discussing doctrine thus became a snare trapping the unwary. Quite often I could not get rid of the impression that the employment of very superficial criteria predestined our lives more than we were aware. The primitive superior, whether judicial or lay, tended to base his decisions on banalities because these were the only criteria he was able to comprehend. When ponytails for young girls became fashionable in Czechoslovakia (about ten years behind the West), the Chairman of the Regional Court in Ústí, Kubánek, ordered all the ponytailed secretaries in his realm to chop off this "demonstration of capitalist decadence." After everybody had complied, Kubánek was satisfied, as he later told me, that he had saved the purity of People's Democracy. Correctness in dress played an inordinately large role in the decisions of the Party functionaries. In dealing with the apparatchiki it was prudent to be familiar with the political vogue of the day, be it to wear or not to wear a tie, to be dressed shabbily or in black (e.g., in March, 1953, the month of multiple mourning), always to avoid tight trousers, etc. Once I wrote to a Local People's Committee inquiring about a litigant's behavior and received this one-sentence reply: "The person in question prefers a tie with a camel[2.] to the heroism of building a classless society." Tie, pants, haircut, whistling the wrong hit, and such-like trivia were the evidence on which many decisions concerning motives, ideas and loyalty were made by men in power. Similarly, it was the manner of speech that constituted the test of a speaker's political character.

A young prosecutor once remarked (in private): "In our country there are only two kinds of people — good actors and bad actors. The former are praised as faithful adherents to the proletarian cause, the latter are condemned as reactionaries." This statement, though overdrawn, is not without truth. The judges, both the predominantly cynical young ones and the opportunistic elders, to a great extent acted out their expected roles. In contrast to these fakes, only the PŠP, actually living their roles, were genuine.

As has been suggested, Party affiliation in a general sense was not all that important. With my non-Party status I enjoyed more confidence than many of my older colleagues who were members. Within a group, however, the Communist label counted heavily. The consciousness of belonging to an exclusive club was very strong among the minority of university students who were organized Communists. For instance, when a student called Forejt, later to become the District Prosecutor at Sušice, got drunk in the dormitory, the Party cell reprimanded him — not for intoxication but for the disgraceful exhibition of "vomiting in front of non-Party members." During our judicial career, however, the distinction gradually withered away, because within five years at most, it was unlikely not to become at least a candidate for Party membership.

To sum up, arbitrary qualities, whether of age or pedigree, predominated over more rational criteria, as I learned when I found myself in the driver's seat of the judicial vehicle.

In 1956, at our Plzeň Regional Court three candidates were subjected to an important test. Several examiners, representing the Regional Court, the Justice Ministry, and the Provincial Party Secretariat, spent eight hours probing into our professional competence and, above all, trying to ascertain whether our political maturity warranted elevation from Assistant Judges to fully-pledged District Justices. Somehow, all three of us passed, and within a month we had received decrees of appointment issued from Prague and signed by First Deputy Minister of Justice Josef Litera. These designated us *independent* judges, responsible solely to the law and our conscience, paid from the monies of the Ministry and subject to removal from office only with good cause.

This independence and freedom of action were largely fictitious. Nonetheless, within one year the life-appointed judges were converted into elected officials.

This change, the government explained, was based on the desire to match more exactly the Soviet model. It was held that the dependence upon the electorate would make a manifold contribution to the democratization of the society. The citizen would know his judge, would hold him accountable for his actions, and would fire him should he fail to interpret the law in the true spirit of People's Democracy.

The election was indirect and for a three-year term. As is commonly known, the totalitarian election is a contradiction in terms. The voter has no choice but to cast a ballot in favor of the only candidate selected for him by the Party. It is also the Party that counts the returns in such a way as to lead to the unerring 99 per cent majority. In our case, the election could be described as "doubly totalitarian." Not only were the voters denied any real choice of candidates, they were even denied the right to vote at all. It was the District People's Committee — a replica of the Soviets in the USSR — that would decide in the name of the people on our fitness to hold office. Nevertheless, the fiction of a democratic choice was energetically maintained. Campaign posters, newspaper coverage, and personal appearances by the candidates were all used to further the fantasy. The prerequisite to standing for election was approval by the Party authorities and the secret police. Thus, while I knew who had approved my candidature, and who would elect me, I did not know — and still do not know — whose candidate I was. Was I nominated by the Ministry of Justice, by the Regional Court in Plzeň, by the District Court at Stříbro, by the "toiling masses," or by whom?

When the time of the judicial elections arrived, the population had had ten years of experience with spontaneous, non-contested spectacles. This demonstration of the "single will of the masses" annoyed the average voter, but as an ex-candidate, I can only say that it aggravated me even more. There I was engaged in a pre-

ordained ritual, and I had to plead, to exhort the non-voting voters
to entrust me with their confidence. The Party arranged a majestic
propaganda drive, and the Ministry of Justice, consistent with its
fondness for statistics and socialist competition, ordered the judges
to conduct their campaign in factories, villages, offices, schools, indeed to campaign everywhere, and to report on the number of appearances, on the attendance, the extent of audience participation,
etc.

As it happened, shortly prior to the election, I had sold my car
and was left with slow and unreliable trains and buses to reach my
apathetic constituents. Once, on the way to deliver a speech to a
branch of the Foresters' Union in Konstantinovy Lázně, I got lost,
wandering for almost the whole day in the woods without ever
reaching my destination. This mishap, too, had to be reported,
causing some headache to the Ministry's official, Dr. Blažek, who
was collecting campaign data for the Plzeň province. Blažek admitted that the drafters of statistical sheets did not anticipate the
variable "candidate lost in woods." He subsequently accepted my
suggestion that the column "lost" be added to the report.

The campaigning judge who did not get lost and reached the
audience faced a formidable problem in deciding on a topic that
could be relevant, interesting, and yet within the Party's expectations. Officialdom frowned upon any tendency toward familiarity
with the audience. Communism is a serious, unsmiling undertaking, where conversational ease is unwelcome and wit is subversive.
We rejoiced only when under orders, as, for example, on the May
First parade, when marching before benign rulers, or at the launch-
ing of a new Sputnik. Even the lowly dogcatcher in the United
States knows that a joke is essential to a campaign speech. Not
with us. Dedication to the cause was a dedication to the struggle,
to the worship of intolerance, and to the condemnation of the
doubtful. Whatever the purpose of an election campaign, it was not
entertainment. The climate would not allow for jokers of the Will
Rogers type. The platform was the preserve of thundering Billy
Grahams.

As the saying goes, the first totalitarian election was staged
in Paradise. The Creator nominated Eve — and Adam, the only
voter, then cast the ballot of his choice. My electorate had the
richness of Adam's choice, but unlike him, the people I pleaded with
for support were disfranchised. The District Soviets were to cast

the ballot on their behalf. The non-voters, however, were left with a sort of a negative vote.

The public could—and was encouraged to—participate through letters, complaints, denunciations, spoken or written, signed or anonymous. The practice proved useful to the Party by providing our phantom democracy with an air of legitimacy, the judges with a healthy scare, and the Establishment with a bulky volume of malicious accusations that one day might be found handy.

I might mention one incident which almost ended my career before I was able to achieve this myself. Before the campaign started I surrendered to the politically imprudent temptation to grow a beard. In those days an unshaven face—even a mini-moustache—amounted to about 51 per cent evidence of insincerity in building socialism, and of vestiges of bourgeois appetites. This was strange logic, indeed, in view of the hirsutism of Marx and Engels. (It should be noted that Fidel Castro still had more than a year to spend before descending from Sierra Maestra to Havana to join the architects of the classless world.) At Stříbro, the local potentates were particularly apprehensive about beard-growing, for a reason I found out only when it was too late. In the pre-Communist days of 1945, the number-one man at Stříbro was a certain Dr. Hrdlička, an eccentric who pledged that, should the Communist Party win in the elections of 1946, he would not shave or change his clothes as long as the Bolsheviks retained their plurality. They won, and from that day until their take-over in February, 1948—the time of Dr. Hrdlička's speedy dismissal—he kept his word, to the discomfiture of everyone except himself. He ran the local government, administered civil wedding ceremonies, and became a kind of Twentieth Century embodiment of the Count of Monte Cristo in his lean years. Now, in 1957, a picture of a bearded candidate for judgeship was posted in one hundred and ten odd communities in the district, just asking for trouble.

The officials of the District People's Committee decided to report me, demanding the removal of the unshaven judge. The complaint reached the Minister of Justice in Prague. The Ministry, in turn, notified the Chairman of the Provincial Court in Plzeň, Adam Pittner, and entrusted him with the investigation. All I was able to improvise for my defense was an accusation that the comrades who had complained exhibited highly un-Bolshevik manners. Instead of informing me about my *nedostatky* ("short-comings," this favorite term in the political dogfight) and attempt-ing to solve the issue in true comradely fashion, they had catapulted the charge straight to the top. Pittner was inclined to agree that the point deserved some thought. In gratitude for Pittner's back-ing, I immediately consented to the closest shave of my life. Mean-while he reported to the Ministry, the Party, and the District Soviet that the charge was based on misunderstanding and, more-over, had been handled in a hasty and improper way.

Clean shaven, I made it and was in due course, in October, 1957, elected unanimously. So was the majority of approximately 1,350 candidates—but not all of them. The election served the Party's purpose in allowing them to withdraw the nomination of judges in disfavor, provided they could be replaced. During the campaign the Party belatedly discovered that a selective purge could neatly be wrapped in the outward pretense of democratic process. Let us imagine Judge X., noted for competence and integrity, though not Bolshevik militancy. A purge might elevate him to martyrdom in the public eye, but a "democratic" election would not. While a tenured judge could appeal—or attempt to appeal—against administrative dismissal, an electoral loser was left with no way out. It was not unknown in such a case for the Party to offer sympathy to the unfortunate judge who had failed to gain the confidence of the people's representatives—omitting to add that these representatives had voted "Nay" under Party order. To sum up: most of the judges were nominated; most of the nominees were elected; and the few casualties acquiesced in their fate. An exception to this rule was a demoted judge in Karlovy Vary (Karlsbad)[3] who committed the perfect suicide by both taking poison and hanging himself.

For the judges elected, there proved to be no marked differ-ence between the times when they had been solely responsible to law and conscience and their new accountability to the "people." When, in the pre-election era, the appointed Judge U. irritated officialdom by wearing only shorts under his gown and taking occasional naps while presiding, he was fired. When the elected Judge H. declined to comply with the Party's "suggestions" to dismiss certain labor law claims, he was also fired, with the only difference that now the dismissal order carried not the signature of the Ministry but that of the Chairman of the District Soviet.

A reading of the 1957 Electoral Act would not disclose any

vassalage of the judiciary to the Soviets. Our only specific obligation was that of delivering semi-annual reports to its Plenary Session headed "On the state of socialist legality in the area of jurisdiction." Beyond that, it was left to the judges' own initiative and sense of survival as to how to handle the tribunes of the masses. The reports were not always written, and a judge who insisted on their delivery was liable to be considered a nuisance by the politicos. This is not to say that the latter had any scruples about intervening in the affairs of the judiciary. We were left alone, not because of a concern on part of our electors to maintain independent courts, but because of the deluge of responsibilities of higher priority.

The first report I prepared for the District Soviet was never delivered. The Plenary Session began at eight in the morning and was expected to last for twelve hours. My presentation was scheduled for 11 A.M. I was amazed to see the range of the agenda, stretching from contributions to the Defenders of Peace Fund to deficiencies in transportation of vegetables to market. The speaker who was scheduled to address the audience before me spent ninety minutes reporting on the production of eggs in the district. During this fascinating account of the heroism of socialist chickens, Oliverius, the Chairman of the District Committee, approached me, suggesting that as a favor I might withdraw from the agenda because of other pressing and more pertinent problems facing the gathered comrades. I gladly complied and pledged, moreover, not to attend the next semi-annual meeting or, indeed, any other subsequent meeting. Oliverius accepted my pledge with unconcealed gratitude.

It was not the Soviet, designed by the law to be our watchdog, nor even the Party as an institution, that caused all the worry, but rather individual Party officials, who would twist our arms when they felt it necessary and found the time to do so. Although I will refer to the Party's interference into judicial work in some detail later, at this stage one brief point at least can be made: the desire of the totalitarian state and its agents—be it the Party, the Soviets or the Secret Police—to control all aspects of public and private life within its borders was so ambitious as to be virtually self-defeating. With only twenty-four hours in any one day, the eyes and ears of the Peeping Toms committed to supervising everything at all times, became blinded and deafened by trivia, and the perception of the essential was lost. In a curious way, it was the little man who benefitted from such an arrangement: he was able to pass unnoticed in a crowd. A more thoughtful, a more discriminating master would have caught him.

---

1. a. First Republic, 1918-1938, the creation of the Versailles Treaty. b. Second Republic, 1938-1939, the creation of the Munich Treaty. c. Protectorate, 1939-1945, under Nazi occupation. c. Postwar uneasy coalition with the Communists, 1945-1948.

2. Wild, hand-painted ties were also one of the belatedly imported hits in the fifties, especially popular among the young males in the rural areas.

3. My occasional use of the German transcription of a locale (e.g., Marienbad rather than the tongue twisting Mariánské lázně) is motivated by reasons of convenience and preference for better known terms, and not on revanchism. Nevertheless, I offer my apology to offended Czech patriots.

LAY ASSESSORS: THE ROLE
OF THEORETICAL MAJORITY 2

The passing of the era of bourgeois justice was signified by more than a turnover of personnel and the promulgation of new basic Codes. Both legal thinking and institutions changed. Also, the jury system was discarded as a capitalist trick designed to confuse the people. The Party could not afford to preserve a system based on adjudication by one's own peers. The jury was a body too unpredictable and anonymous to control. The Party, however, following Soviet practice, was anxious to preserve the lay element in court proceedings and introduced the so-called "lay assessors." An examination of the recruitment, role and importance of the amateur jurists is the purpose of this chapter.

The lay assessors, literally the "judges from among the people," are loyal, trusted, legally untrained, and—as will emerge later—somewhat reluctant participants who, in addition to their regular occupations, take part in trials, sharing the bench as equals with the presiding professional judge, who now bears the title Chairman of the Senate. In the case of a District Court, the senate would consist of a chairman and two lay assessors.[1] With all members having equal voting powers, the representatives of the working class can—and are supposed to—prevent the jurist from acting contrary to the "spirit of socialist justice." This innovation was brought about by the 1948 Act on the Popularization of the Judiciary. While expected by many to be only a provisionary measure, it instead became a permanent feature of the Czechoslovak court structure, even after the majority of the bourgeois judges had been replaced by lawyers of a new breed.

With juries abolished, the ultimate decision on innocence or guilt is left to the "one plus two" district court bench, where the presiding judge exercises his influence to the point of dominating the assessors. The 1948 change has borne strange dividends; replacement of the jury system by the people's judges, instead of diminishing the power of the professional judge, actually enhances it. The "one plus two" pattern does not mean that the judge has to share all decision-making with the same two assessors. The fifteen or so laymen allotted to his court cannot expect to exercise their functions more frequently than once a month.

Before dealing with the court performance of the lay assessors, let us first look at what kind of people they are and how they are recruited. A typical people's judge is a middle-aged factory laborer, a Party member of long standing, with a record of participation in a variety of political assignments—the type of activist called a *funkcionář* (functionary). At the Plzeň court most were workers from the Škoda Industries; by contrast, in rural areas members of agricultural cooperatives predominated.

A totalitarian state, demanding maximum politicization and active participation by the citizenry, always has more "functions" available than people willing to fill them. During the fifties, in particular, function-mania reached its zenith. Performing one's "function" was regarded as a necessary evil, eating up free time and energy. The problem was not so much the avoidance of political engagement—a luxury one could hardly afford—but making the right choice from among all the uncalled-for merchandise. A prudent customer would select the item with the most impressive label and the minimum of contents. The more formal, ostentatiously packaged, and meaningless the function, the better.

With so few Mohammeds forthcoming, the Mountain was obliged to move. The Ministry allocated quotas for provinces and districts and instructed judges to initiate active recruitment. "Persuasion" and "voluntarism" are the magic words in the totalitarian myth of spontaneity. One always volunteers—to work in mines, to give up part of one's salary, to join a kolkhoz—regardless of how injurious the decision may be to one's self-interest.

This time I had to act as "persuader;" a role no less uncomfortable than that of the "volunteer." Also, of course, no one volunteers to be a persuader; the job goes to the junior members. At the Plzeň court this meant Václav Veverka and me, both Assistant Judges.

To illustrate our assignment, let us take an actual day in the spring of 1956 spent peddling our cause to the state retail store managers in the old part of the city. One of our targets was the manager of the hosiery shop, formerly the private firm Zelený, earlier Rudinger, on the corner of Františkánská and Zbrojnická Street.

"We are from the court and want to talk to the boss."

This was greeted with the familiar unfriendly, slightly puzzled look. "Two guys want to see the boss, and they are not from the secret police but from the court."

"Please, wait just a moment, comrades." The salesgirl vanished to a back room to bear the news.

After a while, the manager—his lapel exhibiting a freshly pinned Party button—stood in front of us.

"Labor be honored, comrades. What can I do for you?"

We comrades did not know exactly where and how to begin. We wrestled with clichés about socialist justice and about the masses assisting in building this justice, and, finally, came to the point. "You, comrade manager, were suggested to us by the people's authorities as a very promising candidate for the honor of becoming a people's judge." To assuage the shock of this honor, we then immediately proceeded to the anti-climax, assuring him that this function was more of a pleasure than a burden. Perhaps he would be called to the court with less than the customary frequency. This could be arranged. He would be well advised to accept the offer. He would meet important people, we added, and one never knew when such a connection would be handy. "So, comrade, please sign the application form. That's all."

The comrade in question was no fool. He, like most people, had escaped from this sort of wooing into extra work many times before. Had he not, he would have been long dead from exhaustion. During our talk, he weighed the pros and cons and decided that declining the offer was worth the risk. He excused himself with what we called the "religious variant." Emulating the biblical "Lord, I am not worthy that you should enter under my roof," the fish escaped our net while he was expressing his enormous gratitude for the confidence the working class had reposed in him

by its offer. Unfortunately, he did not feel up to the task. Though
loyal and dutiful, he felt he had not yet attained sufficient political
maturity. He was not worthy that. . . . We countered that undue
modesty was no virtue in a true Bolshevik, at the same time
mentally striking one more potential candidate from our list.

Door to door canvassing of this sort may sound like a
caricature, but it was all too familiar to us. Religious-style pleas
of socio-political unworthiness were frequently used as evasive
tactics. But the portmanteau medical certificate, revealing the
bearer's incapacity to serve in any public position at any time,
was also common.

Once recruited, the freshman lay assessors were sworn in and
received a certificate outlining their new status. Though clearance
by the Party and the police was prerequisite to each nomination,
it was not customary to request from Prague a transcript of the
candidate's criminal record. Although any failure to do this was
more likely to be a bureaucratic oversight than a nefarious scheme
to dress ex-convicts in judges' gowns, the inevitable followed. A
new people's judge, understandably enough, would choose not to
reveal the less illustrious part of his past. At the least suitable
moment—and to the considerable discomfort of the court—the
truth would emerge. Once, for example, a defendant recognized
among the judges a former accomplice with whom he had once
served a long prison term for robbery. The errant lay assessor
was quickly dropped and, at least as far as the Plzeň province was
concerned, from then on a check with criminal records became a
mandatory procedure.

By 1957, the lay assessors, along with the professional judges,
had become subject to indirect election by the Soviets. The Party
cells in factories or villages, or "mass organizations" (e.g., trade
unions or youth groups), nominated the candidates. That year
the Ministry of Justice introduced a self-defeating innovation. In
its zeal to maximize the role of the people's judges, it increased
their numbers. Thus, instead of having only fifteen assessors at
my disposal, after 1957 I had no less than sixty. If the bureaucrats
in Prague anticipated that sixty watchdogs would be more efficient
than fifteen, they were mistaken. Such an arrangement would
only have worked had the composition of the two to one ratio of
assessors and judges been altered accordingly. In this instance,
the real beneficiary was the professional judge, the very person the
reform was designed to curb. The increase in the number of the

assessors served only to dilute still further their potential power. If under the old system each layman participated in court work once a month, the new practice called for appearances no oftener than twice a year. How much influence, for good or ill, could an outsider exercise when he dropped in once in the spring and again in the autumn?

Of the sixty assigned to my civil law senate in Stříbro, most were members of agricultural cooperatives. Almost all had only elementary schooling, half were women, and less than half were organized Communists. The average age was forty to forty-five. The actual power of lay assessors—and the degree of their participation in the judicial decision-making—is greatly misunderstood, not only in the West but also by the general public in the very countries maintaining this system. Often my friends in Czechoslovakia—outsiders to legal affairs, yet individuals not without sophistication—would sympathize with me. They had so absorbed official propaganda that they pictured the poor judge on the bench as always falling prey to the lay element, a slave to the know-nothing Party hacks. "After all," they would say, "there is only one of you and two of them. What can you do against that?"

I have never felt myself to be a victim of the assessors, and I doubt whether any other judge has. Indeed, the opposite view, that the people's judges were useless dummies and mere socialist window dressing, was closer to the truth, with this significant qualification: Whether the lay assessors were active or passive depended almost entirely on how they were handled by the presiding professional. It was generally agreed among the judges that the assessors could be utilized as a valuable source of knowledge concerning matters about which a lawyer would know next to nothing. A case in point would be when I was in charge of a claim for damages in which a worker who had suffered injury in a steel mill was suing his employer. It would be to my advantage to arrange for lay assessors who had some experience with the work in a foundry. Most of the assistance I received occurred during civil law suits involving agriculture. Since I was totally ignorant about farming, almost anyone could have fooled me if I had not had at my side the emergency assistance of a lay assessor who was, himself, a farmer.

The professional judge dominates the proceedings and the decision-making; if he does not, it is nobody's fault but his own.

A judge has several devices at his disposal for neutralizing the troublemakers and for dispelling any doubt as to who is in charge. In the more than one thousand verdicts I have handed down there has not been a single case in which I did not succeed in overruling the opposition of lay assessors, provided there was any. Much more usual was tacit acquiescence in everything the presiding judge said and did. Since I was not an exceptional jurist nor operating in exceptional circumstances, it may well be assumed that my experience was typical throughout Czechoslovakia. Certainly it was verified by all that I heard from fellow judges.

Our headaches—and they were many—were caused by Party intervention, by denunciations, by scheduled purges, but not by lay assessors. We were protected against the latter in several ways. A source of strength was our professional knowledge. The chairman runs the show; he conducts the proceedings. Usually, he has to spend more energy encouraging his lay colleagues to say anything at all than in shutting them up. The judge decides the case and drafts the verdict. The judge's second line of defense is his power to arrange the court calendar and to select assessors for each particular proceedings. Prior to this scheduling it is advisable to go to some pains in working out a sort of ranking order of suitability for the sixty assessors—a time-consuming and never definite project, but one that pays off very well. My practice, not uncommon among my colleagues, was to compile a list of all sixty, including their names, addresses, occupations, personal habits, estimated degree of political militancy, and their personal relationship with me (if any). Armed with this information, I would classify my group into five categories:

A (friendly, helpful)
B (potentially helpful, promising)
C (neutral, not sure yet)
D (potential troublemakers, suspicious)
E (outright dangerous).

Dangerous individuals were summoned only to participate in routine, non-contraversial business where they could do no harm. Authorizing the detainment of a mental patient was just such a case.

Sometimes, instead of pre-selecting cases, I preferred to summon my least agreeable assessor for a date he probably would not be able to keep. If he was a member of the agricultural cooperative, he would be called to the court during the peak harvest

season. If he was in charge of a state retail store, he would receive his summons during the quarterly control period, when he
could not leave the premises. Calling an activist to appear on the
bench on the day he was attending a Party training school was a
good way to ensure his absence. Failure to answer the call on more
than one occasion would result in his being relegated to the inactive list. The way was then open for the judge to suggest to the
authorities that the erring assessor be eliminated from the list on
account of his lack of cooperation and failure to understand the
needs of socialist justice.

It might be useful at this stage to say a word on how I
categorized my assessors. A certain element of unreliability always
existed, but this could be reduced by careful research, utilizing all
available channels of communication, cautious deduction, some
guesswork and, in the last resort, that sixth sense which one may
always develop after, say, ten years of experience with totalitarianism. The strategy was as follows: prior to my transfer to
Stříbro, I had found out (in Plzeň) that there was one person in
my new district whom I could trust. This one person gave me the
names of a few reliable assessors. They, in turn, supplied further
names, along with references and warnings. Thus the outline of
the picture took shape.

If, however, an assessor still was questionable on my list, he
was summoned only in company with someone I could rely on.
Should something then go wrong, we were two against one, and
no harm would be done. Even then, if both the people's judges
suddenly contradicted my intentions on how to decide a case,
instead of calling for a vote I would adjourn the trial on the pretext
of obtaining supplementary evidence. In view of the pressure the
courts were under to speed up their work, we could not wait six
months until the next turn of the troublemaking assessors was
due, and so I would decide the case in question with a more malle-
able couple. Such tactics the Ministry certainly did not foresee
when they increased the number of the people's judges. Instead
of converting them into the guarantors of proletarian ethos of the
judicial process, the system reduced them to occasional passive
onlookers in unrelated court episodes.

Necessity dictated that one not reveal one's true political
orientation to many, if any, of the lay assessors. Even if I could
have fully trusted some of them, there was no assurance of their
being discreet enough to resist passing on the interesting informa-

tion that the judge had no great liking for Communism. The least
sympathy for the regime I found among the women assessors working in agricultural cooperatives. Though their criticism of the
Establishment was frank and often devastating, I pretended not
quite to understand and to interpret their views as "harsh but
healthy criticism that will help us to overcome our shortcomings
on our road to Communism, etc."

Most of the assessors I worked with were politically loyal, at
least in the sense that they identified with the promises, if not with
the reality of the regime. Distinctions between right and wrong,
between just and immoral, were not lost on them. Dedication to
Communism did not imply for every assessor a desire to become
involved in the class struggle. Comrade Nováková, for example, a
gentle elderly lady of long Party standing, viewed her participation at the bench as a kind of social welfare work—helping children
from broken families or reconciling potential divorcees. Nováková
was a reliable standby, always available and always willing to fill
in at short notice. I appreciated her help and would express myself
in this way: "*You* and *I* are trying to build new socialist family
relations. *We* are extirpating maladies inherited from the past. I
thank you, for everything, comrade." Comrade Nováková's response would be to mention at home and among her Party friends
what proud warriors for the new society she and "her" judge were.
Her son, incidentally, was on close terms with the First Party
District Secretary. I made sure that he dropped a kind word in
the right place and even arranged that he, too, should become an
assessor, further strengthening my reputation with the local
apparatchiki. Others, who regarded the assessors' role at the court
a nuisance, but were of some political importance, had to listen
to my insincere assurances as to the indispensability of the popular
element in the judiciary and my appreciation of their assistance.
To make their stay more palatable, an appealing agenda had to
be selected. "Between ourselves, gentlemen, how about a real good
paternity mess? Something, comrades, with a little spice, and
which you haven't yet experienced." Appreciating this opportunity, the assessor would in turn let it be known that the judge
was no stiff bureaucratic egghead, but a warm guy who understood
the toiling masses.

A rather special group among the lay assessors was made up
of the wives of local potentates. Housewives, wedded members of
the New Class, were in lesser need of gainful employment and

participation at the court served both the purpose of token political involvement and of pleasant diversion from the dullness of their existence in uneventful small towns. These social upstarts were susceptible to—and appreciative of—flattery. Genteel allusion to their largely non-existent charms, fictions rarely heard from their overworked husbands, were particularly effective.

The assessors were in general, at least at the beginning of their term, shy and uncertain. Since this feeling of inferiority might backfire and endanger their relationship with the presiding judge, our task was to relieve this initial uneasiness. Thus, if an assessor came to his first trial and forgot to put on a tie, there was always a spare one available in my office. If he lit up a cigarette during the proceedings, he would be told very discreetly to wait until the recess. The presiding judge had to appear folksy and down-to-earth—in short, a regular guy. At the same time, however, he had always to be on top of his job, careful to provide no grounds for doubting his professional competence. The importance of this delicate balance cannot be over-stressed. The least manageable assessors in this respect were those who had once aspired to higher education. Their resentment at their own failure led them to develop a jealousy and vindictiveness against professionals in general —a dangerous attitude that demanded very careful handling.

Special care in selecting assessors was needed whenever the court calendar included a politically touchy case. The choice of meek, compliant assessors would not suffice. The purpose was not only to pass a verdict according to my liking, but to reach a decision that would survive the appeal; more importantly, I might be standing up to extra judicial pressure and investigation by the Party. If, for example, an influential defendant was about to lose a divorce suit because of his adulterous behavior, at least one of the assessors had to be a Party man of at least equal political standing, but also one known for his puritan principles. Should the Secretariat then look into the matter, I would notify the assessor of the problem, indicating that *his* prestige and integrity were involved and advising him to clear up the issue with the Party Secretary and to demand that the investigation be rescinded. This use of proxy, frequently practiced by my fellow judges, offered an unbeatable advantage in that the assessor approached the apparatchiki as a Party equal. The sense of a mission entrusted to him by the judge flattered his ego, and he would defend "our" verdict with redoubled energy.

In selecting the right assessors, the judge had to be mindful of the possibility that the litigants might be personally known to them. Though the law demanded disqualification of any judge, lay or professional, in such an instance, this rule made no sense in a small district, where almost everyone knew everyone else. It was thus invoked rather sparingly, mainly to neutralize an unruly assessor, who might lessen the judge's control over a case.

When the judges retired for deliberation, it was the chairman's duty to summarize and evaluate the findings for the assessors and to brief them on the pertinent passages of the law. "The assessors know about the life; you know the law," we were told by the Ministry. "Familiarize them with the legal provisions applicable in each case and then, together, arrive at a just conclusion." To ensure the assessors' acceptance of his "suggestion," the professional judge would present the legal basis in a somewhat selective fashion. The often contradictory principles of the law furnished justification for almost any decision he had in mind. If, for instance, he favored the rejection of the divorce petition, the assessors would be told about the necessity for curbing matrimonial irresponsibility and the growing divorce rate. Should he favor the petition, the assessors would learn that it was against the spirit of socialist justice to insist upon the continuation of a marriage that has ceased to function as a socially useful unit. The manipulation of alternative legal interpretations was of cardinal importance. A shifting emphasis between the principles of "merciless class struggle" and the "well-known generosity of the toiling masses" could determine whether a defendant was given probation or a long prison term. Similarly, a juvenile finding himself the heir to an agricultural property could face a lifetime drudgery on a kolkhoz unless the judge insisted on the legal maxim of the primacy of the child's own interest as opposed to the principle of the rejuvenation of agriculture.

According to law, the people's judges had to vote first on the verdict (the younger assessor before the older one); the professional judge voted last. This provision, designed to secure unimpaired freedom of decision on part of the lay element, remained on paper only. This is not to say that we "violated" the provision. We simply ignored it. We did not vote in the sense anticipated by the law, and I have not heard of any court which did. After being given a summary of the case and being supplied with the legal basis for the "suggested" verdict, the assessors automatically signed a ballot with the pre-typed caption: "Decision unanimous." It was the assessors themselves who preferred to dispense with the proper voting procedure. For most, any form of voting was a meaningless ritual, while others felt that voting implied mistrust of the professional judge—an inference they did not wish to evoke. Indeed, it was common for the assessors to sign beforehand and unasked all ballots for the day.

Though the assessors abdicated the opportunity to exercise individual judgment, a prudent chairman did not ignore their opinions during the deliberation. If their view would have led to a patently unjust or untenable decision, it was then my task to inform them that though I agreed with their reasoning (or agreed with reservation or disagreed but respected their view) the law, unfortunately, ordered us to decide the case otherwise, i.e., the way I had in mind.

The system of having a majority of lay judges on the bench was an ineffectual device for checking and controlling the presiding professional. It did not impede the freedom of judicial decision-making. This freedom was endangered and often annulled by other means.

---

1. The Senate of a Court of Appeal is composed of three professional judges and only two lay assessors. The minority of the latter would seem to contradict the statement about the controlling power of the lay element. The government explains this seeming inconsistency by referring to the appellate bench as being concerned more with legalistic than with factual considerations.

3 CLASS JUSTICE WITH CONSEQUENCES

Of the two most damaging influences bearing down on the Czecho-slovak judiciary, the Communist Party's interference rated a poor second. In any overall account, the pressures and whims of the apparatchiki were a mere nuisance when compared with the real plague upon our work, namely, the so-called class approach to judicial decision-making. Nothing was more harmful to the pursuit of justice than the insistence on the implementation of the omni-present enigma termed as "classness" (*třídnost*). While the impact of this phenomenon must permeate the whole narrative, all I shall attempt to do at this point is to mention some of its rudimentary characteristics.

According to Marxist Writ, private ownership of the means of production splits the society into antagonist, irreconcilable classes of exploiters and exploited. In such a situation the state becomes the instrument by which the exploiters—the ruling class—preserve their privileges. The rulers employ all means, including the laws and the courts, to oppress the non-propertied majority. Thus in Marxist terms the concept of "blind justice" and "equality for all" is an idealistic delusion. Even after the successful proletarian revolution, the laws and the courts remain the instrument of the new ruling class designed to liquidate the political, economic, and

30

ideological remnants of capitalism. Not until the goal of pure socialism is attained can pure justice and equality emerge.

Viktor Knapp, my former teacher and Czechoslovakia's most influential writer in the field of civil law, has called the class content of law "a brilliant discovery of legal science," confessing that "until then we staggered through an impasse of sterile idealistic speculations."[1.] Those of us in the field who were expected to implement this new policy and who had preserved at least a modicum of self-respect were somewhat less than convinced of the brilliance of this insight. We felt, rather, that the whole class-concept "discovery" was irrational, ambiguous and arbitrary. No one has ever been able—or willing—to define a class enemy. We asked ourselves such questions as: Is class hostility based on former material possessions, on a record of past exploitation, on having held a high office in the pre-Communist state, or is it simply a question of one's state of mind? Can one cleanse himself from the stigma of class hostility by cooperating with the Establishment? What determines the social class of my children? Who is the "bigger" enemy: an atheistic ex-exploiter or a devout Catholic laborer? Should we, when unmasking a kulak, be guided by the criterion of his total acreage, of his mental outlook, or of his position in the village? What will happen to the sons of a kulak after he dies? His property will be divided into, let us say, four parts. Will this mean that out of one kulakian possession we create four middle-sized or even small-sized peasants? If I am an expropriated bourgeois who has been working for ten years as a manual laborer in a socialist enterprise, are my children—ages eleven and nine—of proletarian or ex-bourgeois background, or do I have one of each? What process of social transformation does a teenager undergo, when he defects to the West despite the embarrassing fact that his father is a person of prominent political standing? If the children cannot be punished for the sins of their parents, why was it that in June of 1964 a law was passed cutting down the benefits to orphans whose parents happened to be, twenty years ago, identified with the bourgeois Republic? One could continue with these inquiries *ad infinitum.*

To repeat, nobody in the post-1948 regime ever attempted to work out definite and binding criteria for distinguishing between the enemies and the allies of the toiling masses. This comfortable omission enabled the organs of the state, including the judiciary, to manipulate the enigma for the purpose of intimidation and selective discrimination. There was always the implicit warning that a bad label was available for any person, no matter how immaculate his background, who hesitated to comply with the requirements of the day.

An unfavorable social class designation implied hostile intent. If, for example, a small farmer failed to fulfill the production quota he was to be punished for "non-fulfillment." In the case of a kulak, however, a similar failure was classified as sabotage, because with the kulaks hostile intent to harm socialism was presumed, and hence did not need to be proved. This arbitrary distinction could mean for a defendant the difference between only a nominal punishment and the death penalty. The class label determined or at least influenced the outcome of trials ranging from murder through bodily injury to verbal offense. In the field of civil law, in the adjudication on divorces, alimony, paternities, torts, probates, etc., class criteria also operated. Often references to social background were the sole arguments used by a plaintiff to substantiate his case.

Until 1958, it was a matter of tacit agreement that whereas in the area of criminal law the class dictum should be scrupulously observed, we, the civil law judges, could remain relatively free to adjudicate on the basis of what we considered just and reasonable. This tranquility was to end with an abrupt order summoning us to a special conference held at the Provincial Court in Plzeň. There, the Supreme Court Justice Orlický announced a new line which urged "the most meticulous observance of the class essence in each civil law case." The distinguished comrade lectured: "Comrades, from now on, each verdict of yours must reflect the dialectical unity of the merits of the case and the class profile of the litigants. You must be explicit about this both during the proceedings and in the written opinion. Any decision which fails to comply with this policy will be considered hostile to the interest of the toiling masses, and hence, illegal."

The requirement to unify dialectically the litigants' past with the merits of the suit is something I could not then and cannot now comprehend. It can be done, I admit, but it cannot be done without making a mockery out of the trial and without alerting the parties that something very nefarious is going on; that the judge is either a fool, a prostitute or probably both. Let us assume that one is presiding over a dispute between two neighbors contesting the ownership of a chicken. How does one unlock the "proper dialectical unity" between the bird and the socio-political qualifications of the litigants? Some judges did not feel the slightest inhibition in complying with the new policy. I read, for instance, a number of opinions produced by the District Court at Litvínov in which the analysis of the parties' pedigree, political trustworthiness, and the resulting dialectical fantasies amounted to about eighty per cent of all the reasoning.

It was less awkward to smuggle into a written opinion, after the trial was over, some irrelevant statement pertaining to the unity between the sociopolitical label and the judgement, than to put the interested parties on the stand and interrogate them about such matters in open court. However, this had to be done, because the Justice Ministry officials searched the court records for gaps in "classness." If these gaps were found, the defective case was likely to be submitted to the Supreme Court for annulment on account of alleged illegality.

Let us return to the two neighbors disputing over the chicken. Before dealing with the merits of the case, I was expected to inquire into the backgrounds, the past and present political affiliations of the litigants (though not of the chicken), of their parents and, if I was a particularly dutiful judge, also of their grandparents. This sort of justice failed to impress even the most unsophisticated. Moreover, it provided the unsuccessful party with a convenient rationalization as to why he lost his case. For example, there was one case involving a sale of a horse. The plaintiff, a member of an agricultural cooperative, had bought the animal from a private farmer before joining the kolkhoz. According to the law any defect in a purchased animal which reveals itself within six weeks of the sale entitles the buyer to sue for the annulment of the contract and for the recovery of the price. After having examined all the evidence, I had no doubt that the farmer had sold the horse in bad faith, and I decided the case accordingly. After the pronunciation of the verdict, the loser — who should have lost in any court, no matter whether socialist, capitalist or feudal — left the court room with the following words: "Why did I like a fool bother to come here and expect justice? I should have remembered that I am not a member of the kolkhoz while he is. I am really a fool." This indignant statement was more than welcome. I put it verbatim into the record and at the next provincial conference presented it to the delegates from the Justice Ministry and the Supreme Court. "Comrades, here you have an example in which the class analysis served as a convenient excuse for the loser, encouraging him to question the objectivity of our organs of justice."

The message was self-evident. If militant "classness" was the guarantee of socialist legality, and this legality was retained, one could not expect praise from the public for objectivity and fair judgment. After a prolonged discussion, Supreme Court Justice Orlický summed up the case and advised all of us, "Comrades, class adjudication is a tricky business, and all I can recommend to you when executing this policy is to be discreet with the litigants."

Stalinism in Czechoslovakia succeeded in stripping the law of its certainty and the courts of their integrity, but it failed to convince the average man that he was the beneficiary of the innovation. All the available propaganda techniques could not entirely hide the fact that the merchandise was damaged.

Mr. Smith — Czech style — remained doubtful. He read the 1948 Constitution that guaranteed freedom of speech. He also read the 1950 Penal Code specifying more than a dozen felonies that might be committed by the exercising of this right. The Constitution assured the citizen of his right to leave the country which he was not allowed to leave. The law became conditional — the "law if." For example, the 1950 Civil Code stipulated a host of proprietary and contractual rights, *provided* their exercise did not contradict the "common interest," the "economic plan," or the "spirit of socialist community of life." Promise of a right was enchained by an escape clause securing political expediency.

Mr. Smith's doubts about the sincerity of the letter of the law extended also to the organs administering justice. All he needed to do was to check with the journal *Sbírka rozhodnutí československých soudů* ("Collection of Decisions of Czechoslovak Courts") publishing court opinions of exemplary political maturity. *Sbírka* disclosed to him, for instance, that a Catholic priest, discovered reading a papal message from the pulpit, was found guilty of high treason. Another priest, who expressed his concern about such matters and the somewhat uncertain future of the Church under Communism, was also convicted of a grave political crime.

Mr. Smith learned about the Supreme Court, which exhorted judges to discriminate against bourgeois defendants and to distrust the evidence given by bourgeois witnesses. In a custody dispute, a lukewarm adherent to socialist ideas was disqualified from the exercise of his parental authority, while in a probate proceeding the heir lost only because of an unfavorable report on him from the

Local People's Committee. One year, the public would read about a show trial with its spontaneous admissions of guilt and self-accusations. The next year the villains might be, posthumously, rehabilitated. The law proved to be binding upon everyone except the self-appointed tribunes of the people. Mr. Smith kept wondering.

The judges' responsibility to link explicitly the social and political background of the litigants with the substance of the suit demoted the concept of socialist legality to a contradiction in terms. The public's anemic confidence in the fair administration was labelled — first by the critics of the Establishment and later by the Establishment itself — as "legal nihilism."

One frequent demonstration of this negativistic attitude was the question of the need for maintaining courts at all when it was generally agreed that impartial and independent decisions on their part were impossible. Why, in particular should there be any law schools? During my four years at the University, I do not think that a single week passed without my being asked, "Why do you bother to study law when we don't have any law?" That question was overdrawn and inaccurate. We did have a law, though of a rather peculiar kind. Nonetheless, these repeated inquiries as to why a seemingly reasonable young man would want to become a jurist made me decide never to volunteer a word about my professional orientation.

While the three law schools in prewar Czechoslovakia annually graduated thousands of students, the two schools left after 1948 (Charles University in Prague and Comenius University in Bratislava) produced together only about two hundred lawyers a year. Even by the time I had joined the court the situation had not improved, and the two schools were forced to resort to so-called organized recruitment. The result was that judges were obliged to act as campaigners. The Ministry of Justice ordered us to lecture to the senior undergraduates about the legal profession, proclaiming its advantages and happy prospects.

It is hard to be a respected practitioner of a disrespected profession. A profession without integrity was also without appeal. However, the fact that Bolshevik jurisprudence was unattractive to undergraduates was only a minor symptom of legal nihilism. More important and far more interesting was how the public adjusted to the climate of socialist legality. Some people decided to beat the system at its own game: "The courts discriminate but they cannot discriminate against *everybody*. Someone has to win. Undeserved disadvantages of my opponent may turn to my advantage. Let's feed the judges with their own vocabulary, their politically irrelevant arguments. This is what seems to count."

The litigants — especially those with a weak case, or no case at all — brought "politics" into the court room proclaiming their contribution in the building of the classless world and denouncing their opponents as bourgeois vermin. Ofter the court became a stage for an improvised performance by clumsy actors trying to convince the bench of their Bolshevik ardor. Many who were anything but proletarians would appear at court dressed in overalls and eulogizing the world revolution in the badly-imitated accents of the working class.

As long as this ridiculous impersonation was limited to image building, it did not significantly handicap the trial. However, some of the litigants furnished the court with *evidence* about their opponent's hostility toward the Establishment, and the judge could not afford to ignore it without endangering himself. In one of the divorces I presided over, the husband offered in evidence a letter by his wife to a girl friend. Though the letter indicated the defendant's interest in other men, the plaintiff pointed out the following passage which he had underlined: "My friend and I were out walking and two fellows tried to make a pass at us. They both wore Party buttons. We told them to go to hell. These Communists are so stupid, I can shit on them."

This was disloyal, to say the least, and since it was in the record I was obliged to take some sort of action. I decided to consult the prosecutor, and we agreed on the following formula: My letter read: "To the District Prosecutor: Enclosed please find file X. Please note letter Y on page Z, which might eventually substantiate a criminal procedure under Section 119 of the Penal Code, the Felony of Affront of the Group of Citizens [i.e., Communists]. Sincerely, O.U." The next day the file was back at my desk. "District Prosecutor to O.U.: The file is being returned. This office does not feel it appropriate to initiate any action since the abusive letter, in view of additional intimate points made, was evidently intended to be read only by the addressee. Indication of the writer's intent to inform a wider public about her critical view is notably absent." This statement constituted a rare show of personal courage on the part of the prosecutor. As a result, the plaintiff did not benefit from his wife's rash admission.

Any litigation was potentially a political booby-trap. The reader should not, however, be left with the impression that a Communist court was a place of unrelieved tension. The lesser the sophistication of the politicized participants, the more majestic might be the sweep of their testimony. It would be a pity if posterity was denied the following case in point. The setting was rural, and the issue was divorce. The plaintiff, the chairman of a kolkhoz, accused his wife of having an affair with the animal husbandman from the same cooperative. The alleged sinner, who had recently returned from a year in some sort of school in the Soviet Union, took the witness stand. I asked him: "Tell us what happened between you and the defendant." The witness, though somewhat ill at ease, was not unaware of the impact of Communism on the rules of evidence in Czech courts. He replied in a coarse subdued voice: "Well, what happened was this. She invited me to her bedroom and said, 'F . . . me and tell me about all the wonderful things you experienced in the Soviet Union.' Naturally, I agreed. What's wrong with that?"

Nothing, of course, nothing. Whether or not this testimony was true, I was overwhelmed to discover that adultery must now be added to the list of instruments promoting socialist consciousness. At least as far as this witness was concerned, indoctrination justified extramarital cohabitation. It might be argued that such an incident reveals more about the politicization of life in a totalitarian society than a respectable theoretical treatise.

Subordination of the law to the needs of political expediency yielded another peculiar by-product. The citizenry increasingly failed to consider final and binding an *unfavorable* ruling by any state organs. Thus, an unsuccessful civil litigant in a case, say of damages, was inclined to ignore the legally prescribed means of redress and to write directly to the top. Most probably this would be the President of the Republic or the Central Committee of the Party. The message would amount to an appeal for intervention and annulment of the alleged miscarriage of justice. Such individuals, however, were usually not content to limit their pleas to the matter in hand — they tended to escalate the charge to include the decision-maker himself, alleging evil intentions. This tactic not only provided the petitioner with the satisfaction of potential vengeance against the "hostile" official, but also, he hoped, advanced his own standing with the authorities. The recipient might not view the complaint as an attempt to promote petty self-interest, but as evidence of pious, loyal concern with the general welfare. In short, the citizen might conclude: "I am writing to you, Comrade President, not only because of the injustice I have suffered but above all because of my patriotic duty to report to you that judge X. is the wrecker of socialism and hidden enemy of the people."

These denunciatory practices evolved from the circumstances surrounding the Communist takeover in February, 1948. Too many competent civil servants had been replaced by barely literate Party appointees; orderly administrative processes were frequently breaking down. Irrespective of class denomination, the citizen victimized by the Bolshevik City Hall and frustrated in his futile search for a legitimate remedy would decide, as the last resort, to write to Antonín Zápotocký, the Prime Minister. Zápotocký was thought by many at that time to be the most accessible and sympathetic Communist potentate in the country. With his elevation to the Presidency in 1953 the letters were re-directed to him at Prague Castle, and even under the subsequent occupancy of the far from popular Antonín Novotný they continued to flood this ancient shrine of Bohemian kings. While one can sympathize with the man-in-the-street struggling to secure his rights from an arbitrary state, by the late fifties this graphomania had grown out of all proportion. The trend had shifted from legitimate complaints to malicious and unsubstantiated denunciations. The incompetence and bias of the new bureaucrats, the class struggle and discrimination, only magnified the general moral decline which could be traced back to the disintegration of the State following the Munich settlement of 1938. The promised lush pastures of comradely togetherness bloomed largely with the state-sown weeds of encouraged and demanded class hatred. Exhortation to "progressive animosity" atomized the society and turned the average citizen into a creature more resentful and selfish than even the most revolutionary government could find comfortable. In addition to the ideologically desirable hostility of poor peasants to kulaks, proletarians to bourgeoisie, and toilers to class enemies in general, the social fabric was torn by a host of accumulated ill-feelings, such as those between educated and non-educated, well-off and less well-off, car owners and bicyclists, those with relatives residing abroad and those with no one from whom to receive chewing gum, between youngsters with smooth skin and those with acne, and so on *ad absurdum*. Resentment fed on itself, aided by envy, jealousy, and cynicism. As the story goes, the Archangel Gabriel descended to earth and travelled from country to country, offering to fulfill three wishes. The typical Czech had only one request: "Please, Gabriel, make my neighbor's goat perish."

Citizens not only wrote complaints and denunciations to the President, the Prime Minister, other Ministers, Party organs and Soviets at all levels, but they also communicated with the secret police in letters either signed or anonymous. The Party, while on one hand concerned that the inflationary trend of complaints to the top was by-passing the prescribed hierarchy of decision-makers, on the other hand welcomed them for a number of reasons. The letters promoted the image of the people's state; they ventilated accumulated grievances on the part of the populace; they kept the leadership in contact with the "masses;" they could lead to correction of "shortcomings" otherwise secure under the protective umbrella of the Kafkaesque bureaucracy; and, finally, the complaints helped to keep the bureaucrats on the alert, insecure, and thus, in turn, more compliant.

According to information I received, the average number of complaints each year against any judge was about six. Thus, every other month one could expect a new, fresh *malheur*.

Being cleared of a charge did not mean that one's reputation remained intact. The more uncomfortable aspect of these complaints was their unpredictability. The least probable suit, the most innocent, well-intentioned remark was blown up into a serious affair by a litigant the judge would consider most unlikely to stir up trouble.

The Party encouraged, or at least tolerated, this sort of mob rule — acquiescence in undeserved, unsupported causes and often outright malicious accusations served as a substitute for impartial and binding rule of law. Petitions, complaints and denunciations were a false cure for the totalitarian ailment.

---

1. Viktor Knapp, *Předmět a systém československého socialistického práva občanského* (The Object and System of the Czechoslovak Socialist Civil Law), (Prague: NČSAV, 1959), p. 29.

4 JUDGE THE COMPETITOR AND PRODUCER

We shall now examine the effects upon the courts of criteria derived from the manufacturing industry. To execute this operation, some interesting exercises in semantics were called for. To the Marxist fundamentalist, words served a preordained political purpose. In his black and white understanding of "the material reality," certain terms were the property of the Angels, whereas others denoted the doomed. Our law professors informed us, for example, that the Devil (the domestic or the foreign enemy) could never qualify for the adjective "courageous" (*statečný*). He could only be described as "cowardly" (*zbabělý*), or, should he in the most exceptional cases defy fear, be labelled "cynical" (*cynický*). Similarly, competition within the capitalist orbit was called *konkurence*, while competition in socialism read as *soutěžení*. The former accelerated the doom of the exploitative society, the latter opened the gate to terrestrial bliss, provided honor for the meritorious and a standard by which to measure one's own social worthiness.

It is nearly impossible to enumerate all the areas in which we competed, or to be more accurate, were ordered to compete. Our *soutěžení* involved the recruitment, training, activism and attendance of lay assessors; the hours of manual labor the professional judge dedicated to the community; the number of working days

40

spent in our favorite agricultural cooperatives; and the degree of involvement in public life generally. At the end of each month the judge compiled his activity report — strangely resembling reports some American colleges require from their faculty. The report was sent from the district to the Regional Court, where a summary was drawn up and submitted to the Ministry of Justice. Judges competed with judges, district courts competed with district courts, regions with regions. Only the Ministry was spared, and thus it was able to direct its energy to criticizing its agencies for not competing hard enough.

Had *soutěžení* stopped short of affecting judicial work proper, it would have been no more than nuisance. The Ministry attempted, however, to impose upon adjudication all the characteristics of industrial production — time sheets, output targets, quotas, etc. The assumption was that this change would lead the progressive intelligentsia of lawyers to an approximation of the mental outlook of the toiling masses. Since the proletarians had to be on time at their plants, the same applied to the judges. At the larger courts time cards were introduced.[1.] At all the courts, the so-called *výrobní porady* ("production conferences") came into being. Each week we gathered to discuss not the intricacies of law and decision-making, but rather "production," "norms," and the "fulfillment of the plan."

The Ministry of Justice, and its chief Václav Škoda, in particular, tried their best to supply the Party leadership with ideologically pleasing statistics on the progressive decline of court activity. The Scriptures revealed that with the steady approach of socialism the volume of adjudication would drop accordingly. The facts frequently refused to confirm this prediction. Pilferers, drunks, criminals in general, divorcees and other civil litigants refused to toe the line of historical inevitability.

The officials from the Ministry made periodic "check-ups" (*prověrka*) on the utilization of man-power at the courts, spending days evaluating the work load of each judge and comparing it with data submitted previously to Prague. The Ministry also exhorted us to contribute to our own withering away. It became the judge's duty to participate in "educational campaigns" on the prevention of criminality and reduction in the volume of civil law litigations. The effects of too much talking to the masses, however, could be unexpected. A colleague of mine, a vigorous lecturer, found himself out of job when, for this or some other reason, a sharp decline occurred in his agenda of civil law cases. Some of the judges anticipated the possibility of campaigning themselves out of existence. One colleague in Marienbad even went so far as to advise the public of the advantages of judicial settlement — an exercise in self-preservation for which he was savagely criticized by the Ministry.

In 1958, Kubánek, the Chairman of the Regional Court at Ústí and one of the most militant judges of proletarian vintage, started a campaign, called "Challenge from Ústí." The challenge was supposed to be a short-lived experimental competition between the courts on the amount of verdicts *produced* and the overall dispatch of their proceedings. As expected, all the judges accepted the challenge "spontaneously and enthusiastically." June of that year proved to be the best season on record for divorce hunters. A trial that earlier would have lasted for months became a while-you-wait operation. The judges, racing for honors, produced. Ústí province won the competition; we at Plzeň were second, while the Slovakian regions and Prague ended in the cellar. The winners were promised a substantial financial reward, and the competition from Ústí would then be over. As it turned out, however, no one collected a cent, and the "Challenge," instead of being terminated, became a permanent feature of judicial work and a yardstick of our performance.

The judge was thus faced with two unsought problems. He had to justify his existence by insuring a full work load while at the same time disposing of this load at a rate deemed appropriate by the Ministry. Luckily, Prague was not *so* doctrinaire as to set up uniform production quotas for all the courts in the country, but took into account specific characteristics of each area. As one might expect, the divorce rate in metropolitan Prague far exceeded that in the predominantly Catholic Slovakia, and the booming industrial city of Ostrava enjoyed a higher rate of rowdyism, alcoholism and prostitution than other regions. There were also marked differences within each province. Within the Plzeň province, the district Klatovy, despite having more than twice the population, had a lower volume of civil actions than my court at Stříbro. The Justice Ministry therefore, settled for a compromise and fixed the production quotas for each court by combining its previous output with the national average, subject to annual review. The output figures in the Stříbro court were fixed at 120 criminal cases and 420 civil cases (240 contested and 180 uncontested litigations) per year.

Some additional and rather routine professional engagement on the part of the civil law judge, had, as far as the Ministry was concerned, almost no bearing on the evaluation of his performance.

These norms became the criterion of our social usefulness, the cause of our distinction or disgrace. Awkward labels became commonplace, such as a "judge of ninety per cent productivity" or a "comrade with one hundred and fifty per cent output." Experience taught us that the one hundred and twenty per cent output was the one to aim for and the best label to bear. Such a judge fulfilled the plan, surpassing it neatly but with caution. Overzealous production might have invited an undue amount of attention from the Ministry and brought on suspicion that the figures were fabricated —or that they betrayed hastiness and superficiality on the part of the judge, or neglect of his extramural obligations to lecture and prevent crime and discourage litigations.

For the resourceful judge, there were some ways to alleviate the burden. Suppose for example, a criminal law judge failed to fulfill his monthly quota — instead of adjudicating ten cases he had only managed to dispose of five. But the fifth case submitted to the court by the prosecutor was an indictment of four drunkards injured in a brawl. In normal times such a case would be registered with the court under one entry and tried as a single case. However, because of the quota system, each accomplice would be tried separately, one indictment sliced into four, with four trials bringing the judge's performance closer to the fulfillment of the plan. Some judges overdid themselves in this respect, as, for example, a colleague in Slovakia who atomized an indictment against a band of twenty pilferers of socialist property into twenty unrelated trials.

To our considerable relief, meeting the norms did not require a settlement of each case by a final verdict. In civil adjudication any solution would do, such as withdrawal of the claim, reconciliation, or transfer of the suit to another court. Since final figures and not thoroughness of work counted, the tendency to maximize output with minimum effort gave birth to a score of questionable practices.

According to law, the jurisdiction over a divorce petition was determined by the last common residence of the litigants. A citizen came to my court requesting legal assistance and help in drafting the claim — a service provided free of charge. As I dictated the petition to the clerk, it became evident that the last common residence of the couple was not in my district. In the pre-norm era, I would have sent the claim straight to the appropriate court. Now, however, the petition first had to be entered into the court register, where it received a file number. Then the absence of jurisdiction was "discovered." Lastly, the clerk would type the "Resolution on the Transfer of Jurisdiction," an undertaking lasting at most two minutes. Then I signed the resolution and the file was disposed of so far as I and my quota were concerned.

In a similar case, let us assume that the jurisdiction of my court was established. After listening to the story of the potential plaintiff, there was no doubt the claim was too weak. Again, in the pre-norm era I would have informed the party about his slim chances and advised him to abandon his petition. Now, whoever came, on whatever pretext, had his case recorded and was allotted a file number. Once this number was duly registered, it was up to the judge to persuade the petitioner to withdraw the claim. Many quota-happy judges, however, overreached themselves by intimidating litigants and threatening to call in the prosecutor if they did not comply. Another pretext for bolstering one's output was provided by a law which barred a judge from presiding over a case in which his relation to one of the parties might put his impartiality in doubt.

The following case demonstrates how the quota system, designed to speed up adjudication, might on occasion produce the opposite effect. If I disqualified myself from conducting a trial and shifted the case to a colleague within the province, it was up to the Provincial Court to decide the eventual dispute over the jurisdictional responsibility. If the courts involved were not from the same province, such a decision was passed by the Supreme Court in Prague. In civil law matters, in particular with "continuous cases," e.g., those involving supervision of minors from broken families, the case could be conveniently disposed of if the participants moved out of the district. Among the shifting files there was one upon which the Supreme Court passed by mistake a rather odd decision: A mother of many children who were under supervision of the District Court at Rýmařov in Northern Moravia, moved to Stříbro. The judge in Rýmařov promptly declared his lack of authority and forwarded the file to my court. Having studied the file, I did not like it a bit. That prompted me, before accepting the jurisdiction, to request from the police a statement as to whether the mother in question was registered with us for *permanent* residence. This "excessive formalism" as it was called, paid off, and since the reply was negative, I sent the file back to Rýmařov. Rýmařov returned it to me, stating that factual and not permanent residence determined the place of jurisdiction. Though I felt fairly sure I would lose, I forwarded the case to the Supreme Court. In about a month the file was back on my desk. The judgment of the Supreme Court read: "Jurisdiction over the case is vested with the District Court of Rýmařov." I could not believe my eyes. When, however, I started to read the lengthy opinion, all the reasoning pointed to the conclusion that it was not Rýmařov but Stříbro where the case belonged. What apparently had happened was that the Supreme Court clerk had made a typing error which the Judge failed to notice before he signed the document. Having advocated formalism in this dispute from the beginning, however, I had to remain consistent, and since the judgment clearly stated "Rýmařov" and not "Stříbro," I returned the file once more to Rýmařov, anxious to discover whether my frustrated Moravian colleague would retain it, or if he refused, how the Supreme Court would reverse its own final decision. Another month passed before the remarkable judgment reached me: "The jurisdiction over the case vested with District Court of Rýmařov is to be read as vested with the District Court of Stříbro." This was the end of the quarrel, an exercise in bureaucratic pettiness and a brainchild of the production era.

The judge was, to a certain extent, able to accommodate himself to the role of producer. But some aspects of the assembly line justice were difficult to accept — in particular, the "speed norms." To cite a few figures: the norm for a contested civil action was two months, except for paternity claims and damage suits of socialist legal persons against their employers for mishandling of entrusted funds; there, the norm was six months. A case not finished on time had to be reported to the Ministry as "unfinished business" with an accompanying explanation of the delay. According to the terms of the Ústí Challenge, judges were not expected to permit the number of cases pending to be more than double their monthly norm. Thus, if the norm was set up at thirty (100 per cent), a "good" judge could not afford to have more than sixty (200 per cent) awaiting decisions. Norms were calculated on the basis of the volume of the previous year's agenda. If in 1958, my average monthly input of new cases was twenty, the 200 per cent limit set up for 1959 was forty. Suppose, as happened in 1959, the amount of new claims grew from twenty to thirty, then keeping up with the plan was far more difficult — by one half, to be exact. The increase of the volume of the cases in the current year was considered irrelevant. Somehow the judge had to find a way to speed up his decision-making if he was to avoid joining the ranks of the indolent producers.

The prosecutors, too, had to wrestle with quotas and competition. In order to empty their in-trays, they would submit at the end of each month as many indictments as they could muster. The only result was to transfer the load to the pending tray of the judge. In the beginning, judges pleaded with the prosecutors to be more sensible; later they complained to Prague, but after neither brought any results they resorted to a mild form of cheating. Thus, if the prosecutor sent a file, say on the twenty-fifth of the month, the court would acknowledge receipt as of the first of the next month. Such a procedure would pertain even though their offices were separated by only a few feet.

The only beneficial aspect of the Ústí Challenge I can think of was that it encouraged the abrupt resolution of picayune litigations that did not deserve to be on the court calendar in the first place. A senior citizen, for example, sued a Local Utility Enterprise for 19 Kčs (*Koruna*)— about one dollar and twenty cents at the tourist rate of exchange. The plaintiff, an elderly woman living in the home for the retired and exempt from court fees, presented a claim for an overcharged electricity bill, dating back several years. When I took over the case, a considerable number of witnesses had been heard, none of them supporting the plaintiff's allegations. Yet the old lady was indefatigable, requesting the testimonies of more and more people who, as it turned out, had no idea of what on earth was going on. Compensation paid to the witnesses for travel expenses and lost income — all paid from the monies of the state — greatly exceeded the amount of the claim. Under the impact of the Ústí Challenge, I put the case on the calendar and dismissed it — not in a matter of minutes but in seconds. "In the opinion of the court the claim is a product of the imagination of an old person who, in her solitude, has nothing better to occupy herself with than pestering the authorities." Once so ruled, our plaintiff, who up to then had protested everything during the litigation, accepted the decision and did not appeal. The irksome case had been written off.

Sometimes it almost seemed as though the Ministry of Justice's prime concern was not so much with the actual record of our adjudication but rather with the way we reported it. Besides a monthly public activities notice, we also reported on the number and nature of cases pending and decided and had to wrestle with semi-annual and annual reports and a score of ad hoc statistical summaries. The Ministry was interested in everything, and in particular in the social class background of the litigants. The standard report accompanying each criminal case consisted of perhaps a hundred items, each to be filled in. It is not an exaggeration to state that occasionally a statistical data sheet required more effort than the trial itself. No matter how hard we tried, about every fifth report was returned by the Ministry for revision as incomplete.

The usefulness of data-gathering is not on trial here. The government was certainly justified in asking for information relating to the trends in criminal behavior and civil law disputes. My criticism is directed against the inflated proportions of this task, the undue paperwork and the emphasis on data of questionable relevance. According to one unflattering definition, statistics is an accurate account of inaccurate information. The air of unreality associated with the data we submitted was particularly obvious. The class warfare dogma asserted, for example, that in the process of building socialism, law-breaking by the toiling masses would decrease and deviant behavior would become the monopoly of the members of the deposed ruling class and their accomplices. The criminal law judge was caught in a dilemma: the dogma called for the punishment of class enemies, but those convicted by his bench were mainly of proletarian stock. Should Prague find out about this inconsistency, he might be accused of defective class consciousness, of aiding the enemies and of alienating the ruling class. The statistics, therefore, had to be engineered to make it appear as though members of the bourgeoisie and not of the proletariat had been punished. However, a mere re-classification of the clientele did not dispose of the problem. The Ministry could have noticed that the so-called bourgeois culprits were sentenced with the leniency reserved for proletarian wrongdoers — which is what they actually were.

The Supreme Court had warned the lower benches that identical crimes called for varying punishments in accordance with the socio-political classification of the defendants. Where a laborer would receive a suspended sentence, a bourgeois would not even be granted probation. Both the statistics and the punitive measures had to be adjusted to satisfy the dogma. With a worker on trial, the judge would find an excuse to re-classify him as a class enemy and would give a stiff penalty, proudly reporting to Prague the ideologically correct result.[2] Once again, dogma proved superior to reality.

The Ministry of Justice reached the zenith of its folly in 1959, when it ordered the "re-organization of production quotas." From then on, the entire spectrum of judicial activities was translated into norms, specifying hours and even minutes required for execution. Fortunately, I had not much time left to experience this innovation, which was to be abolished in the early sixties.

Tardiness in adjudication, with court calendars as clogged as those in America, can be seen as one extreme; our pattern of production norms represented the opposite unpalatable alternative. As far as I could observe, the majority of our judges — including the former proletarians — regarded the attempt to immitate the assembly line as an idle exercise. We did not benefit from it, nor did the public, nor did "Justice" — which, after all, is what the whole thing was supposed to be about.

1. Just as they were in some research institutes, hospitals and clinics, producing the lamentable picture of a noted surgeon chasing the clock to perform an operation the government would then eventually brag about to the world. The time cards, however, were impractical and not enforceable at the smaller courts with only a handful of staff and at a comfortable distance from the superior controlling authority.

2. Opportunities for re-classifying a proletarian defendant into a bourgeois were unlimited: an unfavorable report from his employer or the Local People's Committee; a second cousin who defected to the West; a grandmother-in-law who owned a candy store at the time of Emperor Franz Josef—these all would do.

5 EXTRACURRICULAR OBLIGATIONS

The criteria that determined a Czech judge's competence and his chances for political survival bore some resemblance to those for the typical American college faculty. While hired for one activity, his success depended on another. The capitalist pedagogue had better publish; a Communist judge had to demonstrate "public engagement."

These engagements were manifold. First, in order to redeem ourselves from the stigma of belonging to the quasi-parasitic intelligentsia, we had to strive to acquire a reputation for "positive attitude toward manual labor." Recognition of such an attitude was an indispensable part of one's dossier. When, for example, in an economy drive the Plzeň court dismissed a stoker, the judges took over the job of stoking the boiler themselves. The more coal they shoveled, the brighter glowed their future and the more illustrious became their dossiers. As a rule, however, political muscle-building was a spare time activity and took place outside office hours. Clumsy bureaucrats could be seen in the evenings and on weekends collecting and cleaning used bricks, digging ditches for purposes not always specified, or tearing down dilapidated buildings. A Marxist will agree that destruction must precede construction; in this sense we were not good Marxists, because I am afraid we were wreckers rather than builders. My only contribution to constructive work involved the sewage link between the municipal swimming pool and the bridge at Stříbro and the improvement of the sport stadium.

The often useless exercises were generally disliked even by those who admitted that occasional manual diversion was beneficial to one's health. In the first years of the Communist regime the most popular method of avoiding open air participation was a medical certificate prohibiting undue physical exertion. Gradually, however, the statements of somatic misery became too commonplace and their terms so inflated as to impugn their credibility. As the basic rule of dialectic materialism states, accumulated quantity brings about a change in quality. Thus my collection of alleged illnesses, assembled over the years, testifying to a heart condition, suspected epilepsy, suspected Parkinson's disease and some other maladies, only resulted in convincing the authorities that I was in perfect physical condition.

The last time I called for the help of a medical certificate was on May 1, 1956, and it did not work. Two volunteers were required to carry flags in a parade of the judicial personnel. No one volunteered. I was equipped with a medical report (not a forgery but a genuine phony certificate supplied by a friendly physician) testifying to my inability to lift heavy objects. A flag pole certainly qualified under this category. It was to no avail. The Party organizer, also sporting a certificate, assigned the two youngest members to the honor. I was one of the two. I did benefit, however, in that I carried the Czech flag, while the other junior judge, with no document, had to sweat under the burden of the Soviet banner.

The ailing collectivized agriculture necessitated regular help from the townspeople. This assistance was called, for reasons unknown, a "brigade" (brigáda). From the point of view of our superiors, any prolonged period of brigáda work served the additional purpose of helping them to unearth our genuine political attitudes, which in normal times were securely hidden by a thick layer of caution and the Bolshevik jargon. It was quite possible to learn more about an individual's real feeling concerning the new society while he was struggling with mud and manure than over years of detached office contacts.

The brigade came in handy for other reasons. Perhaps it was a coincidence, but in the last days of October, 1956, at the high point of the Hungarian revolution, most of the court personnel at Plzeň was evacuated and sent to dig potatoes at the *Rudá záře* ("Red Glow") kolkhoz at Pernarec.[1.] Only the most trusted Party members were left behind, were issued pistols and ordered not to leave the court, day or night. The stay at Pernarec—which at that time was honored as an exemplary kolkhoz—exposed me once more to the sad reality of collectivization. The most revealing aspect of this experience was the utter lack of interest shown by the farmers in their work. For example, we had been collecting potatoes all of one day, and by six in the evening were about ready to return with the harvest safely loaded on the trucks. We left, but the potatoes stayed. "Why?" I asked. "You can't leave them here overnight. They'll freeze and be ruined and all our work will have been for nothing." "We know," was the cheerful reply, "but don't forget, comrade, it's already six o'clock." As expected, frost destroyed the loaded crop. The next day the same experience was repeated.

Our assistance to collectivized agriculture was also supposed to be spiritual: to inoculate the peasants with enthusiasm for the socialist cause. The Party District Secretaries, under criticism by the higher echelons for lagging collectivization in some areas, decided to assign stubborn villages still opposing "the socialist mode of farming" to assorted professional groups. Representatives of the latter had to pledge that within a fixed term in their assigned village a kolkhoz would be established, or they would be held responsible for the consequences. Our court at Stříbro, along with the local branch of the State Bank, shared the responsibility for persuading the peasants at Radějovice to give up private farming. Before I could be drawn into the "Operation Persuasion," it had been accomplished, thanks to an indefatigable pair of missionaries, bank manager comrade Štěpánek and criminal law judge Lev Tanzer. Tanzer subsequently explained his success at a conference of fellow judges in the following terms: "Comrades, I simply came to the village, went to the first household and announced, 'Here I am, my name is Tanzer and I am your judge. I am here to convince you about the advantages of socialist agriculture and of its superiority over private farming. I shall not leave this room until you sign up voluntarily for membership of the kolkhoz.' The persuasion campaign was a total success."[2.]

Crash programs and the overcommitment of resources—those perennial twin maladies of the System—obligated us to be a corps of versatile Socialist shock troops. Detached professionals in the morning, ardent pea-pickers after lunch. On the one hand I was responsible for the court's production quotas and for the swiftness of its proceedings, but at the same time I was also held accountable for the wheat harvest. The race for top priority did not always turn out to my liking. "Comrade Secretary," I admonished, "you want four people, and that is all I have available today, and there are five trials scheduled. Litigants have been summoned, the people's judges are here, and the hall is full of waiting witnesses. I just can't close up shop." "You certainly can. Cancel everything. That is my last word." I cancelled. Scores of people were annoyed, the witnesses and lay assessors were reimbursed out of court funds, a total sum at least several times the value of our output that day in the fields.

Our only consolation was our awareness that the refusal to comply with the demands of local Stalins was impossible. Requests from other sources were more irritating. They came from zealots bent on proving that pestering one's fellow citizens was not the monopoly of the Party. One such gentleman was the local high school principal, Antonín Macháček. Head of the school in Stříbro, he had suffered a mild heart attack. After his return from the hospital, equipped with a certificate exempting him from all manual work, he informed the staff that they had volunteered to demolish and rebuild a stable at the Otročín collective. The teachers had to spend their next twenty weekends on this project. The courage to protest against this deprivation of free time for almost five months was missing. One brave soul, however, did point out that none of the pedagogues was an architect, which fact, perhaps, might have some relevance. This assertion Macháček brushed contemptuously aside, reminding his audience, "For a Communist nothing is impossible,"—a proposition precluding all debate. So the teachers labored at Otročín. Not without accidents, they managed to demolish the old building just in time to learn that the project had been called off as impractical. Notwithstanding this, Macháček acquired such a reputation as a man who really cared about the well-being of socialized agriculture that my nominal boss Lev Tanzer began to envy him. Inevitably, Tanzer, too, suggested that we build (i.e., destroy) a stable. Luckily for us, the idea coincided with Tanzer's sudden purge—an incident to be described later— and after his dismissal the project was quickly forgotten.

Another extracurricular responsibility was public lecturing.

The quota varied from two to four performances a month, mainly sponsored by the "Society for the Dissemination of Political and Scientific Knowledge" better known as the "Society with the Long Title." Characteristically, the lectures became bureaucratized, standardized and constrained. The speaker first had to present the so-called "delegate's authorization form" to the representative of the audience. In most cases this would be the Chairman of the Local People's Committee, who then inserted the following information: date, name of lecturer, topic, number in audience, extent of audience participation, duration of proceedings, evaluation of the lecture ("political-educational impact on the masses") and any additional comment which occurred to him. This report was then submitted both to the Society with the Long Title and to the Regional Court Administration for their evaluation, to satisfy their statistical cravings and to engage in the favorite game of socialist competition with other districts and provinces.

The data were largely imaginary. For example, I arrived at the village of Holostřevy to lecture to the peasants about the virtues of the socialist family. The talk was scheduled in the local inn. Though the place was packed to capacity, the only two persons attracted there by me and not by alcohol were the Chairman of the village Soviet and his Secretary. Unable to entice the crowd, we decided to join them, and between drinks the Chairman filled out the report, approximately as follows: Talk—43 minutes; 32 persons attended; 18 comments from among the audience; the lecture fulfilled its purpose and it helped us to understand . . . etc. The figures were to a greater or lesser degree *always* engineered, though usually not as blatantly as in this village.

There was also an attempt to recruit me as a lecturer promoting "scientific atheism," a suggestion I flatly rejected, pointing out the injury suffered recently by an advocate of such a cause. Somewhat surprisingly the assailant had been the Chairman of the local Communist Party cell, who had accompanied his violent response with these words: "Christ was the first Communist, and I will not permit anyone to speak to our comrades opposing religion!" In the light of this charming incident, my objection was accepted as perfectly legitimate.

It is not my intention to imply that campaigns aimed at "enlightening the masses" were doomed to failure. Putting aside their political orientation, the fault was not so much with the lectures but with the demands they made on time. Not only the

courts, but also Czechoslovak-Soviet Friendship Society, other
friendship groups, Defenders of the Peace, local Soviets, the Communist Party itself, agricultural and dozens of other groups tried
their best to rob the people of all their spare time. Frequently I
arrived at the village brandishing my "delegate's authorization"
only to find that in the room reserved for the talk were one, two or
more representatives of different causes all scheduled to speak and
arguing about the merits of their prepared messages. Attendance
was understood as a civic duty, as evidence of political maturity,
and thus it was imperative for the public *not always* to stay away.

Anyone with any stake in the society had to be "involved."
Most of the functions were purely formal. The more formal and
imaginary the function, the more it was sought after. In the early
years of Communist rule, a reluctant functionary could take advantage of his dual loyalty to both the place of employment and
the place of residence. A prudent citizen, if asked by his employer
to accept the function of a collector of "voluntary" contributions for
the Korean orphans, would inform him, happily, that this honor had
already been bestowed upon him by the local Soviet at his place of
domicile. If, on the other hand, comrades from his neighborhood
were the first to offer him the distinction, they were told about
his heavy political involvement at the office (factory, school, etc.).
I benefitted from such inexactitudes for almost ten years, but by
1958, we had to report on all the functions held and degree of our
participation in them. Thus, in addition to my vice-chairmanship
in the Society with the Long Title, I had to shop around for roles
that did not require too much of my time, could not be easily
controlled, and would sound impressive to the superiors. After a
great deal of deliberation I chose a seat at the District Committee
of the Defenders of the Peace—a purely nominal body serving
mainly to provide a livelihood for the most incompetent and
otherwise unemployable Party devotees. I also accepted the chairmanship of the chapter of the Czechoslovak-Soviet Friendship
Society at court. I decided on this job because of the rumor—
which turned out to be false—that functionaries in this organization would have a priority right to travel to the West. My remaining function was on the Committee for the Solution of the Gypsy
Question. In the opinion of the Regional Court Administration I
did not rate too highly. It was assumed, though nowhere specified,
that the right number of functions a good judge should perform
was seven—and I had only four.

Since the multiplication of "involvements" could not be accompanied by an equivalent extension of the number of hours in a day, a functionary, including those who took their tasks seriously, had to compromise on attendance, frequency of participation, and the overall degree of activism. Experience taught me that it was prudent to attend every other meeting and not to miss more than three times in a row. If the by-laws or custom called for checking the attendance before and after each meeting, one would plead for the abolishment of the second check, emphasizing that such a stringent rule was offensive to the spirit of spontaneity and voluntarism of the participants. With the practice of one signature only, the citizen could sign in and then quickly disappear to preserve some free time for himself.

Functioneering was a dull, time-consuming routine, an organizational *l'art pour l'artism* a mere incantation of phrases. But functions like death and taxes were inevitable and inescapable save for those in prison, and even there the inmates were expected occasionally to get "involved." As the saying goes, Prussia starved herself into greatness. We, accordingly, tried to talk ourselves into socialism.

1. A more plausible explanation may have been that the Party remained sensitive to the events of June, 1953; in Plzeň, as described in Part Two.

2. Tanzer's story was not quite a masterpiece of objective reporting. The villagers surrendered under the impact of various pressures. Punitive taxation by itself played a greater role than the judge's evangelic fervor.

6 HOW THE SYSTEM PAYS

If salary alone were the criterion, the Czechoslovak judge would, at best, be only a marginal member of the elite. As is true of all societies, there are other factors besides income which determine one's social standing. With totalitarianism, influence, access to those in power, the infinite web of nepotism and mutual favoritism outweighed a fat bank account. One did not have to worry about purchasing a car or a villa if these could be *issued* to him. Citizen A., who could afford a vacation abroad, would be obliged to remain at home if the secret police did not approve the trip. His airplane seat would be taken by B., less affluent but more trusted; or even better, by C., who would enjoy the sea resort at the State's expense. It was not income but patience and influence which made the National Health Service available. In 1957 I went to the Plzeň University Hospital as an anonymous patient, waiting my turn along with the rest of the toiling masses. After we had wasted about six hours, during which time no physician appeared, a nurse sent us away, telling us to return the following day. Benefitting from this experience, I called up a friend, and in no time a comrade professor and two assistants were in attendance upon the provincial V.I.P.

I suppose that some form of mild corruption will always take place where goods are scarce and services miserable. Whatever the reason, in Czechoslovakia the consensus so condoned the use or abuse of one's "power and connections" that it was difficult to draw the line between necessary cleverness and outright corruption. It is a truism to state that the more sensitive one's political position the less chance one had of keeping it until retirement. The resulting sense of insecurity, however, was offset by day-to-day advantages which went with the job. Everywhere one had "friends" eager to assure themselves a credit balance for services rendered. These people repaired cars and plumbing, traded goods in short supply, operated state laundries, or were members of Regional Abortion Commissions. While judges as a group were the beneficiaries of a variety of favoritism, instances of their accepting outright bribes were almost non-existent. The only certain exception I know of involved a high-living judge in the District Court of Aš, who was sentenced to ten years. In another case, Judge R.K. was also convicted, but I have good reason to believe he was the victim of a frame-up.

The salary scale of judges was only slightly above the national average. A miner, a laborer in a foundry, a bus driver and other skilled workers enjoyed higher incomes. Once I talked with Dr. Štěpanovský, a relatively important official of the Ministry of Foreign Affairs, about this peculiar arrangement. He said, "In Poland the professionals are well paid because there aren't enough of them. In East Germany, the intelligentsia are well paid so that they won't defect to the West [this conversation took place before the building of the Berlin Wall]. In our country we have got more of these people than we sometimes need and there is no way for them to escape. This is your explanation."

To this essentially accurate assessment one should add, first, the Justice Ministry's lack of interest in promoting the salaries of the judicial personnel, and second, the feeling of guilt and inferiority imposed upon us in the latter years of Stalinism. "It is the worker, the manual laborer, who produces and who creates values. You do not contribute. Though you are still a necessary part of the state structure this does not prevent you from being the somewhat parasitic elements in society." This was the reasoning, more implicit than explicit, of the Party functionaries who naturally never doubted their own usefulness. The apparatchiki also did not fail to mention that in prewar Czechoslovakia, the judiciary had been overpaid by their bourgeois masters, and the socialist austerity offered them the opportunity to redeem the stigma of past opulence. This policy, of course, victimized all judicial personnel irrespective of age or class origin.

My first monthly salary as an Assistant Judge netted 789 Kčs —probably an all-time low for a university graduate in the country. After my promotion to full Judge in 1956, the salary was set at 1,750 Kčs, within the scale of district civil law judges (1,620- 1,780). Judges on the appellate court received between 2,000 to 2,500 Kčs. Had I left school at fifteen and trained to become a machinist, I would have been earning at least as much as any judge before leaving my teens.

Until 1957, a judge's income was controlled by the Ministry. With the transformation of the judges from appointed to elected officials, the authority over salary matters was decentralized. The Regional Court Administration was allotted a lump sum and, within broad guidelines, was free to decide the rate of judicial compensation. Income was supposed to fluctuate according both to the quality and the quantity of the adjudication and the degree of one's involvement in political life. This approach generated a considerable amount of animosity within our ranks. Everyone felt, justly or not, that he was being underpaid. Each demanded an increase, but since the Regional Administration operated on a definite budget, it could—and did—raise the salary of Judge A. only by cutting the income of Judge B.

There was only one source of extra money available to the Administration, in view of the way the social security system operated. In case of illness, health security benefits were paid from Trade Union funds and not from the budgeted accounts. Thus illness left the Regional Administration with a surplus of money earmarked for the absentee, but not actually expended. Money accumulated in this way during the year was distributed as bonuses to deserving comrades on the occasion of Czechoslovak festival days, such as the anniversary of the 1917 Bolshevik revolution. The districts, as ordered, nominated their candidates for the rewards, but their recommendations were almost invariably ignored by the Administration, which would go on to select candidates of its own choosing.

Low judicial salaries were partly due to the indifference of the Minister of Justice, whose method of work could be illustrated by a campaign in 1956. As in other countries, the judge used to deliver his written opinion some time after he had given his verbal verdict in court. However, Minister of Justice Václav Škoda decided that this was a bad practice. First, he reasoned, the written opinion was drafted in the solitude of the judge's office, leaving the lay assessors with no say as to its contents. Second, according to Škoda, the educational impact upon the participant in the verdict was impeded by the fact that the oral statement was not immediately followed by the distribution of a typed opinion. From this Škoda concluded that after the court reached its decision, the judges should collectively compose the written opinion then and there, which the presiding judge would deliver simultaneously with his verbal presentation. Only in extraordinarily complex cases would this innovation not apply, and the judge be left to draft the opinion in the tranquility of his office. The Ministry decided to award 1,000 Kčs to whoever of the judges would volunteer to implement this new, progressive, socialist form of judicial procedure.

The reaction among the judges to this proposal—which within a year turned from a "suggestion" into a required practice—was generally negative. It was unrealistic to expect that the opinion could be the product of teamwork between the jurist and two laymen. For a great number of the people's judges, signing the voting protocol was the apex of their literary accomplishments. Also, not every professional judge was an outstanding stylist, able to dictate extemporaneously to his clerk an opinion faultless in form and substance. His judicial reasoning and evaluation of evidence had, after all, to survive the scrutiny of the Appeal Court. Even if one were endowed with such felicity, its employment would take time. Under the old practice the parties had to wait for the decision an average of ten to fifteen minutes (i.e., time for a cigarette and for the judge to inform his lay colleagues of "their" decision); the new mode à la Škoda required hours of waiting. The legal counsellors in particular did not enjoy spending their time freezing in the unheated corridors.

Despite these objections, which in time proved their validity, a handful of judges, myself included, volunteered to try the new method. Škoda congratulated us on our understanding of the "new methods of work" (also one of the beloved phrases of the System) and added that the Regional Courts had been authorized to present us with the promised 1,000 Kčs. Škoda knew, and we knew, that the Regional Courts had no spare funds to pay us.

In the late fifties the Ministry of Justice, reflecting the

current policy of the regime, instituted a campaign that could be described as "economy at all costs." In the past when I needed a pen, a pencil, or stationary, I went to the secretary, picked up these bureaucratic necessities, and that was the end of it. From 1958 onwards, however, each new pen, pencil and other paraphernalia I needed required my signature in quadruplicate. These "documents" were then gathered in Plzeň (a task which called for one extra full-time employee) and forwarded to Prague (no doubt to occupy a number of supplementary staff). We estimated that if all the judges stole all the office supplies they could get their hands on, the state would have lost about five times less money than it had to spend on the salaries of the administrators in charge of this new measure.

Our complaints about inadequate salaries and rigid budgeting led nowhere—that is to say, they did not reach farther than the Regional Court. The sympathetic Adam Pittner used to give us advice somewhat at odds with the presumption of monolithic unity and totalitarian consensus and rather reminiscent of a pluralistic society. He would say: "Comrades, you are not living in a vacuum. You know people, and some of them are important. Plead your cause. These outside pressures may help." They did not. It was after all, asking a lot of any public, especially one having to live under a somewhat dubious system of justice, to get excited about the well-being of its practitioners.

7 THE JUDGE AND THE APPARATCHIKI

Only the insiders knew for sure whether or not the Party ran the courts. There was neither total independence nor unqualified subordination. The practice of the apparatchiki varied from leaving the judges entirely alone to drafting verdicts in the Party Secretariats. In about ninety per cent of the court agenda there was not the slightest sign of interference in our decision-making. This observation, however, does not warrant the conclusion that some sort of "ninety per cent judicial independence and integrity" existed. Both the sorry experience with the remaining ten per cent and the awareness that someone might at any time inflict his "suggestion" upon us, conditioned *all* our adjudication. One had to distinguish between "hints" and "orders." One had to weigh the importance of the interfering apparatchik against the issue involved. The judge confronted with the dictates of the Party was circumscribed by a number of variables, notably those of time, place and personalities. Also, the impact of sheer force of circumstances had to be taken into account. The fluidity of the relationship between the Party and the court was accentuated by the absence of any specific written rules that would spell out the subordination of the judge to the Party Secretary. Nevertheless, the law made the judges responsible to the "spirit of the people's

democracy"—or, later, to the "spirit of socialism." The interpreter
of the spirit—and indeed the spirit itself—remained the Party.

While the main factors that determined the intensity and
frequency of the Party pressure were rather unstable, there was
at least one fairly constant element—physical limits. As pointed
out earlier, the number of hours in a day made for a conflict between the appetites and the digestive capacities of the would-be
supervisors. The means available to them were ludicrously inadequate to the enormity of the task. Battalions of apparatchiki
will always fall short of their ideal goal of total control over the
myriad facets of life. This limitation compelled them to decide
among priorities, and the judiciary, fortunately, did not rate at
the top of their attention. From time to time, the promotion of
such causes as atheism or the harvesting of hops were of greater
urgency. Periodically, however, the Party would drum up a particular issue within the realm of the judiciary, such as the
liquidation of kulaks, or pilferage of socialist property, or such
"anti-social acts" as alcoholism.

Stalinist doctrine dictates that any trial, including the most
innocuous civil litigation, should be regarded as a political affair,
justifying scrutiny by Party bureaucrats of any item on the court
calendar. Not unexpectedly, however, the apparatchiki meddled
mainly in anti-state crimes. The Party also reserved the final say
on capital punishment in general criminal cases.

This interference was explained—if it was explained at all—
more or less euphemistically in terms of the "higher interest of the
toiling masses." At times its application strained credulity. What
possible "higher interest" was involved in the following case related
to me by a Supreme Court Justice in 1959? A deranged mother
in Eastern Slovakia had murdered her daughter, dismembered the
corpse and buried the remains in the cellar. The court-appointed
psychiatrists examined the defendant and testified that she was
incapable of grasping the meaning of her action. She claimed that
"nasty tiny devils" had visited her nightly and had ordered her to
butcher the child. Despite pressure from the Party officials, the
court refused to disregard the findings of the medical experts and
ordered the defendant confined to a mental institution. The Party,
however, did not give up; the Prosecutor was forced to appeal the
verdict, and the Court of Appeals, surrendering to political pressure, condemned the deluded murderess to death. The sentence
was carried out.

The degree of Party interference tended to fluctuate with the seasons. The leadership utilized the "scientific method of dialectics" as a means of avoiding their own responsibilities. Dialectics exculpated inconsistency. Life, according to the Writ, consisted of "phases." A phase of severity followed a period of moderation, and so on. If the Party promised lower prices and the prices went up, the housewives would be told that the surprise development was due to the advent of a new phase and not, as someone might think, of duplicity or inefficiency. The Party also employed dialectics in dealing with the judiciary. We, too, were subject to phases.

Experience taught a judge that defiance of an apparatchik's "recommendation" was a health hazard. Yet, in 1956, after Khrushchev's secret speech at the Twentieth Congress, our good Party attacked compliant judges for "excessive responsiveness to local pressures." If we did not "respond" prior to 1956, that was the end of us. If we had responded, the Party, bursting with indignation, now informed us of our unscrupulous, unprincipled, detestable nature.

These sermons on judicial morality were held simultaneously in all provinces. At the one I attended the representative from the Regional Party Committee in Plzeň barked at us about our lack of personal honesty. Significantly, no one in the audience dared to suggest that the Party, too, was "co-guilty of the shortcomings." Nevertheless, it was my great pleasure to observe the expression on the faces of those with the most cooperative records.

The magic of dialectics did not die out in 1956. What was true that year vanished into oblivion the next. By 1958, my colleague H. was swiftly purged for not being at all responsive, i.e., for indulging in behavior inappropriate until 1955, laudable in 1956, but reprehensible again two years later.

The Party's desires were usually transmitted to the judiciary informally. The Secretary of the District or Regional Committee would "suggest," "advise," or "plead for understanding," rather than "order." The distinction between the two alternatives, however, was often lost, since disregard of a "suggestion" brought retribution almost equal to the punishment inflicted upon those refusing to obey an order on the battlefield. Given the lack of any set procedure or recognized chain of command between the Party and the judiciary, the personal relationship between the apparatchik who urged and the person who was urged was of major importance.

Generally speaking, no one could earn the permanent good will of the Party. Some, notably the prewar judges, could only hope to achieve a temporary deferment of their purges. The Secretary, in dealing with a person handicapped forever by his bourgeois past, would make it very plain that compliance was the currency with which he could purchase a further lease of life. The prewar jurists were most vulnerable and, therefore, most compliant. At my court, when the Party sneezed, the ex-bourgeois judge Tanzer felt it politic to suffer pneumonia. When, at the same court, Tanzer's successor, proletarian Josef Kugl, was visited by an interfering low-rank apparatchik, the judge felt no qualms in literally kicking the intruder out of the office.

Some of the lowly officials of the Party could be thwarted without a great deal of sophistication or courage. For example in Plzeň, in 1956, I presided over the damages suit of State Bakeries against the former manager. The defendant, it was claimed, had mishandled the entrusted funds. Though she was contractually liable for all losses, it was far from certain that she had stolen anything from her employer. The store she had managed was located on the busiest street (at that time still named after Stalin), the daily receipts had run high, and her entire staff was an uncontrollable collection of dubious honesty. After the first hearing was adjourned and I was about to leave the court room, a husky, tall fellow approached me, saying: "I am the husband of the defendant and I am also a member of the Regional Party Secretariat. My wife is no crook, and I am just reminding you that I am from the Party apparatus. I don't wish to threaten you but only warn, that's all."

It was the first time I have been exposed to such overt, crude pressure. Thinking the matter over, I went to the office of my immediate superior, the PŠP man Miroslav Tlapák, and told him what had happened. Tlapák, a touchy, conceited fellow, lent a responsive ear. Because of this attempt to intimidate one of his subordinates, he himself felt humiliated and decided that it was necessary to respond in kind. The clumsy, interfering husband (actually a nobody in the Party regional apparatus) lost, thanks to the proletarian judge's imagined challenge to his prestige. It is far from certain, however, that the outcome would have been the same if the judge involved had been one of the ill-starred pre-war generation.

On one occasion in the late fifties I attended the funeral of František Houdek, a people's judge, a respected Party member and a dear friend of mine. One of the cars the Establishment had made available for the mourners was occupied by the head of the Department of Education of the District People's Committee, Miroslav Juda. It was suggested that I share the car with him. During the ride, Juda brought up the following subject: "Mrs. Cvrková is suing her husband for alimony at your court. I urge you to decide in her favor." Juda, I think, did not really mean what he said. But once he said it, I had to respond in kind. "Comrade Juda, I am appalled. You have just violated the Constitution and several laws I could think of. You are attempting to corrupt my independent judicial judgment." Juda belatedly recognized that his strategy was off key. His Party standing was clearly not sufficient to intimidate me. Mrs. Cvrková, in fact, had no case with or without Juda. Even supposing a favorable verdict, however, Antonín Novotný himself would have been incapable of seeing the claim through to the satisfaction of the plaintiff; the aged, ailing husband was hopelessly indigent.

Since Juda tried hard in 1957 to have me fired, I was not entirely unhappy to play a small part in his eventual purge. When his position with the Party became shaky, my description of what had happened on the way to the funeral seems to have hastened his downfall.

Though centralism and uniformity ranked among the outstanding features of totalitarianism, I was not the first or the last citizen of a Communist country to suspect that the state functioned as a confederation of miniscule principalities run by local despots. Such an observation was unlikely to occur to the man in the street but was not unfamiliar to those who constituted the Establishment on the local level. Anyone in my position, or a comparable one, could feel the imprint of the person currently in charge of the nearest Party Secretariat. In some of the provinces the degree of Party intervention in judicial work was markedly more profound and more consistent than in other areas. More than that, even within each province there were so-called "soft districts" as opposed to the "hard districts," depending upon the temperament of the apparatchiki in residence. Within our province, the Party bureaucrats in the district of Blatná were particularly nosy. When, for example, the manager of the Tractor Station there drove a car while intoxicated and caused considerable damage, pressure from the Secretariat forced the prosecutor to shelve the charge. When, again in the same district, two potentates were accused of drunkenness and homosexuality, the Secretariat suppressed the indictment. A prosecutor assigned to Blatná was pitied by his colleagues, while my appointment to Stříbro brought relief to me and congratulations from my friends. I was told that I was entering a world of "reasonable comrades."

Among the many means employed in the search for harmony in the provinces, at least three deserved mention. First, there were numerous interdepartmental conferences attended by the representatives from courts, prosecutor's offices, People's Committees, Party Secretariats and the police. At such gatherings the participants not only learned about the current Party line, but also had the opportunity to air their grievances and discontents with "other comrades." Occasionally, even the Minister of Justice, the Minister of the Interior, and some other prominent personality from the Party Central Committee would be present.

A second device for reducing the area of potential conflict between the judges and the apparatchiki in the districts was the practice of reporting to the Regional Court pending court cases, both criminal and civil, which might prove politically sensitive. We in the field rather welcomed this innovation. If we were dutiful in our reporting, it offered us a certain shield of security from ex post facto charges that our verdicts were stabs in the back to the Party's interest.

A third frequently employed and effective method by which the judiciary avoided open conflict with the Party was to arrange the transfer of touchy cases from one court to another out of reach of the interfering local potentates. The chairman of the Regional Court might also arrange the transfer of a pending litigation to another district as a preventive measure of broader political implication. A case in point which I well remember involved the Secret Police Officer Němec, married and the father of two. Němec had been shifted from Plzeň to take over the command of a remote outpost, leaving his family behind. In the place of his new assignment he became acquainted with the District Prosecutor, Miss Válková, a spinster whose main physical distinction was a magnificent display of acne. Against all logic, the good looking and seemingly intelligent officer fell in love and impregnated this "guardian of socialist legality." Moreover, he proudly acknowledged his fatherhood of the child and insisted on divorce—to the great embarrassment of the Establishment and to the glee of the more malicious elements of the informed public. Not even the threats of the provincial secret police commander, Lt. Col. Jindřich, succeeded in dissuading Němec from petitioning for a divorce. Not to aggravate the circumstances of this unfortunate affair, the Regional Court and the Party agreed that the case be shifted to the neutral territory of my court at Stříbro, where the participants were not known.

In this case the change of venue was easy to understand. But sometimes we received a suit from outside for reasons which were unfathomable. Take, for instance, a claim of alleged injury from Tachov. In Tachov, Stříbro's neighboring district, an old woman accused the local physician of malpractice. She claimed that negligent treatment had led to the paralysis of her arm. The contents of the file provided me with no clue as to why this suit should be extraordinary in any respect. Soon after I took over the case, the Chairman of the Regional Court, Adam Pittner, called me up, inquiring about the date of the hearing and advising me to handle the trial with the utmost care. He neither elaborated on the reasons for his interest nor said anything that might be read as an infraction of my judicial independence. During the subsequent proceedings, which were attended by Pittner and two unidentified apparatchiki from Plzeň, it was proved beyond a shadow of a doubt that the claim was without any merits. The case was swiftly dismissed. After the trial I had a talk with Pittner and the two taciturn Party bureaucrats (who did not bother to introduce themselves). Significantly, not one word was uttered about the trial. After the exchange of a few meaningless pleasantries they left as they had come, and I never found out why three potentates had driven all the way there and wasted half of the day because of a trivial, unsubstantiated claim of an obscure misanthrope.

De-Stalinization in Czechoslovakia followed a somewhat zigzag path. At the same time that we were denouncing the great despot for his fondness for violating socialist legality, our Ministry of Justice confronted us with the following policy: each week, the judges, along with the prosecutor and the commanding police officer, were to gather at the District Party Headquarters to discuss with the First Secretary the "area problematics of socialist

legality." In other words, the new line called for the institution-
alization of the Party's primacy over judicial affairs—the only such
attempt made that I know of.

During these meetings ("consultations"), which I attended
for almost two years, the initial discussion usually dealt in general
terms with local issues troubling the district, such as alcoholism,
traffic accidents involving tractor drivers, failure to fulfill the
delivery quotas of agricultural products, and the like. Invariably,
however, instead of discussing general issues, individual cases pending at court came up. It was at these meetings that decisions were
made on conducting trials "before organized public," better known
as show trials. At these weekly gatherings the Secretary occasionally also "transmitted the desire of the Party" on how individual cases, both criminal and civil, were to be decided.

As mentioned earlier, there were "hard" and "soft" districts
and I functioned in one of the latter. Vojtěch Horák, our burdened
First Secretary in Stříbro, was not interested in taking matters of
justice into his own hands. But as the periodical sessions went by,
Secretary Horák grew interested in judicial affairs to a degree not
to my liking. Fortunately for me, however, I discovered that Horák
was quite human in his frailties, allowing me to take advantage of
the situation. One day he called me up and wanted to know about
the divorce case Solařová versus Solař. He "suggested" that I
should report to his office, file in hand. In disregard of the law,
which prohibited the exposure of court files to outsiders, the independent judge ran to Horák with the requested papers. The
story of the Solař couple was ridiculous enough to be of interest
even to an overworked apparatchik. The case concerned a childless couple. The wife was an elementary school teacher; her
husband, formerly a candidate for the Catholic priesthood, held
a white collar job with the state railways. Both were members of
the Communist Party. At the court, and also in public, the husband complained that his oversized penis handicapped the pursuit of his matrimonial bliss and, in addition, his wife irritated him
by reading a book during their sexual intercourse. Perhaps this
was the reason why the First Secretary took such interest in judicial matters. At any rate, Horák liked the contents of the file very
much and expressed a wish to read more of the same genre.

Realizing that this local potentate's interest in sexual peccadil-
los could be helpful to me, from then on I continued to supply him
with materials relating to the bedroom antics of his charges. This

somewhat restricted fare tended to blunt Horák's revolutionary consciousness and to decrease his meddling in the rest of my court agenda. I shall refer to the one very unpleasant exception to this rule much later in this narrative.

The Party Secretaries, in their search for total control, were aided by a particular mentality that had also developed among the judges themselves. Responsiveness to the Party's wishes — expressed or only presumed — was not due solely to outright orders and pressures, but rather to our calculations and self-imposed controls. It was not so much the order to this or that that mattered, as the knowledge, feeling, or at least suspicion that our necks were at stake and that at any time someone might come and accuse us of "violation of socialist legality and aiding the class enemy." A few years of practice with totalitarianism taught us to react in the same way cows react toward an electrified fence. This preventive adjustment in our behavior made, in fact, total control unnecessary. In other words, our concern with survival, conditional to a large extent upon the state of mind of the First Secretary, molded our actions in such a way as to conform to the apparatchik's desiderata. Like a newsman who, living with censorship, becomes his own censor, the judge adjusted his actions to the anticipated response of the Party. Here, totalitarianism appears at its best. The judge becomes his own apparatchik. If there was anything certain in the relationship between the Party and the judiciary, it was the second fiddle we were holding with our sweating fingers.

8 THE ART OF MARX-MANSHIP

In the traditional world of bourgeois Central Europe, servility to superiors and arrogance towards subordinates were the preconditions for a successful and stable career. How simple, unexciting and enviable! The totalitarian metamorphosis complicated these matters beyond recognition. Among the definitions of "art" which Webster offers, the most applicable would be "the employment of means to accomplishment of some ends." Yet survival was not solely an affair requiring the participant's skill, artistry, imagination and adaptability. Too many unknowns had to be reckoned with. Say, for example, the mother-in-law of a careful citizen quarreled with her neighbor and broke his skull. Suppose the victim happened to have been a close friend of the local man in power. The careful citizen could find himself in grave trouble through no fault of his own. Or, suppose the government ordered a fifty per cent reduction of the white collar personnel in establishment X. This sudden, unpredicted and unpredictable action had to find its victims. The survival game had to be played not only by those indifferent or hostile to the regime, but also by its staunch adherents. The System treated with severity violators of the rules, whether they were infidels or true believers in the Cause.

The discussion which follows is based mainly on my experience

as a member of the judiciary during the nineteen-fifties, but it could
be quite fairly extended to include most other contemporary pro-
fessions. True, the judges, because of the political sensitivity of
their office, were more vulnerable than the average citizen. But,
on the other hand, individuals in many other walks of life had to
live with an equally shaky tenure and had to follow the rules of
the game with similar attention. Anyone with any stake in society
— a job, an apartment or a child in college — had to play the game.

Loyalty alone did not suffice as a means of survival. As mentioned earlier, superficial criteria determined political maturity.
The System placed a premium on correctness in manners, on right-
ness in sloganeering. Spontaneity, and thus sincerity, were posi-
tively dangerous. Also, good luck outweighed "good thought," and
it is not only my personal case that proves this point.

Apart from sheer luck, the foremost prerequisite of survival
was a sound understanding of human psychology. Unless a citizen
developed keen perceptions and an ability to penetrate through the
jargon to the real thoughts and values of his contemporaries, sooner
or later he would slip up, misjudge an opponent and occasion his
own downfall. For many people a useful way to acquire these skills
was through the game of chess. A diligent study and participation
in the game provided us with the ability to detect the strategy and
tactics, protective lies and potential double-crossings of our socialist brethren. In life, as in chess, it was recommended that one be
at least one move ahead of his partner. Perhaps it is no accident
that we Slavs are among the best chess players in the world.

Prudence recommended that one start from the premise that
all men were essentially unreliable and therefore could not be
trusted with anything. Then one proceeded through careful probing and testing to eliminate this presumption of wickedness.
Usually we had to stop somewhere in the middle of the road. The
risk involved ruled out magnanimity; one could not afford to give
the person under scrutiny any benefit of the doubt. Consequently,
we had a great number of acquaintances and very few true friends.
In an atomized — and demoralized — society, even the rare friend
was a potential liability. Though you finally decided to trust him,
you could never be entirely sure about the care with which he had
selected his *other* friends.

This may sound to the reader as a rather too conspiratorial
and perhaps even hysterical picture of totalitarian existence. Such
an impression may possibly be remedied by reference to the fact

that according to the best estimates available, one adult in twenty in Czechoslovakia worked (involuntarily, in most cases) as an informer for the secret police.[1] I knew of individuals who underwent irreparable trouble because of their failure to subject their would-be-friends to a thorough psychological X-ray. These casualties would hardly consider the foregoing caution unduly excessive.

The critical screening of one's fellow citizens was a two-way process. The task was not only to ascertain who *he* was but to prevent him from finding out who *you* were. This image-building required consistency and self-discipline. To repeat once more: form prevailed over content. One's overt performance — meticulous adherence to the manners, slogans and Party textbook values of the day — was what really mattered.

I have observed that after several years of practice in image-building, the actor takes pride in a faultless performance and still further delight in seeking to perfect it. It becomes a kind of a sport to ponder what constitutes just the right time to start and end one's contribution to the rhythmical applause at a public meeting; how loudly and with what fervor to sing the Internationale; when to introduce one's meaningless comments to the gathering of comrades, and so forth.

Let us imagine two strangers, both equally adjusted to the rules of the game, who happen to meet, and "open a discussion." What develops is a verbal exercise about nothing, with just the right amount of political prose on both sides and with a few carefully planted traps to probe each other out. An outsider or a layman in totalitarian behavior would hardly appreciate the delight of a perfect performance in such a situation when one had discovered some flaws in the opponent without revealing a jot or tittle of one's true self. A strange political *l'art pour l'artism*, indeed. This preoccupation with form, this need to probe, obscured the real issue — loyalty to the regime — until it became almost irrelevant.

Suspension of one's role in bed with a mistress, for example, was not advisable. Other good actors shattered their images because of alcohol. We used to consume vast quantities of wine and hard liquor, but even when one's body had collapsed under the load, "the loyal mind" had to function to the very last conscious second.

This sort of mind, naturally, had to be trained. I had a particularly difficult problem because of my habit of talking rather loudly in my sleep. An uncontrolled tongue could only invite disaster when one had to participate in agricultural "brigades," live among forest workers and spend nights in one room with other comrades. With the reader's indulgence I would like to claim that I managed to train myself to experience loyal dreams and emit safe cries from my mattress. I do not know whether the experts in the field would accept or refute the possibility of this subconscious self-discipline, but at any rate, it worked for me.

A helpful and easy device in building a correct image was to become involved in a non-political though officially supported cause. It was useful to acquire the right kind of hobby — not that of a stamp collector, which was too individualistic, and certainly not gliding, because one might be suspected of entertaining the idea of flying away (as some did). But if, for instance, one played soccer— a healthy and politically harmless game — he proved that he was no ivory tower intellectual who shrank from contact with the toiling masses. More importantly, however, the Party would assume that one's preoccupation with his hobby reduced the danger that he would concern himself with undesirable thoughts or actions. As one Catholic priest confided to me, "I am now a big fisherman. Now that I am participating in this approved folksy activity, the Party is much less suspicious about my spreading the gospel of God." However, not all sports would do. Tennis had not yet been cleared of its bourgeois associations, though table tennis was considered to have an unimpeachable proletarian ancestry. In contrast to the decadence of golf, volleyball was held to be the epitome of socialist recreation and was the standard choice for what was aptly identified as "organized relaxation."

A good, consistently successful actor tended to become overly confident and might tempt the hand of fate. Any indulgence in double talk, innuendo or irony was playing with fire. It was very difficult on occasions to resist the temptation to smuggle some slight irony into court decisions. What often happened was that the joker, after initial successes, began to underestimate the adversary. The latter, suspecting the joker of stepping out of line, feigned ignorance and thus encouraged further folly. Before long the joke was on the joker.

Another risky enterprise was the attempt to play off one part of the System against another. For example, Tanzer, a prewar lawyer and a Party member, was also an active functionary in the minute surviving Jewish community — an agnostic during office hours and a religious man the rest of the time. Malicious voices even claimed that Tanzer was such an obnoxious character that the Germans had refused to put him in a concentration camp. This was a rather macabre allegation, but after knowing him for years, I was prepared to believe anything. Tanzer, the most mediocre of lawyers, a clumsy and transparent actor, outlived skillful performers. Tanzer developed the habit of visiting, uninvited, the District Party Secretariat and demanding political guidance for his judicial decision-making. If the Party said five years, Tanzer gave ten behind bars to some unlucky defendant. Occasionally the victims of such treatment appealed, and the Court of Appeals reduced the sentence to more reasonable proportions. The touchy Tanzer would then run to the Secretariat, complaining that the court in Plzeň had sabotaged his pursuit of a rigorous class warfare policy. When reprimanded by the judges from the superior bench for his super-militancy, Tanzer would argue that the comrades from the Party had forced him to be so bellicose. The reader will hardly be surprised from the tone of these lines to learn that the relationship between Tanzer and myself was something less than affectionate. Thus I was not entirely surprised when Tanzer, adding to his reputation for militancy, decided to unmask me as an enemy of the people. All I needed to do — and did — was to drop a word to the Secretariat and another to the Appeal Court. The comrades at both places met and inevitably discovered that Tanzer was a rather insincere Bolshevik. His demotion followed.

Survival depended on the sense of proportion. Militancy may be compared to medicine. If you take too many pills the drug turns into a poison. If you do not take a sufficient dosage, the medicine will be ineffectual. The same applied to well-acted dedication to the cause. For example: according to the Party, our revolutionary times called for the replacement of the old-fashioned greeting *Dobrý den* (literally, "Good Day") by the more up-to-date "Labor be Honored" (*Čest práci*). I was not an exception to the rule in having considerable difficulty in adjusting to the change and getting these two new words to cross my lips. This deficiency had to be remedied. So I started to practice. A friend of mine, Prosecutor B., put me in front of a mirror, where I tried to utter the slogan with just the right amount of zeal, neither overdone nor underdone. When he felt that I hit the right degree of enthusiasm, he would give me a candy from a supply smuggled from Switzerland.

Soft-selling one's loyalty invited suspicion of inadequate commitment to the ideals of the classless world. Equally, the Party saw insincerity in cases of authentic loyalty, when over-done. This is how the boomerang worked. A colleague of mine, M., found out that his brother was involved in an anti-state conspiracy and promptly informed the police. The brother was sentenced to death and the informant to demotion. My colleague's act was too good to be true, and, after all, how could the Party retain in its ranks people with such detestable relatives? Or, to take another, less drastic case: When Stalin died in March 1953, his statue was displayed in all state offices, and each employee had to spend some time (usually half an hour) as part of the guard of honor. Josef Hluže, a prewar trained civil law judge, used his secretary's face powder to produce pallor in an attempt to prove how distressed he was at the passing away of this illustrious humanitarian. Three years later, Hluže was summoned before the Party Committee and severely reprimanded for his excessive preoccupation with the cult of personality.

Anything like permanent gratitude was alien to the dialecticians of the Party. Neither informant H. nor histrionic Hluže deserved any, because both of them had violated the rule of proportion. Significantly, it made no difference that Hluže was a scared opportunist and the informer a genuine zealot. Their sins were the same — they had failed to make their zeal seem credible.

Another rule of the game concerned protective alliances. Favoritism lubricated the totalitarian machine, and mutual services got things done. One had to have connections in the right places, with this important qualification: specific personal contacts, if advertised, meant an irrevocable commitment and thus became a potential liability. If I had had access to, say, Rudolf Slánský, and this had become known in the profession, the liquidation of Slánský would have most probably torpedoed my career. Instead of boasting about avenues — real or imaginary — to the top, it was better to let a rumor circulate about one's access to an unidentified potentate. In my case, a number of people were convinced that I had an in with the top echelon of the secret police. This fable even appeared in my dossier, as I discovered through my unauthorized knowledge of the combination to the court safe. Nobody dared to ask me directly about this matter, and I, of course, confirmed or refuted nothing. Such carefully and modestly nurtured illusions discouraged one's enemies. Everybody had plenty of them.

On the local level, too, it was advisable not to be too closely

identified with a particular person or clique. Since one might back
the wrong horse, the best policy was not to bet at all. Take the case
of Šlapák versus Průcha. The new Housing Act of 1956 allotted
each person a certain number of square meters of living space and
stipulated that any space in excess would be subject to rather heavy
taxation. One day, Šlapák, a second echelon comrade in the local
Party hierarchy and the head of one of the departments of the District People's Committee in Stříbro, entered my office to demand a
legal opinion and recruit my support on the following issue: Šlapák
occupied a large apartment and in order to avoid the tax he claimed
his niece as a member of his household. "According to the law, is
my niece a member of the family?" he asked. Before answering I
inquired why he wanted to know and whether, perhaps, there was
anyone who might happen to disagree with him. It emerged that
the person in disagreement was Milan Průcha, Mayor of Stříbro,
who was responsible for the imposition of the disputed tax. Under
these circumstances I decided to be neutral. Thus, my "legal advice" turned into this empty non-commitment: "Comrade Šlapák,
I do not see any clear-cut reason why you should not eventually be
right." I did not endorse Šlapák, a drunkard and a fool. But I did
not endorse Průcha either when he came to me the following day,
notwithstanding the fact that I rather liked this pleasant and intelligent Bolshevik. Intuition warned me to stay away from this
seemingly trivial affair, which I suspected to be only a pretext for a
long lasting feud. I was right.

The Šlapák-Průcha argument gradually developed into a bitter
behind-the-scenes fight, splitting the Stříbro potentates who had to
take sides in the conflict. One evening as I was dining in the restaurant Evropa with the District Prosecutor Stehlík, Kupka, the Secretary of the District People's Committee and a backer of Šlapák,
came to our table to announce that Průcha was through. "This
morning when Průcha attempted to enter the town hall, our people
stopped him and told him to go home if he didn't want to be locked
up on the spot." The PSP prosecutor, Stehlík, then asked rather
mischievously, "How could you demote an official duly elected by
the people?" Kupka, more conscious of my presence than of the
irony inherent in the question, retorted angrily: "You know quite
well what we all know and what we also told Průcha. 'The Party,
not the people, put you in office, and now the Party has decided to
kick you out.'" The Party later set up an ad hoc investigation

committee to look into the "Trotskyite" activities of the deposed Mayor. Prŭcha was a doomed man, and had I taken sides in the dispute, the victors might also have split my skull.

Despite all precautions, a man in a totalitarian state is bound to stumble. This happened to me occasionally, such as with the simple case of declaring a person legally dead. An elderly woman came to my office and told me her story. She was of Czech origin, born and raised in the Soviet Union. During the collectivization drive in the thirties her husband, a veterinarian, was arrested by the OGPU, and he disappeared for good. All attempts by the family to learn about his fate led nowhere. Now, in 1957, the wife — and widow, presumably — petitioned to have her husband declared legally dead. This was the way I recorded the facts in my protocol. The next step in the procedure was to have a notice printed in the Official Gazette of the Ministry of Interior. Only when it was too late did I discover that my secretary (also a repatriate from Russia) had filled out the form for the Gazette using a verbatim transcription of my protocol, and that I had idiotically signed the papers for the Ministry without reading the text. Thus, through my letter and signature, the Ministry of Interior (i.e., the police) were told that their Soviet teachers were killers. Nonetheless, this manifestly dangerous episode went by without causing any harm. I never found out why the Ministry did not react to my blunder. Perhaps it was an oversight, perhaps not. Who knows what would have happened if the author of this "provocation" had been a judge of prewar vintage.

Some people simply had no hope of redemption. Whatever they did, they were always wrong. They were forced to pretend loyalty, fully realizing that no one believed them. The enemy had to join the parade and hail the leadership. When he did, he committed the sin of hypocrisy, and the Party would then declare, "We would prefer honesty to this sneaky attempt to exploit the confidence of the toiling masses." However, if the enemy did not march, the Party would be equally angry, this time because of stubbornness and provocation. "We gave him a chance, but he doesn't want to change." With the prewar judges, the situation was not quite so bad as that, though sometimes I had my doubts.

The last nation-wide purge I experienced took place in June, 1958. By then the purge had lost its clandestine, semi-conspiratorial aura. Instead, it had become an ordinary campaign, no longer to be talked about in whispers. It had become as natural as the harvesting of the cauliflower or the cementing of our friendship with Outer Mongolia. The head of the Provincial Court, Adam Pittner, accompanied by the chief of personnel, Škaloud — the ex-cobbler and former admirer of Thomas G. Masaryk — travelled from one district to another, where they invited each employee, separately, to have a friendly chat. The person in question was then informed either that he had just been purged or that he had been given the privilege "of not being purged just now." What amazed me most was not so much the amiable tone of the message, but the seeming readiness on the part of the people to accept the inevitability of such a fate.

Discovering foolproof rules in the survival game and the faultless implementation of these rules were goals attainable only by the victims of self-deception. The survival kit included items such as diligence in psychological probing, fundamental distrust, alertness towards trivia, consistent image-building, modesty and sense of proportion, nurturing of protective alliances, and a certain lack of scruples. These had to be weighed and studied with the sophistication and self-discipline of a chess player, who, however, could never lose sight of the fact that he was staring at a rigged board, playing by rules always subject to instantaneous alteration by his opponent. It was the power of the unpredictable that usually counted in the final run. The participant in the gamble profited from his mastery of the rules only if luck guided his decision on when and how to employ them.

Thomas G. Masaryk once allegedly remarked that a stay in the vicinity of a pile of manure tends to make one stink. This is certainly true, especially if the stay happens to be a prolonged one. Yet, no matter how smelly one becomes, one does not necessarily turn into manure. As far as we were concerned, we could survive, less stained perhaps than is generally believed. Generous display of militancy in words and gestures could often be substituted for nastiness and can even take the place of harmful deeds. Good acting and prudence were wisdom, whereas impulsive courage was its negation. Reckless defiance of the Establishment was self-destructive and helped no one. When, for example, I saved a child from the servitude of a kolkhoz, proclaiming my sense of "courage" or "dignity" would not have done the job. Fair play in foul circumstances made little sense.

To return for a moment to manure. It took me a full year after leaving the country to rid myself of the compulsive need to lie. My habitual role-playing, practiced for more than a decade, took considerable time and effort to be overcome. Return to normality was abnormally strenuous for a generation of consistent impersonators from the Stalinist era.

1. This figure was given to me by a highly placed secret police official in the middle fifties.

9 SECRET POLICE: RUSSIAN ROULETTE OR CAN THE GAMBLER BEAT THE HOUSE?

The purpose of this chapter is not to present a complete picture of the secret police and its operations, but merely to show how this organization affected the judiciary and played a role in the survival game. The secret police formed the most formidable audience any actor was called upon to face.

One Monday in the summer of 1956, at the District Court in Plzeň, the telephone in my office rang: "Is this Dr. Ulč? This is *Krajská správa.* Please, come to see us a week from Thursday, at 2 p.m. Ask the receptionist for Novák." This was a very unwelcome sort of call. *Krajská správa,* literally "Regional Administration," was an euphemism for the Secret Police Headquarters. The Headquarters was located in the city's most modern building, popularly known as the Gestapo Palace, because — what a coincidence! — during World War II it had housed the secret police of the Nazis. I had never been in that place, nor had I ever met or heard of the caller using Novák, the most common Czech surname, as his cover.

The reader will recall that my telephone summons fell midway between the two traumatic events of the memorable year 1956. In February, Khrushchev had delivered his secret speech divesting Stalin of his divinity. A few months later, revolution would break out in Hungary. In Czechoslovakia the secret police were still at the height of their power, and enjoyed the deserved reputation of being the most dangerous and least accountable force in the country.

I knew that other colleagues had received calls similar to mine. Even now I do not know whether it was a check up or a frame up; whether an exercise in periodic bureaucratic control or the prelude to an intended purge.

First, I had to try to decipher the telephone message. "Novák" had called me *Doktor* Ulč. This was far too formal compared with the warm, intimate "comrade judge," but still better than the frigid *pan* (Mr.). Second, I was reasonably sure that the police had set up the date of our meeting for ten days ahead (i.e. "next Thursday") not to enable me to prepare my defense against "anything" but to torment me with insecurity during the interim. This was as far as my deductions could go. Any conviction that I was innocent and therefore safe was out of the question. That much at least I knew about the secret police. From their point of view, everyone was *somehow* guilty. Even comrade President Novotný was not immune from their suspicion. The secret police had a dossier on him — if one could believe a story I was told, two years later, by an intoxicated plainclothesman.

That Thursday, I entered the Gestapo Palace. The receptionist contacted "Mr. Novák," whom I then followed from the lobby through deserted corridors into an empty room on the third floor. Mr. Novák was in his early thirties, neatly dressed, and not too communicative. In the spotless room the only furniture was a round table and three chairs — plus, I imagine, some monitoring devices. The third chair was occupied by a character similar to Novák, who claimed his name was Vojáček. We each lit a cigarette and started to talk. The talk lasted for over six hours — mainly about nothing. The comrades started with the weather, mentioned the sporting season, touched *en passant* on my being a judge, and, all along, observed me.

It was both a kind of a Kafkaesque trial and a chess game. The comrades waited for me to make my first wrong move and violate the rule of proportion. To their disappointment, during the three hundred and sixty minutes, I did not embark upon any patently political theme of praise for the Establishment. Avoiding the topic, I knew, would help to promote my image as one so convinced of the righteousness of the regime that he does not feel compelled to prove it to anyone, not even to the secret police. As I tried to

explain in the foregoing chapter, the attitude, if applied consistently, could be very damaging; on occasions even the most initiated
had to advertise their devotion. For my purposes, however, and as
a short run tactic, it was the appropriate move, and it impressed my
interrogators.

During the interview I was careful not to smoke more than
they did, to go to the bathroom only when they had to respond to
the call of nature, and to pretend to be quite at ease, not bothering
about the waste of time. "After all, comrades, what does it matter
whether I sit in my office or in yours?" On the other hand it would
have been unwise to have given the impression that I was enjoying
the meeting. "I don't mind" was the right response, in keeping with
the proportion rule. I also anticipated that an indication of slight
disrespect might help. "I say, you two guys, you really have a good
life. But I wouldn't trade with you. Why? Well, why should I tell
you everything? Find out for yourselves, if you want to. After all,
it's your job." This was a judge speaking, a comrade who had nothing to hide or fear. After this fitting digression, we resumed our
serious talk — still about nothing. Since I continued to play the
game well, Novák suggested that it was time (i.e., after eight in the
evening) to stop and meet again — sometime.

The game dragged on for about two months. During this
period, the secret police tried several tricks with me. For example,
at one of the following sessions, they mentioned, as though by accident, an episode from my past; a detail that was intended to convince me of their omniscience. "Do you remember the New Year's
Eve 1951? You were, we think, in the company of five, and X.
brought up a joke about the wife of comrade President Gottwald."
Undisturbed, I retorted. "Well, well. You really know. Good for
you. I've heard that joke a dozen times. Haven't you? I think it
is in bad taste, anyway. Do you think...?" etc.

The rationale behind this move by the secret police was to
mesmerize the victim, forcing him to conclude that if they
know such *details* they must know *everything*. They were in-
vincible, and it was, therefore, futile for him to hide his sinful
thoughts or actions. Actually, the secret police had a long way to
go before becoming an encyclopedia of universal happenings. It
sufficed for me to test Novák and Vojáček on the spot. In the discussion that followed, I intentionally mixed up two of my cousins,
and the comrades noticed nothing because they did not know
enough.

In many cases this substitution of *pars pro toto* worked miracles. Many targets of the secret police's attention gave up further resistance after they were made to feel that the "Nováks" not only knew everything but were *everywhere*. During the testing period, the citizen, as though by accident, runs into his investigators on the way home, to the office, or to his favorite cafe. These engineered encounters magnify a man's sense of helplessness and engender the belief that the entire secret police machinery is occupied with nothing else but catching him out. Novák, Vojáček, and later some others used to cross my path almost daily. After two months' probing, all this enervating annoyance stopped, and the comrades shifted their attention to the thousands of other potential victims waiting in the wings.

Contrary to the rules of a cautious game, I became very attracted to the idea of learning as much as possible about this ominous organization — and in particular about the mental horizons of its members. My job by itself was not of much help in this respect. Among the Czechoslovak jurists, only prosecutors were in regular contact with the police.

A distinction should be made between the secret police (*Státní Bezpečnost*, "State Security," known as STB, and a replica of the Soviet KGB) and the regular police (*Veřejná Bezpečnost*, "Public Security," the VB). Both STB and VB were part of the Ministry of the Interior, and their territorial organization followed the structure common to the Communist Party, People's Committees, the judiciary, etc. That is, along with the nineteen Regional Party Secretariats and Regional Courts, there were nineteen regional police headquarters, and in each of the three hundred or so districts throughout the country was a corresponding number of police posts. On both regional and district levels, the commander of the secret police was also the top authority over the VB regulars. The STB men were mainly occupied with investigating grave political offenses, while the rest of criminality was combatted by the VB. However, the former was authorized to take over any case it chose, such as particularly juicy sexual offenses.

It is perhaps a worldwide phenomenon that the plainclothes policeman, by virtue of the uniformity of his dress and habits, is not really as secret as the name implies. For example, the Russians call him, with good reason *zelyonye shlyapy* (green socks). In Czechoslovakia, the STB men were also far from inconspicuous. Besides green socks, they sported khaki overalls — the white shirt was reserved for higher ranks only — and a dark blue cap. Their features and manners betrayed their working class origin, and no security man I have ever met was over fifty.

The STB in its official capacity had no connection with the civil law adjudication of which I was in charge. Yet many security men sought out my office, not because of their calling but because of personal trouble. Some were worried about their marriages; others were plagued with *alimenty* (support) for children fathered both in and out of wedlock. These misfortunes, and the desire to do something about them, produced in these men a certain humility. It was not a dreadful STB gunman who stared at me across the desk but a little fellow not unlike scores of ordinary citizens trying to cope with similar adversities. I pretended not to see this temporary lowering of the status of which they were so conscious, and they in turn were appreciative of my tact. I tried to give them the best advice I could. It should be noted, however, that this taking of sides in a conflict was not inconsistent with the warning against involvement mentioned in the preceding chapter. I was insulated from any conflict as long as the litigation was filed at another court, which was usually the case. When there was danger that a case concerning the Stříbro STB men might fall under my jurisdiction, I claimed lack of objectivity and had the dispute transferred elsewhere. Thus, I could offer advice with impunity, and if something went awry, the blame lay with some distant unknown judge.

Discussing parental sorrows left little room for meditation about politics. After a time, however, I succeeded in selling the STB an image of a loyal, though not excessively sloganeering, comrade; a male who understood the troubles of fellow males and treated them as intellectual equals. Here were these boys, badly educated and painfully aware of their shortcomings. Their proletarian background determined their upward social mobility, but once they reached a status of a sort, their pedigree started to bother them. An invocation of right ancestry was good for the Party meetings; it embellished one's dossier, but it lent no spiritual comfort to these pseudo-bourgeois busybodies.

Rather than trying to emulate their warped proletarian outlook, I chose, with their ready compliance, to elevate them as my educational peers. "After all, comrades, we're all in the same boat, aren't we? We both work with the law. In real life what does a bit of paper from an university mean? What counts is performance, and here there's no difference between us." The comrades loved to hear that. They were grateful and started to refer to me as "our doctor," as someone who appreciated their largely imaginary mental qualities. Moreover, I was always ready with a supply of dirty jokes and willing to take part in safe entertainments such as soccer or ping-pong. To fortify this image of a true comrade one could occasionally tease them a little, though this indulgence could only be permitted rather sparingly.

A diligent performance and careful acting could produce many dividends: relative security, familiarity with the outlook of the STB, and some interesting information. Thus, for example, after a year of image-building I was taking a walk on the outskirts of Stříbro and happened to pass the new police headquarters, undergoing the final touches of construction. Several officers were already moving in furniture and I, like a true comrade, not afraid of manual exertion, offered my help. Subsequently, STB man Bozděch took me for a tour through the premises. In the basement, where they were fixing the table for the inevitable game of ping-pong, I noticed a number of what appeared to be separate bathtub cubicles. Though I had some idea of the purpose of this architectural oddity, I feigned ignorance: "I did not know you cared so much about hygiene," I said. Bozděch, who was far from the most stupid in the outfit, proceeded to explain that these were bathtubs originally installed for drowning suspects who proved reluctant to confess their guilt. He went on to add the rather informative complaint that since the death of Stalin it had become not always easy to obtain permission from above to employ these efficient methods. I wasted no time in sympathizing with his frustrations, alluding to the narrowmindedness of the superiors in general.

The STB men sinned against the vow of silence on more than one occasion. Through Hrůza (a surname which translates as "Horror"), the officer in charge of the "religious issue"—a gentleman who prior to joining the STB had headed the Office of Religious Affairs attached to the District People's Committee—I learned that the aged Father Forst, as well as being a venerable Roman Catholic priest, was also a STB informer. Such a piece of intelligence would have been of vital importance to anyone confessing to Forst, but I was unable and unwilling to take the risk of passing on this interesting secret. Some years later, safely in the United States, I saw the movie "The Counterfeit Traitor," in which the Gestapo replaced a father confessor with their own man in order to hear an admission of guilt by poor, doomed Lilli Palmer. While the audience shivered in horror at this unwholesome totalitarian device, I could not resist comparing the scene with the improved practices employed in a small Czechoslovak town.

A further insight into the nature of the secret police may be obtained from the following story. In the Kdyňské Strojírny factory at Kdyně, in the district of Domažlice, an unknown hand was scribbling anti-state slogans in the ladies room. The STB installed a camera in this place of seclusion, which, as they emphasized, was taking a number of very undignified pictures. Though the culprit was not found, the operation was not a total failure. What photographs! How exciting and rich life could be! Naturally, when I was told, I roared with laughter, bursting with admiration for the inventive genius of our STB brains.

Yet the brains in question did not take anybody or anything for granted, and it was my good luck to have grasped this fact in time. No judge, no matter how folksy, bawdy or ping-pong-minded, could be safe from the occasional well-laid trap. A visitor came to a colleague of mine to give him a letter from an old friend, who some years before had defected to the West. The letter requested the judge to provide the bearer with food and shelter, which he did. The bearer turned out to be an agent provocateur, on the payroll of the STB. The host was subsequently sentenced for espionage. Another colleague, Dr. H., was approached by a nice old lady who asked legal advice on the criminal responsibility of withholding information from the police about an anti-state offense committed by a close relative. Dr. H. recited the letter of the law to the visitor who, thanking him, left. Imprudently, he chose not to report the incident to the higher authority. The nice old lady, of course, was working for the STB. She later testified against H., who was charged with the crime of undermining the state. Then came my turn.

Jaroslav Langmayer was a teacher at Stříbro, a lean, nervous young man, married and the father of one child. During the uneventful hot summer of 1958, there was a sudden rumor that Langmayer was in a serious trouble. Through an acquaintance, X., I learned that this educator had been caught in an intimate encounter with a student. Since the girl was under age (she was twelve) and since Langmayer was her teacher, the affair constituted a grave felony punishable by up to ten years of imprisonment. Langmayer was arrested, but in a matter of days was set free. To my request for an explanation of this extraordinary lenience, X. disclosed that the STB lacked an efficient informer at Langmayer's school and that the accused and the police had made a deal. The lewd educator was to fill the vacancy. To my further question as to what assurance the STB had that Langmayer would live up to the agreement, X. pointed out the obvious. If the new informer did not produce desired results, the original charge could always be re-opened, and since this danger served as a sufficient deterrent the issue would not arise.

A few months afterwards, Langmayer came to my court requesting a private talk. By that time his divorce—an ugly and violent affair—was still pending. He was brief: "How much does it cost to have my divorce pushed through as quickly as possible?" I pretended not to understand his question and reminded him that he had already paid the court fee of 400 crowns. When, afterwards, Langmayer openly offered me a bribe to speed up the litigation, I threw him out of the office. Luckily however, unlike judge H., I did not let things lie there. I went across the hall to prosecutor Stehlík, told him what had happened and, following his advice, wrote a memo addressed to the prosecutor: "J.L. has offered me a bribe but in view of the absence of any eye-witnesses or other evidence I do not suggest further action against the culprit." As expected, the secret police checked with the prosecutor whether or not I had reported the incident in writing. Had I failed to do so I might have been compiling this narrative in prison. It should be added that I never found out which of my table tennis partners had arranged the trap.

The STB people were of a quite different calibre from their VB colleagues. The latter, to some extent left-overs from the pre-war police force, in adjusting their political affiliation to the new times had not necessarily changed their professional outlook. Owing to their experience with law enforcement, they were considerably more efficient and competent than the political appointees within the secret police. One incident will illustrate the disparity in the performance of the STB and the VB: a package was found containing a handwritten message, "So shall perish all Communists," and, as evidence of the writer's sincerity, a severed head. Naturally, the STB took over the investigation, and after months of futile search for an underground conspiracy, American agents, etc., they reluctantly handed the case over to the VB detectives. With the help of a graphologist, the VB solved the crime on the spot. There was no political motivation involved; the murderer was the wife of the deceased, and it was she who had written the bellicose pronunciamento to fool the police. As far as the STB was concerned, the trick certainly worked.

The secret policemen felt particularly frustrated in small places such as Stříbro, where an incognito operation was out of the question, and where, in any case, we were really rather short of spies, saboteurs and sundry other traitors. Once, Bozděch—the bathtub elaborator—stopped me and complained, "I am quitting the force and switching to the VB. Most of the work we are supposed to do, you know, is nonsense. Look at the kolkhozy! When something goes wrong there—which means all the time— the brass sends us to find saboteurs instead of accepting the plain truth that the people in the cooperatives are lazy and don't work. I've had enough of all this," Bozděch, indeed, was transferred to the VB as deputy district commander.

My experience with the STB was not thorough enough to provide me with a satisfactory answer as to why anyone would want to join their ranks and become, eventually, a torturer. What I did learn—and learned well—was to belittle the hypocritical claim we Czechs never tired of making that we were people with a "dove-like nature" (holubičí povaha). This nation of doves, literally overnight, had produced legions of individuals eager to make violence and other assorted misdeeds their fulltime vocation. Apparently, any country on this blessed planet is quite capable of offering enough of the dissatisfied, the frustrated, of those who feel that the currents of time and fortune have passed them by, who have convinced themselves that the world owes them a living. All that keeps them from becoming practitioners of state-sponsored violence is the lack of opportunity.

10 OMBUDSMAN SOCIALIST STYLE

The public conferred several ill-fitting titles upon the occupants of the Czech bench. *Pan* ("Mr.") or *soudruh prokurátor* ("Comrade Prosecutor") were most frequent. The failure to call us *soudce* ("judge") was due not so much to the inability to distinguish between the accuser and the bench, as to the popular belief that it was the prosecutor who had the ultimate power over judicial affairs. Thus, occasionally, a litigant ignored my protests and persisted in referring to me as "prosecutor," much as a polite European flatters a Major by calling him a Colonel or promotes all busboys to the rank of headwaiters. It will be noted later that the assumption of a prosecutor's superiority over a judge was to some extent substantiated.

The institution of prosecutor in Czechoslovakia was modeled on the Soviet *prokuratura.*[1] It consisted of a tightly centralized organization maintaining offices on the district and regional level with its Headquarters, called the "Office of the Prosecutor General," in Prague. Unlike the judges, the prosecutors were not even nominally independent. If, for instance, a District Prosecutor declined to submit an appeal in a particular case, he might be ordered to do so by his superior of regional standing. No such overt subordination applied to the judges.

The range of authority vested in the prosecutor exceeded that of a District Attorney in the United States. Prosecution of criminals was only one part of his job; it was his responsibility to supervise the observance of the laws by both the citizenry and the organs of the state. He, like his Soviet counterpart, was somewhat pompously referred to as "the guardian of socialist legality." This guardianship empowered the prosecutor to look into any misdeeds committed by anyone—provided the Party did not say otherwise— and the public was encouraged to bring to his attention any grievances that might arise.

Through the years the prosecutors acquired the reputation of Stalinist knaves. True, they could never hope to match the blood baths of the Great Purge in the Soviet Union during the thirties, but they certainly tried their best. Though we did not produce a specimen of the stature of Andrei Y. Vyshinsky, the late Prosecutor General of the USSR, a number of our own mini-Vyshinskys—such as Vieska, Čížek, Brožová and Urválek, to name only a few—became household names for Czechoslovak terror. Invariably, if a defendant developed hostility in court, it would be directed towards the prosecutor rather than the judge, although it was the latter who would produce the verdict and deliver the sentence. The prosecutors were often critical of this, in their opinion, irrational attitude. "Why blame us, and not the judge?" they would say. "He did the sentencing, not us." Notwithstanding the apparent logic of this complaint, the defendants, their families and the public in general continued to think otherwise.

The overlord and direct superior of all the prosecutors was Prosecutor General, appointed by the Party for seven years, holding the rank of cabinet minister. At the time of writing, this office has been held for many years by the bourgeois political chameleon Jan Bartuška, a prewar rightist and, during the war, suspected of collaboration with the Nazis.[2] If a willingness to forget past misdeeds applied to the magnificent impersonator Bartuška, it was certainly not so with his subordinates. As the result of purges, more thorough among prosecutors than among the judges, they were clean almost to a man. When I joined the judiciary in 1953, colleagues with a record of prewar judgeship were still quite common, but the ranks of the prosecutors had already been cleared of any bourgeois elements. And with regard to Party affiliation the "guardians" were also far ahead of us. During the fifties, in our Plzeň province at least twenty-five per cent of the judges had not yet joined the ranks of the Party. Among the prosecutors in the same province, only one non-Party member remained.

Within the New Class, we the judges were clearly outranked by the prosecutors; their social background was purer, their politicization profounder, and their salaries higher. Their offices, unlike ours, were equipped with "hot lines" to provincial Head-quarters and to Prague. The object of the judges' particular envy was the ID card issued to each prosecutor by Bartuška. In totalitarianism the possession of such a document—popularly called the "magic icon"—worked wonders. Such a card, flashed for a fraction of a second in front of startled eyes, made people tremble and locked doors open. A man with no more than an average taste for self-importance longed for the "icon." Once in 1957, a group of friends and I were disporting ourselves in the best Plzeň bar, at the Hotel Continental. An Army private, consider-ably more drunk than we were, decided to join our company. Our somewhat unrestrained behavior attracted the attention of a high-ranking military man, who decided to arrest the merry warrior. As it happened we had among us not one, but two prosecutors, who, brandishing the "icon," quickly discouraged the zealous officer. He apologized in awe and left the premises. I clearly recall that my having had no such card filled my intoxicated mind with pro-found envy and self-recrimination.

What distinguished the judiciary most of all from the pros-ecutors was the easy access of the latter to the centers of power. Their contact with Party Secretaries was much more frequent and their relationship more cordial—truly "comradely," so to speak. While the judge could never entirely divest himself of his question-able image of an independent arbiter between the interests of the people and of the individual, the prosecutor—despite his Ombudsman-like responsibilities—was regarded as a direct, front-line defender of the Establishment. Moreover, the working class background shared by the majority of the prosecutors and of almost all of the apparatchiki facilitated smooth cooperation between them.

The prosecutor, in dealing with the criminal calendar, handed over the responsibility for the investigation and preparation of the preliminary indictment to the police. However, he was empowered to intervene in their work, to take away their authority over the case, or to return the file to them as incomplete. Such interfer-

ence was always resented by the police and led in some instances
to rather strained relations between the two. This is not to say,
however, that the prosecutors were excessively concerned with
legalistic niceties. After all, it was their crude disrespect for the
law which in the first ten years of Communist rule earned them
their harsh reputation. While the maxim "guilty until proven
innocent" was not explicitly stated in the books, it was widely
practiced. Vyshinsky's formula that confession was the supreme
form of evidence encouraged the torturing of suspects by the police,
and the prosecutors, pressed to fulfill the planned quota of convictions, did not find it inconvenient.

Although this is not the place to examine the mechanics of a
trial it may help to point out some outstanding differences between
Czech and Anglo-Saxon practice. First, the prosecutor does not
make deals of any kind to secure the cooperation of the suspect.
The prosecutor submits charges as he sees fit and promises nothing.
It is up to the bench either to re-classify the offense or hand
down an acquittal. The no-deal policy does not necessarily presume
that the prosecutor is principled, but stems rather from the fact
that all but a few defendants confess to the crime—the police
having already taken care of that, either before or after 1957. The
prosecutor, however, may decide to drop the charges or limit himself to what translates as a "chat," a verbal reprimand that involves
no further action. Such a chat is justified only if the wrongful act
poses an "insignificant danger to the interests of society."

The second example constitutes another, equally preferable
difference from Anglo-Saxon practice. The picture of the prosecutors as being always obsessed with punishment regardless of the
merits of the case is not entirely accurate. Occasionally, a prosecutor would side with a defendant. This may be illustrated by a
story involving my fellow judge, the embittered spinster Dr.
Krabovská. Once she presided over the trial of a swindler who,
under the false pretense of intended marriage, had cheated nine
would-be-brides. Though the total sum extracted was negligible,
the judge felt pretty strongly about the issue and passed a verdict
of nine years of imprisonment without probation. The prosecutor
supported the defendant's appeal, and the higher court reduced
the sentence to more reasonable proportions.

The public was gradually becoming aware of the prosecutor's
role as "guardian of socialist legality." This even seemed to apply
to prisoners already on the receiving side of the prosecutor's

initiative. Once while I was walking the corridors of the Plzeň court, a tall, one-armed man stopped me to ask where he might find the prosecutor's office. Since I happened to be in a rather talkative mood, I inquired why he was so eager to see this dreaded official. The visitor told me a story which later I was able to verify. His name was Bulka, and as a Gestapo informer he had been sentenced to death shortly after the war. Bulka, however, had cheated the executioner in the best traditions of horse opera: with the rope around his neck, he was saved by a presidential pardon. His sentence had been commuted to one of life imprisonment. Having benefitted from some of the amnesties, Bulka, after ten years, was eventually set free. The fact of physical freedom, however, did not erase the stigma of guilt, and consequently no one would employ him. With nowhere left to go, he turned for help to the prosecutor, who, after a few phone calls, arranged the much needed job.

While the prosecutors monopolized the right to initiate criminal trials, their participation in civil suits was only selective. The law entitled them to enter into any civil law suit as an "indirect participant" with the right to offer evidence, question the parties and witnesses, and even to appeal the decision. The prosecutor was authorized to intervene whenever he thought the case might affect the interest of the state or of the society at large. Since the state was interested in everything, this restrictive clause was meaningless.

With the introduction of socialist competition and its attendant quotas, the prosecutors also became "producers," very active in civil law suits. The race for statistics, however, reduced their actual participation to a nominal level. For example, though I had six litigations a day on the court calendar and the prosecutor was a party in five of them, he was physically in attendance at none.

As has been stated, the perennial ailment of totalitarianism is overcommitment of resources. Desire outruns performance. The prosecutor, far from being a menace to the litigants or the bench, was usually absent either in person or in mind. Instead of being the *spiritus movens* of the proceedings, he relegated himself to the role of an essentially inert observer. There were, of course, numerous exceptions to this rule, depending on the kind of suit, the type of litigants, the relationship between the judge and the prosecutor, and most of all, on the degree of militancy of the latter. An outstanding zealot could make the life of a judge pretty miserable. I was very fortunate in this respect, because Prosecutor Stehlík in Stříbro was not only a "reasonable comrade" but also a man with a rudimentary sense of justice. For instance, he was capable of siding with the individual against the state, arguing that at times the interest of the whole is best protected through the preservation of the justified rights of a single citizen. Stehlík's participation served also as insurance for me should anything go wrong. On more than one occasion I was glad to shelter behind his reputation within the Party.

If the main motive behind the prosecutor's participation in civil proceedings was to watch the judge, I personally did not feel this, and I believe that my opinion was shared by the majority of my colleagues. Certain frictions were, however, unavoidable even among friends, owing to the contradictory directives coming from Prague. For example, the Ministry of Justice and the Office of the Prosecutor General differed on the question of defining a kulak. Though no final definition was ever coined by any authority, the Prosecutor General advocated a more militant approach than did the Justice Department. His directives were binding on his subordinates, and this led to a clash with the bench on the issue. As far as my adjudication was concerned, the most frequent disagreement arose over the financial liability of a member of a bankrupt kolkhoz. Contrary to our rather restrictive interpretation of the individual's responsibility, the prosecutors were ordered to argue in favor of full liability. This particular dispute continued for years.

In addition to the prosecutor's involvement with criminal and civil law, a third area became his concern after the death of Stalin. This was entitled *všeobecný dozor* (general supervision) and can be seen as roughly comparable to the work done by the Scandinavian Ombudsman. The prosecutor was empowered to receive complaints from the public regarding the actions of state economic and administrative—though not political—organs. If he so desired, he could challenge any decision he considered out of keeping with the spirit of socialist legality. This responsibility entitled the prosecutor to attend the meetings of the People's Committees (the judges had no such right) and to probe into the performance of a number of state authorities and enterprises, such as Homes for Juvenile Delinquents, State Farms, Housing Offices, and the Industrial Safety Departments. By the late fifties, however, this Ombudsman role was still in its infancy. My experience was that the public still preferred to complain to the President, the Party, or the secret police rather than to the prosecutor.

That part of the public willing to seek out the "guardians" seemed to be confused about this novelty and, on occasions, looked to the court for assistance. Even the representatives of the state themselves did not always have a clear picture. Thus one day in the spring of 1959 I received a call from a village policeman, who informed me that in his community a cow had been found in an abandoned tenement and that neither the State Farm nor anyone else was willing to claim ownership. The policeman requested advice, threatening that if he received none the animal would be delivered to the court for safe keeping. Since I felt neither authorized nor qualified to take charge of the beast, I informed the prosecutor about the problem, reminding him of his responsibility of "general supervision." Thus prodded, he was able to find suitable accommodations for the troublemaker.

My contacts with the prosecutor mainly concerned agricultural affairs. Since I shall deal with agriculture as a separate topic later on, at this point I will limit myself to one illustration—the strike at the Malovice agricultural cooperative. It was in August, 1958, that both the Prosecutor Stehlík and I were summoned to the office of Chairman of the District People's Committee. It seemed that the villagers at Malovice were staging a strike demanding the return of U., the daughter of one of the farmers, to agricultural work. They resented her exemption from field labor. The strike, by definition a touchy affair under socialism, was even more delicate because of the fact that she was a secretary (and mistress) of Kupka, the second-ranking man at the District Soviet. A car whisked us to Malovice from whence it appeared at first, we would not get away unharmed. Fortunately, an insincere compromise calmed the crowd. They resumed work satisfied that U. would soon join their ranks. U., in the meantime, changed her job to become secretary to the second-ranking man at the District Soviet at Toužim.

To sum up: the prosecutors, compared with the judges, were more closely identified with the Establishment, were more trusted, and, I believe, were more genuinely loyal to the cause. Though we belonged to the same family, the judges were only junior members. At least we were "in," however, unlike those Cinderellas of socialist justice discussed in the next chapter.

1. Hereafter I shall refer to these officials as "prosecutors" rather than "procurators" though this term is occasionally found in English language texts.

2. Bartuška's book published during World War II, hailing the Third Reich, was a collector's item—to my knowledge, two copies were owned by Bartuška's enemy, Professor Václav Vaněček of the Prague Law School. In one of his postwar publications, Bartuška acclaimed Stalin as the Founding Father of Czechoslovakia in 1918. More recently, the Prosecutor General has become an outspoken anti-Stalinist.

11 THE DEFENDERS

The changed political climate, while catapulting the prosecutors into prominence, arranged for the attorneys at law a shift in an opposite direction. The counsellors, known as *advokáti*[1] were the first and most serious casualties in the search for socialist justice. The Stalinist concept, with its stress upon class struggle and its implicit preference for the conviction of a hundred innocents to the acquittal of one who was guilty left little room for the *advokáti*. Accordingly, the call for mandatory representation by a counsellor before the court was sharply reduced and the number of *advokáti* left in the country dwindled to about seven hundred—about one per twenty thousand of population—of underpaid, mistrusted, aging practitioners.

The Party policy towards the *advokáti* went from a gradual imposition of controls to the complete abolition of all private legal practices and the subsequent re-organization of the profession into cooperatives. In each province the "Office of Legal Advice" (*Advokátní poradna*, hereafter referred to by its commonly used initials AP) was set up with branches in the subordinate districts. In addition to the AP's, a central office was established in Prague—the supervisor and actual employer of these fictionally cooperative and profit-sharing lawyers.

Only a small fraction of the *advokáti* survived the purge that started immediately after the coup in 1948. The majority switched —or were switched—to posts as legal counsellors for state enterprises, to clerical jobs unrelated to the law, to manual labor, or to jail. The developing system of the AP's could not be staffed from within by worthy Bolsheviks because revolutionary attorneys-at-law were rather scarce. The Party, therefore, had to select personnel from those available. On the whole, the chosen ones appeared to be less aggressive, less imaginative, less competent, and somewhat more dishonest than their dispossessed colleagues. In prewar Plzeň the telephone directory had listed dozens of more or less prosperous private law firms; the cooperative reorganization contented itself with about ten lawyers. The district branches, as a rule, consisted of only one member.

The popular criticism, especially in the West, of socialized services usually revolves around the "no choice" issue. The citizen, allegedly, is deprived of the right to choose his physician, lawyer, undertaker, etc. Concerning the *advokáti* in Czechoslovakia, such a charge is only partly true. The resident of a provincial town could choose from among some dozen counsellors, but in the district not more than one lawyer was available. Moreover, the attorneys were very reluctant to appear at courts other than those within their place of residence. Invariably, and often without informing their client, they empowered the local member of the AP to substitute for them, even if the "distant" court was no more than twenty miles away. A client had no protection against these practices, because the counsellor's unlimited right to use a substitute was stated explicitly in the Power of Attorney signed by the client. Even in the large cities such as Prague, Brno, Bratislava, Ostrava and Plzeň, where the citizen had a choice of attorneys, he could never be sure whether his counsellor would appear in person at court or whether he would send a substitute.

The reputation an individual AP member enjoyed with the public determined to a great extent the number of his clients. Thus, the busiest *advokáti* would often employ as substitutes colleagues less well-established or trainees lacking many skills of their craft. When a prospective client approached the AP and expressed no preference as to who should represent him, the head of the AP selected one of the under-employed bench-warmers who more than likely could not have attracted a client on his own. A counsellor was not able to do much for his party in a socialist court, but many managed to bungle even what little assistance they were allowed to give.

That the attorneys were indifferent to those who called on them is another misconception. Indeed, the *advokáti* cared a great deal, because they were paid according to their "productivity." As noted earlier, the AP's were officially labelled as "profit-sharing cooperatives." Since under socialism the overriding goal was the fulfillment of a plan—any plan—the attorneys, too, had their quotas, production targets, and incentives. The plan for the AP members was computed on the basis of the monetary value of services rendered. According to a Ministerial Ordinance, uniform for the entire country, each activity of the counsellors had its own price. There was a price for preliminary consultation, for pleading the case before the judge, and for drafting an appeal. The fees varied between and within criminal and non-punitive law. Within the latter, the fee was either fixed (e.g., paternity) or fluctuated according to the amount of monetary value *contested*—not won—in the litigation.

The basic monthly salary of an attorney was below the national income average. Thus, he had to fulfill his production plan (about 10,000 Kčs a month); and if he surpassed the target, he received a bonus, which in the case of an energetic lawyer might double his earnings. The salary depended on the performance of the service and not on actual payment by the client. The attorney was only concerned with reporting the service rendered, not with whether the accounting division of the AP actually received any money from the party. In other words, he might have performed beautifully—say, to the value of 20,000 Kčs—and have been awarded high bonuses, with the AP never having received a cent from the client.

To the confusion, no doubt, of an economist, such practices did not hamper the pursuit of justice (of our sort, of course). The beneficiary of this arrangement was the indigent citizen. Since the performance of the lawyer was divorced from his collection of a fee, he did not need to discriminate between an affluent client and a pauper—no mean achievement in view of the prevailing practices under capitalism. In fact, the attorneys, worried by their production quotas, admonished the judges to assign to them *ex officio* non-paying clients to meet the targets. We used to comply with these requests with considerable benevolence. According to the law, in both criminal and civil matters—provided representation of the accused by a counsellor was not mandatory—the judge was entitled to appoint an attorney if the party was unable to afford one, or if, in the opinion of the court, justice would be better served, either because of the litigant's lack of intelligence or because of the complexity of the case.

The common practice of supplying counsellors with non-paying yet profitable clients continued until 1958, when the Ministry of Justice launched a stern warning that the judges must evaluate very carefully a party's material situation, the complexity of the suit and, above all, the social and political background of the person applying for legal aid. The Ministry specifically forbade us to consider assistance for applicants of bourgeois pedigree.

The *advokáti* were hurt in ways other than the restrictive Ordinance of the Ministry. The law abolished mandatory representation by a counsellor in *all* civil litigations. The result of this was that an AP member pleading a non-punitive case became the exception rather than the rule. In criminal law cases, mandatory representation was limited to indictments carrying a punishment in excess of five years and all cases involving minors. Compared with prewar years, more people under the present system could afford to hire a lawyer, because he became less expensive. He also became far less effective. Stressing the interest of the state over the rights of the individual resulted in the counsels' becoming a marginal and somewhat irrelevant appendix to the judicial process.

The public reacted to these developments with the easy generalization that the *advokáti* only cost money and were good for nothing. Representation by a counsellor, however, was not always an exercise in futility. Several variables were involved; notably, the time of the trial, the nature of the charge, and the skill, courage, prudence and political insight of the *advokát*. Certainly the year 1952 was more unfavorable to a decent defense than 1962. Certainly a counsellor in a political show trial was much less effective than in a mundane family law affair. Assuredly, too, the attorney Mrs. Turečková, wife of the prominent Communist Dean of the Prague Law School, could dare to say more on behalf of her client than could an ordinary bourgeois left-over.

The difference between the role of a Czech attorney and that of his equivalent in the United States predated the socialist regime. As we shall see in the next chapter, a trial of continental legal tradition is not a contest between competing lawyers, presided over by a mute umpire. The judge is not a caretaker of order in the court room, at the mercy of the whims and ignorance of a jury. There being no jury, attorneys are deprived of the opportunity to demonstrate their histrionic skills to sway the lay element. The full use, or misuse, of the power of the counsellors is further impeded by the essential informality of the proceedings. The trial is focused not on the procedural refinements, but on the substance of the case. The question before the court is not whether the evidence is admissible, but rather what actually happened. A testimony cannot be torpedoed by the crippling "Objection, Your Honor." Nothing can be stricken from the record. The presentation of the evidence is not limited to the initiative of the contestants. The judge himself may call for the introduction of evidence or the hearing of witnesses not called by the parties in the case. And, in my biased opinion, justice, though not necessarily the attorneys, can flourish under such an arrangement.

Communist practice went a great deal beyond this. Along with the court and the prosecutor, the defense counsel was made co-responsible for ascertaining the "material truth" (i.e., guilt or innocence of the client) and for restricting himself to what was described as "justified defense." The official interpretation of this term went as follows:

> What is the interest of the accused? . . . In our country building social-ism, the interest of the state is identical with the interest of the entire society. The interest in the security of the state and of the society is identical with the interest of every citizen. These interests require, (1) that the culprit be justly punished. This interest of every citizen is also the interest of the accused and the counsel must defend it as the justified interest [of his client]. . . . If, however, the defendant desires to avoid the punishment or tries to get away with mild, un-deserved punishment, this is not the interest the counsel is allowed to defend.[2]

In other words, the defender has to see to it that his client be duly sentenced, though not in excess of the penalty prescribed by the law.

As we have seen in the previous chapter, the prosecutor was in charge of the pre-trial procedure and would rarely file an indict-ment to the court unless he had secured a prior confession from the accused. Once the defendant has admitted his guilt, there is not much left for his attorney to do. Thus, instead of challenging the merits of the charge, the *advokát* attempts to ameliorate the bad image of his client by pleading the defendant's ignorance of the law, referring to his clean record, orderly life and, above all, his liking for socialism. This ancillary role hardly titillated the counsellor's ego, but nevertheless it could be of substantial importance to the defendant. The existence of mitigating circumstances, if accepted by the court, could save the culprit from the gallows, could convert a sentence into a suspended one, or could lead to a verdict of "guilty" without imposition of a penalty at all.

In important trials with the highest stakes, such a plea tended to count little, provided the defender bothered to speak up in favor of his client. In the early fifties, for example, I attended an anti-state trial where the defendants were charged with high treason and espionage. One of the counsellors defended his client in this manner: "It is beneath my dignity and professional integrity to say a word in defense of this man. I respectfully request that he be sentenced as charged." It should be added, however, that not every AP member was authorized to defend in political trials. The Ministry of Justice kept a list of selected attorneys who alone were entitled to do the job. Characteristically, the criterion for selection was political compliance, not professional competence.

By and large, the interest of the client was better served by quiet work outside the court room than by dramatic appeals within it. The conscientious *advokát* would instruct the party on how to dress, how to behave at the trial, how to address the bench, how *least* to irritate the judge and the lay assessors, which facets of his past to stress most in the image building, etc. The court room lawyer, in American parlance, had shrunk into an office lawyer. This self-effacing strategy was also advisable in civil litigations where no prosecutor or threat of punishment was present. Insofar as I am able to speak for the civil law judges, we were far more impressed with a convincing written brief than with verbalistic bravado during the proceedings — and the counsellors were well aware of it.

It is my speculation that this profession may achieve some restoration of respectability, depending both on the improvement of the political climate and a rejuvenation of the personnel.

---

1. The literal translation of this term, an advocate, does not seem to be widely used, and I have avoided it. Instead, I have chosen to employ the Czech word or terms such as attorney-at-law, legal counsel, or counsellor.
2. D. Císařová, "K úkolům socialistické obhajoby," (On the Tasks of a Socialist Defence), *Socialistická zákonnost,* VIII, No. 7 (1960), pp. 432-4.

12 THE COURT ROOM

So far we have considered the *dramatis personae*, the range of permissible behavior, and the caveats the judge had to remember. Now it may be helpful to sketch in the stage-setting for the trial and to point out some of its general features.

Though I shall refer in the course of this chapter to criminal and non-punitive adjudication concurrently, I should like to stress a significant difference between the two at the outset. The penal calendar, owing to its lesser complexity, was easier to handle. Knowledge of only two Codes (those of substantive and procedural penal law) would suffice. The small demands made upon judicial knowledge, however, were complicated by the heightened attention given to the performance by the apparatchiki.

The criminal trial was not so much an undertaking to establish facts as a ratification — or, at best, verification — of findings secured in the pre-trial period by outside agencies, i.e., the police and the prosecutor. Along with the indictment, the judge received a bulky file, to which all he was required to add was one thing — the verdict. Accordingly, trials consisted of a survey of previous findings and a brief recapitulation of the already established facts. Almost no room was left for any surprises, and whatever drama remained tended to involve characterization rather than plot. This may also help to explain the deference and frequent hostility of the accused towards the police and the prosecutor, rather than towards the judge. The bench, after all, "could do nothing but pass the sentence." The accused could spend weeks and months with the pre-trial agencies, but he faced his judge for only an hour or so. Sixty minutes was about the average length of criminal proceedings, although this rule allowed for exceptions, notably show trials or those involving complex charges, multiple defendants or expert witnesses.

In contradistinction to his criminal law colleague, the civil law judge was his own policeman and prosecutor. He had to build the case from scratch, seek out his evidence and, because of the diverse nature of non-punitive adjudication, familiarize himself with a host of laws, ordinances and ministerial decrees. A civil law trial was rarely a one-shot undertaking with only one hearing. What could be accomplished at the criminal bench in one afternoon might drag on for a year or more in the civil dispute.

Socialist competition, introduced in the mid fifties, left a substantial imprint on the techniques of preparation, organization and conduct of all trials. It was especially with the civil law judges that concern with output prevailed over thoroughness, and improvisation over procedural rules. For instance, the law stipulated the use of a court interpreter to translate the testimony of a non-Czech-speaking witness. Conformity with this rule would have led to one extra adjournment to summon the interpreter. Pressed by production quotas, the judge could ill afford this waste of time. Thus, if he knew the foreign language in question, he preferred to do the translating himself.

After a litigant had filed his claim with the civil court, the judge first transmitted a copy to the defendant, instructing him about his right to respond in writing within two weeks. (Fifteen days was the time limit most frequently used by the courts. This also determined the period for an appeal in both civil and criminal matters). Because of production goals, the judge would not delay further action. Instead of waiting for the expiration of the fortnight, he would feel free to schedule the first hearing. The correct arrangement of the calendar was a demanding exercise in logistics.

In order that the proceedings might run smoothly, and people not be kept waiting, certain rules had to be observed. For instance, it was advisable to schedule the most complex and least predictable case last. Some of my colleagues, the older ones in particular, were

rather insensitive in this respect and did not care at all if the court
corridors were packed with a freezing, frustrated crowd.

Proceedings were often slowed down by the sloppy service of
the post office in rural areas. No case could be heard if the party
or parties were not present and the court was not in possession of
the blue postal return slip signed by the litigant evidencing his
receipt of the summons. Often we did obtain the slip but not the
litigant because, as it turned out, the return ticket had been signed
by the mailman in the name of the addressee. Occasionally, the
mailman, finding no one at home, would leave the summons at the
doorstep, to be drowned in mud or devoured by some wandering
domestic animal.

A reluctant litigant or witness could be both fined and brought
to court under police escort. Though I used to employ the latter
measure quite often, I invariably waived the fine. It was a sad
testimony to the impoverishment of the agricultural population
that most of these delinquents failed to respond to the summons
only because they could not afford to pay the bus fare to town.

Let us now have a look at the court room itself. A visitor
would not see anything particularly Bolshevik in character there.
The walls were empty except for the picture of the Head of State —
and of Stalin, until his removal — and the State emblem. No flag
was in view. The bench was situated on a foot-high stage at one
end of the room, usually opposite the entrance. In my day, the
chairs and the rest of the furniture, in most instances, carried a
capitalist trade-mark dating back several decades. At most of the
courts I visited, these chairs were in a pseudo-Gothic style and up-
holstered in leather. From the bench, on the judge's right was the
prosecutor or plaintiff's table; on the left was a similar desk reserved for the defendant in a civil law suit and his attorney. The
accused would sit at a bench about fifteen feet away, facing the
judges. The rest of the room was taken up with accommodations
for the public — if any. The Czech court houses were usually at
least a hundred years old. The Renaissance edifice in Stříbro was
four times that age.

The judges' official gowns, called *taláry*, were black with violet
trimming, leftovers from the pre-Communist age. Initially, the
Party banned them, claiming they were pretentious regalia, alien to
the masses, a symbol of exploitation, and totally incompatible with
the modern concept of justice. After all, it was asserted, the judges
in the Soviet Union wore mufti. Notwithstanding this, Czechoslo-

vakia in 1953 saw the unsung comeback of the *taláry*. There was no public explanation for this *volte-face*, but some of the initiated said they had heard from the Party that the return to the old garb might help to promote the respect of the masses for their representatives on the bench.[1.]

An attempt to combine working class folksiness with the stern image of State majesty was bound to lead nowhere. After years of experimentation the court ceremonial settled down to a code not very different from the conventional bourgeois court. Thus, "All rise" was in order when the judges entered or delivered the verdict. A litigant spoke only with the judge's permission. No one was entitled to smoke in the court room or in any way to disturb the proceedings. Though the judge had no power to declare a person "in contempt of court," he could order the trouble maker — litigant, defendant, spectator, attorney or anyone but the prosecutor — removed from the premises, fined, and, in serious cases, even arrested and charged with a felony.

The order kept during the trial often left very much to be desired. No one but the presiding judge was to blame for this state of affairs. Some judges, and the lay assessors in particular, took an occasional nap during the proceedings. Others, in order to avoid the charge of being "contemptuous of the toiling masses" turned the trials into comradely anarchy.

Because the courts did not employ ushers to instruct the public on their expected behavior at court, it was up to the prosecutor or the counsellors to give this advice, and if none of them was present, the judge himself had to take on the task. The enforcement of the ceremonial posed no great difficulty, except for the question of how to address the court. The traditional term "pan" meant not only "Mister" but also "Master" — a connotation hardly appropriate in a classless-bound society. On the other hand the progressive "soudruh" (comrade) was also out of place. The judge, confronted by a mass murderer, certainly would not relish being called comrade. The older generation avoided both, choosing instead "pan rada" (loosely translated "Your Honor"). Unhappy with all three alternatives, we instructed the parties to address us as "lidový soude" (Court of the People), a term vague enough to offend nobody. Characteristically, the warm "comrade" was reserved only for use by the prosecutor. In turn I would also call him a "comrade," while the counsellor had to be content with the noncommittal "pan doktor" (Mr. Doctor). The *advokát* cognizant of his lowly status refrained from comradeliness; for him the judge was "pan předseda" (Mr. Chairman). This all may sound unimportant, but an insider, conscious of the power of words and of form in totalitarianism, would disagree.

The advice to call us "Court of the People" was not, however, entirely a product of Communism. It reflected the basically impersonal notion behind the judicial process. It was not the individual judge who ruled, but the judicial apparatus *per se*, the authority of which was exercised through some of its officials. The verdict was pronounced "In the name of the Republic" (*Jménem Republiky*) because it was the State and not the judge that passed sentence. The judge was merely its instrument; he did not "discover" law but was only responsible for its interpretation and application.

The atmosphere of the trial was rather casual, depending, of course, on the gravity of the charge. The presiding judge opened the hearing with the following formula: "This is the criminal proceeding against the accused (name, date and place of birth, occupation, marital status, last home address) charged with the commission of the crime X." He would beckon to the prosecutor to read the indictment. The defendant would stand and listen to the charge. Afterwards, the judge would ask him: "Do you plead guilty?" Irrespective of the answer, the next step — and the very core of the trial — would be the presentation and evaluation of the evidence.

At this point I would like to repeat and emphasize that Continental legal procedure, both of the non-Communist and Communist varieties, is free of the kind of formalism characteristic of the common law systems. Form is subordinated to substance, technicality cannot prevail over the merits of the case. Objections such as "inadmissible evidence," "a leading question," or "hearsay," customary in the Anglo-Saxon trial, are unknown. A witness is made to feel at ease and left to testify in his own words, unharassed and uninterrupted as long as he does not become too irrelevant. It is then the responsibility of the presiding judge to stop the witness and lead him back as close as possible to the point at issue.

The Czech judge was not a passive referee presiding over a contest of articulate attorneys; he was in charge of the proceedings. He chose the evidence; he questioned the witnesses; he passed the judgment. However, after the completion of each testimony, the lay assessors, the prosecutor, the attorney, the defendant, or the litigants (in the civil law suit) were given the opportunity to question the witness. The initiative in presenting evidence was not monopolized by the parties. As we shall see in subsequent chapters, sometimes the outcome of the trial was determined only on the basis of evidence introduced by the judge. These practices, certainly unpalatable if not outright repulsive to any proponent of common law virtues, were here justified in terms of the "pursuit of material truth." All participants, and above all the presiding judge, were obligated to discover the "truth."

It was up to the discretion of the judge whether or not to accept the evidence offered. When I was a freshman Assistant Judge I once drafted a divorce petition for a jealous husband who claimed that his wife had committed adultery with an employee of Škoda Industries. At the time of the trial, the alleged miscreant was stationed as a technical advisor in North Korea. I requested that this crucial witness be asked to testify. The judge, naturally, ignored the motion. Yet a judge was also free to disregard any evidence offered, even if the prospective witness lived across the street from the Court House.

Anyone present at either civil or criminal proceedings was automatically disbarred from any subsequent testimony in the case. This rule was motivated by a concern for the objectivity of prospective witnesses. Therefore, in order to avoid disqualification of such persons by default, the judge, before his opening statement, would address those present, ordering all witnesses to leave the room and wait elsewhere until they were called.

The oath was then administered by the presiding judge. The witnesses were not allowed to sit, but had to stand facing the judge throughout their testimony. The term "oath" (přísaha) needs, in the context of an atheistic state, some elaboration. Instead of the old-fashioned obscurantist přísaha we labelled the obligation to tell the truth as slib (a binding, solemn promise). The judge simply admonished the witness to "tell the truth, the whole truth and nothing but the truth." This was to be achieved without assistance by any God. The witness was warned that a conscious distortion of the truth constituted the grave offense of perjury.

The right to decline to testify was rather narrowly circumscribed. The witness was entitled to keep his silence in cases involving a possible breach of state secrets, in cases of likely self-incrimination or in the incrimination of close relatives. The right of silence was, however, suspended if the relatives were implicated in a grave political crime. The litigants in a civil law suit might be put on the witness stand. This did not apply to the accused in a criminal proceeding. The defendant was always questioned, but he had to be simultaneously informed by the judge of his right to choose any kind of defense he felt to be appropriate. Because of this accepted and admitted right to lie, the accused could not commit a crime of perjury. However, the judge was obliged to inform him that a truthful statement constituted an important mitigating circumstance which the court would take into account when deliberating upon the verdict.

In the overwhelming majority of criminal cases, the defendant would plead guilty to the charge. The defense's main task was to draw attention to the mitigating circumstances and to try to excite the compassion and magnanimity of the judges. Such proceedings were swift, though at times rather monotonous. This was because of the bulk of testimonies being read by the judge from the voluminous file. If, say, the case was based on the testimony of twenty witnesses, the court would hear only two of them, while the statements of the rest were recited from the prosecutor's record. Contrary to popular belief, the burden of proof did not rest with the accused. "Guilty unless proven innocent" was never an officially, explicitly, sanctioned axiom, but, admittedly, it reflected the attitudes of the organs of investigation and, in cases of political urgency, the attitudes of the judiciary also. I shall speak more about this subsequently.

Court records (the so-called *protokol*) were of more importance in civil than in criminal trials. While the latter consisted of a brief list of references to the file prepared by the prosecutor, in civil actions the *protokol* was expected to reflect in detail all the activity in the court room. We had no skilled male stenographers at our disposal. Instead, on the presiding judge's left was a small desk at which sat a female clerk equipped with an ancient, noisy, manual typewriter. The judge dictated his accounts of the proceedings to the clerk. Testimonies were recorded not verbatim but in a condensed form. Since the *protokol* was supposed to be a vivid description of the proceedings, the judge was empowered to record rather impressionistic observations on the behavior of the parties and the general climate in the court room.[2]

In the absence of the verbatim transcript of the trial which the courts in many countries transmit to the parties, in Czechoslovakia the litigant was well advised to compile his own notes during the proceedings. The court clerk typed several copies of the *protokol*, one of which was usually handed over to the prosecutor. The counsellors, in order to obtain a copy of the *protokol*, had to ask for it in advance and supply their own stationary, a practice illustrative of their diminished stature.

After the hearing of all the evidence, the parties were given the opportunity to present the final plea to the court. In criminal proceedings the defendant — and his counsellor if any — enjoyed a rare advantage over the prosecutor. As a result of the assumption that the last speaker leaves greater impression on the listener, the law stipulated that this privilege be given to the accused. This rule was consistently applied. If the prosecutor wished to make a supplementary statement after the hearing of the defendant's summation, the defendant still retained his right to have the last word.

At many courts the judges' "retiring to deliberate" was only a figurative exercise. Sometimes there was no antechamber to which to withdraw, and the court room had to be cleared to allow the judges privacy. Only the judges and the court clerk were permitted to stay. Though I experienced instances where the judge unlocked the door of the antechamber in order to consult the prosecutor — instead of arranging an assignation in the men's room — the rule of undisturbed seclusion was rarely violated. There was no need for violation. Outside pressures influencing the court were applied before, not during, the trial.

After his lay colleagues gave the decision he required, the presiding judge rendered the verdict. Then the chairman of the bench beckoned the audience to be seated and delivered, from a written statement or extemporaneously, the reasoning behind it. With copies of the decision in the hands of the parties, the trial at the court of original jurisdiction ended.

To this account of the rudimentary features of a trial I should perhaps add a final comment on the prevailing policy towards the spectators at court. According to law, all adjudication was public except for cases in which state secrets might be endangered or public decency outraged. While the former injunction was adhered to very meticulously, the latter injunction was rarely used. I remember, for example, that in 1951 our law school class — over a hundred students—attended a divorce hearing at the Prague court. The core of the trial centered on the question of who had left an imprint of a hearty kiss on the rear of the defendant. Ignoring the embarrassment of the woman involved, the judge permitted us to stay and divert ourselves listening to the increasingly piquant evidence.

The right to bar the public was seldom applied since on the whole there was no one to be barred. Prior to the proceedings my secretary would post on the court room door the day's schedule for the benefit of the litigants and the public — that never dropped in. It was not so much interest as time, however, that the public lacked. One who was obliged to spend the whole morning in the futile search of a sack of onions was not likely to be in the right mood to witness, for the rest of the day, socialist justice in action.

1. The state was peculiarly negligent in accounting for the *taláry*. While on the one hand all the property entrusted to us—pens, stationary, ink, etc. —was meticulously guarded against misuse on our part, nobody controlled the gowns. Each of the judges inherited a great number of them to accoutre the lay assessors of varying sizes. Since the *taláry* were made of a fine pre-war fabric, some of my colleagues had them converted into ski pants. My utilization of the socialist cloth was less objectionable: it served me as an extra bed cover during cold nights.

2. The *protokols* offered a treasure house of verbal gems to any interested observer. Some were no doubt intentional, though many, I am sure, were genuine malapropisms on the part of semi-articulate judges. Some of the more sporting members of the judiciary were inclined to keep a file of such sayings. I did not, but I can remember this fabulous rationalization of adultery recorded in a case at the District Court at Hořovice: "My wife is a cruel person. She verbally abused our goat calling him 'a miserable beast' and therefore I decided to go to bed with Mrs. Moháčková." Indictments and court opinions, too, provided for interesting reading. Once the court in Prague passed a very lenient verdict against a photographer who used to supplement his income by producing pornographic pictures. The justices reasoned: "It is the belief of this court that the defendant will divert the lenses of his camera from female private parts to the proud sweating face of a Stakhanovite happily fulfilling the production plan and therefore. . ." The third and last sample was the creation of the District Prosecutor in Karlovy Vary (Karlsbad). According to the 1950 Penal Code, Sect. 245, par. 1, "Whoever takes possession of things in socialist ownership, in order to handle them as his own, shall be punished etc." The said prosecutor charged an employee of the municipal slaughterhouse with the felony of pilfering socialist property because of his "having stolen bull's testicles to handle them as his own."

PART TWO. CRIME AND PUNISHMENT

13 MY FIRST EXPERIENCE
WITH THE CRIMINAL COURT

As much as I disliked the decision of the System that turned me
into a judge, I still thought I could live with this lot provided I had
only civil, non-punitive law to administer. My wish was realized,
but not immediately. In August, 1953, fresh from law school, I
presented my articles of appointment as an apprentice judge to the
former railroad laborer and present Head of the District Court in
Plzeň, Miroslav Tlapák. My title was Assistant Judge, assigned to
the criminal bench under Tlapák's supervision.

If the majority of jurists lacked enthusiasm for criminal law,
it was because this law lacked respectability. Actually, the record
of Czechoslovak penal policy under the dictatorship of the proletariat was mixed. Occasional hanging of the innocent coexisted
with magnanimous treatment for some of the guilty. The more the
System punished, the more it pardoned the condemned. The growing number of sentences was often accompanied by a declining
severity. While on the one hand the courts interpreted a political
joke as a grave felony of "incitement," on the other hand the maximum legal sentence — short of death itself — was reduced from
life to twenty-five and, finally, to fifteen years' imprisonment. If
the imposition of a sentence served not only as revenge on the part
of the society but also as an attempt to rehabilitate the offender,

then the fifteen years' limit makes more sense to me than penalities calling for forty, or ninety-nine or more years of servitude found in some Western countries.

The relative moderation in punitive practices was motivated by doctrinal rather than humanitarian considerations. Criminality, according to Marxist reasoning, is a characteristic of a sick society. The abolition of exploitation disposes of class antagonism and, in the long run, eliminates all violation of the law. Criminality remains only as a relic from the past; the act of the deposed bourgeois and his ally, or of the genuine worker still the prisoner of capitalist mentality. Accordingly, the Criminal Code of 1950 (Sect. 17) stated that the purpose of punishment was: first, to render harmless the enemies of the working class; second, to prevent the wrongdoer from committing further crimes and reeducate him towards observance of the socialist way of life; and, finally, to leave through adjudication an educative imprint on the rest of the society.

The emphasis on rehabilitation was matched by the government's concern for preventing violations of the law. The stress on prevention went so far as to require the courts to impose equal sanctions on crimes committed and crimes merely attempted. On occasion, nothing more than the intent to violate a law was subject to criminal prosecution. In the cases of class enemies — that elusive never-to-be-defined category — evil intent did not need to be proved, it could be presumed. Fortunately for my peace of mind, the role of an Assistant Judge required more learning than performing. My first weeks were spent reading files, only to discover, as I imagine any law school graduate from any country does, that school had taught me very little that was of practical use.

My duties included being present at the trials and drafting the supervising judge's court opinions. Since our patrons were often of ex-proletarian stock, badly in need of assurance of their mental excellence, they loved to harass their better-educated trainees. True to form, Tlapák gave me a hard time. Though his grammar and style betrayed a grade school horizon, I was always eager to tell him how much I appreciated his guidance and benefitted from it. After about a month, Tlapák began to approve my drafts without comment. I began to feel that he did not even read them any more. To test this suspicion, one day I made up a verdict in which I sentenced Tlapák to death. Next day, the verdict was back in my tray with my supervisor's signature verifying the ruling.

As an Assistant Judge, I was not entitled to a private office; all that I was provided with was a small desk. I did not care about its size, but I did mind its uneven surface — it was riddled with bullet holes. Two months before I started work at the court, the table had been used to fortify the entrance to Tlapák's office against the efforts of some uninvited citizens to break through. To discourage the intruders, Tlapák and his fellow Judge Fikerle had engaged in a shooting exercise. Its after-effects kept me busy for several months. The events leading to the holes in my desk can be regarded as a case study of subordination of law to the Party's interest, of reality to doctrine. This was the Plzeň revolt — a rather extraordinary incident the outside world did not quite notice.

Czechs are not noted for feats of martial courage and pathological heroism. Yet, as it turned out, the Czechs were the first among the people's democrats — over three years before the Hungarians and not quite three weeks before the well known upheaval in the *Deutsche Demokratische Republik* — to suspend, temporarily, totalitarianism through violence. The suspension was brief, localized, but it existed.

The direct cause of the June 1-2, 1953, revolt in Plzeň was the promulgation of a single law — the Currency Reform Act. This wiped out overnight a substantial part of people's savings, annulled the state's debts to the people, but retained the debts owed by the individuals to the state. While this sudden impoverishment was quite upsetting, nothing would have happened in Plzeň had it not been for additional local Party duplicity.

Rumors of an eventual monetary coup had been circulated for a long time. By May, 1953, the feeling that "something was in the air" was particularly intense. Thus, when the management of Škoda Industries changed the paycheck policy by increasing the advance wages, the employees began to inquire about the reasons behind this shift. Suddenly receiving more money than usual, they requested assurance of the durability of the *koruna*. The Party dispatched spokesmen to calm the worried. "Our currency is firm. Trust the Party, comrades. Any rumors about a reform are nothing but lies; a slander spread by the domestic class enemies and Western imperialists in order to set back the building of our socialist future."

With these guarantees, the workers left for home, only to be informed by Prague radio on Saturday afternoon, May 30, that the feared law had just been promulgated. On the following Monday, the Škoda employees went to work as usual, but the majority of them refused to start until they received a satisfactory explanation for the new measure. The Party sent in badly-briefed propagandists with the impossible task of persuading the workers that they had not been cheated by their government. This time the oracular authority of the Party did not work. The toiling masses were ready to listen but in no mood to be convinced. In many instances the workers' attitudes were articulated by those intellectuals who had been demoted to manual labor and who easily outwitted and ridiculed the propagandists. The Establishment's slogans failed to restore work and discipline. Instead, the word spread to walk out and demand a convincing explanation from the Mayor of the city. (Significantly, in 1953 the city hall was still considered to be the center of local political power. Today, the people would march straight to the Party Secretariat.) Not everyone succeded in leaving the factory. In the Doudlevce plant more workers got out than in the Škvrňany division, where the "Workers' Militia" barricaded the entrances. Some of its members panicked and shot into the crowd, causing the first casualties.

About three thousand workers, now joined by some bystanders, began to march toward the City Hall — a distance of about two miles. They were in a rebellious mood, but at this stage their feelings did not go beyond resentment over lost savings. Yet the totalitarian syndrome of social atomization was running thin. As they became part of the crowd, the workers rediscovered their sense of solidarity. Initial slogans criticizing the currency reform escalated into cries attacking the regime itself. The most popular shouts seemed to be *Plzeň černá, Benešovi věrná* (Black Plzeň is faithful to Beneš) and *Bude zase hej, přijdou hoši z USA* (We shall have good times again; the boys from the USA will return).

When the demonstrators reached the City Hall, they found its massive gate locked. By that time the protesting crowd assembled between this Renaissance structure and the Gothic dome of St. Bartholomew on Republic Square had been augmented by thousands of spectators. Here the local potentates made another mistake. Caught by surprise, the "vanguard," without guidance from above, refused to talk to the "masses." The situation began to slip out of hand. Young laborers, many of them in their teens, seized the initiative. A few managed to sneak into the building through a window, and unlocked the gate. The angry toiling masses surged forward. Party posters, propaganda material, busts and pictures of leaders were torn from the walls and trampled underfoot. The rioters also found their way to a microphone to address the gathering in the square with bellicose denunciations of the currency fraud, of the government, and of Communism in general, at the same time cheering for Beneš (by then dead five years) and for the American troops who had liberated the city in 1945. The crowd was especially enthusiastic when some uninhibited youths seized upon that traditional Bohemian form of political protest — defenestration. Only this time, instead of pro-Hapsburg Catholics and imperial scribes, busts of Stalin and Gottwald came flying out of the windows.

While this premature liquidation of the cult of personality was going on at City Hall, another seat of State authority was under attack — the court building, No. 40 Veleslavínova Street, a mere block away. The demonstrators' attention had been drawn to the judicial headquarters not so much through resentment towards its official occupants as by anger aimed at a single symbol of a hated profession. Votruba, a secret policeman, had been apprehended earlier at the corner of Solní and Dominikánská streets. He was manhandled, but being fast on his feet, he had managed to escape and find refuge in the court building. After his hasty retreat, the gates had been locked after him, only to be demolished by a huge log swung by the irate pursuers. Votruba was finally caught inside the building and was dragged out to the nearby river Mže to be drowned. The unexpectedly low water level in the stream, however, threatened to deprive the execution of its desired dignity, and the enterprise had to be called off. Votruba was allowed to limp away while his captors returned to the serious business at the court.

There, the now-familiar scene of mayhem was re-enacted. Besides the busts and portraits, judicial robes, typewriters and a number of filing cabinets were thrown into the street, doused with gasoline and burned. As it turned out, the destruction of the files proved to be of little value since only records of Family and Probate Divisions were affected. The flames did not devour documents relating to the prosecution of political crimes because nobody managed to find these important papers.

By this time, a huge demonstration was going on in the streets. A jeep ornamented with Czechoslovak and American flags was followed through the city by thousands of protesters. Pictures of former Presidents Masaryk and Beneš and all kinds of flags (including that of Chiang Kai-Shek's China) except those displaying the hammer and sickle appeared in windows. Visible symbols of the System, notably Party posters, were torn down and burned. As the witnesses later recalled to me, it was quite touching to observe octogenarians laden with bottles of gasoline feebly climbing ladders to arrange for the annihilation of the Party advertisements.

When the rebellion reached the level of fist-fights it had become predominantly an affair of the young. The only weapons used by the demonstrators — and that with admirable skill by Škoda apprentices — were knuckle-dusters. (One of the most prominent exponents happened to be the son of the cadre chief at the Škoda Works.) The targets most eagerly sought out were members of the STB secret police, militiamen, and whoever still happened to be wearing the Party emblem. Some of the young warriors even volunteered their services to others. To mention an actual case: a fragile old lady approached a worker in the street, asking him, as a favor, to beat up a man standing not far away, who, she claimed, was a mean Communist. The request was promptly complied with. Inevitably, some fists reached wrong jaws, owing to mistaken identity. Many teenage laborers, for example, wore the blue shirt of the Communist Youth Organization (ČSM), with an insignia on the left breast, as a part of their ordinary working clothes. This was for a variety of reasons, but respect for the Organization was not one of them. The Party always criticized this habit of desecrating the uniform. On June 1, the blue shirt workers, actually disrespectful of the ČSM, were mistakenly taken for defenders of the regime. Opponents of the Party thus unwittingly punished on its behalf many nonconformists.

Demonstrations, fist-fights, burning — though no looting — continued into the next day. The rebels had no organization and no leadership. From beginning to end, the entire affair was undirected, the product of a multitude of spontaneous acts. Even more striking, however, was the response of the state authorities: for forty-eight hours they did virtually nothing. An Army detachment equipped with submachine guns and under order to clear the streets did show up at the court house at one point, but the crowds were not to be deterred, and some individuals even moved closer to the soldiers, challenging them to "shoot workers' bullets into workers' chests." No violence took place, and eventually the commanding officer ordered his unit to leave.[1.]

Local officialdom was paralyzed by the unexpected turn of events, and reference to Marxist Writ offered no instant wisdom.

Party functionaries and the secret police disappeared from the streets. The regular uniformed police (VB) were visible but remained passive. The only group ready to defend the regime was the Workers' Militia, which engaged in most of the shooting and also suffered most of the casualties. According to a secret report I later saw, among the seventy-some persons seriously injured during the course of the revolt, the clear majority were militiamen and secret police. To round out the picture, it should be added that the fire department—an institution traditionally ridiculed in Czechoslovakia—paid its token of loyalty to the government by trying to disperse the demonstrators with fire hoses. However, someone cut the hoses before the effectiveness of this method could be tested.

In short, utter confusion on both sides characterized the two-day revolt. The rioters and the local authorities were equally taken aback that such events could ever come to pass. If initial success induced in the demonstrators a state of euphoria that left them incapable of organizing purposeful activity — for example, attempting to take over the radio station rather than burning Party posters — the sequence of events likewise incapacitated the Establishment. The only practical action undertaken by the latter was the dispatch of secret police informers into the streets to mix with the demonstrators, take pictures, and remember as many faces as possible.

When the rebellion was finally quelled on the second day, it was the accomplishment not of the Plzeň authorities but of the units of the Interior Guard (*Vnitřní stráž*, at that time a branch of the Ministry of the Interior) and a contingent of the Workers' Militia, both sent from Prague. A curfew and martial law were proclaimed, and about two thousand people were arrested.

The revolt in Plzeň did not spread beyond city limits. With no access to the air waves, it could not aspire to being more than an episode of local dimensions. It also brought no tangible positive results. Party policy hardly changed; if anything, its methods of waging the class struggle became harsher. The injured police agents recovered from their wounds, and the only real casualty on the government side was the STB regional commander, Major Bálek, who was dismissed and made traffic commissioner of the Regional People's Committee. Nevertheless, this bizarre example of disobedience did contribute in a small way to the history of totalitarianism, demonstrating that the all-powerful Behemoth could be knocked out—even if only for forty-eight hours—by the fists of the proletariat.

This humiliation cried for revenge. The Plzeň potentates were furious, both on account of their poor performance in adapting Bolshevik genius to meet the emergency, and because all this had happened in their city and nowhere else. The court building, one of the main targets of the demonstrators, soon became the scene of their nemesis. The judges' displeasure with the revolt matched that of the apparatchiki. While Tlapák and Fikerle were occupied with shooting from a safe distance, some other colleagues had gone into hiding. A woman judge, Eliška Synková posed during the critical moments as a cook in the cafeteria, and District Prosecutor František Herger contracted cramps in the course of spending several hours locked in an uncomfortably small ladies' room. The only actual casualty of the courthouse engagement was a clerical employee, Havel, a Party busybody, who was caught and thoroughly maltreated while trying to leave the premises by the back entrance. Later on, I happened to sit on a committee which turned down his claim to a medal for bravery.

Arraigning and punishing the culprits posed a delicate problem. A workers' revolt against a workers' government was an "unhistorical" fact. As most of us would agree, one normally does not revolt and employ violence against himself. The original suggestion to place the blame for the rebellion on Plzeň's social democratic tradition or on the presence of the United States Army in 1945, was brushed aside as inadequate. After a week of cogitation, the Secretariat of the Party Central Committee in Prague came up with the following formula: the rebels were not workers, but bourgeois vermin dressed in overalls. Thus, any punishment meted out would be just and proper because imposed upon the class enemy. The Party also supplied some semantic guidance. To alleviate the unpleasantness, the happenings in Plzeň were not to be regarded as revolution, counter-revolution, uprising, revolt, rebellion, or demonstration but *události* ("events"). Prague also decided that the affair should be settled with no publicity, no show trials and no executions. Capital punishment, the reasoning went, would hamper the official attempt to disclaim the gravity of the "events."

On the one hand, the working class defendants were damaged through their reclassification as bourgeois elements; on the other hand, they gained through the decision that none should be charged with the most serious felonies, such as high treason, sedition or sabotage. The Party consulted the jurists to find the most suitable crime. The choice fell on the two which follow:

Section 154. Assault on Public Organs
   (1) Whoever uses violence or the threat of violence with the intent to influence the exercise of the jurisdiction of a people's committee or a court, shall be punished by imprisonment for a term of one to five years.
   (2) Equally he shall be punished who takes part in any gathering of at least three persons for the purpose of the commission of the crime under paragraph 1.
   (3) An offender shall be punished by imprisonment for a term of five to ten years,
      (a) if the act described in the paragraph 1 is committed with a weapon, or
      (b) if there is any other aggravating circumstance.

Section 177. Assault on a Public Official
   (1) Whoever uses violence or threat of violence
      (a) with the intent to influence the authority of a public official, or
      (b) because of the exercise of the authority of the public official, or
      (c) against any third person who attempted to protect a public official,
shall be punished by imprisonment for a term of one to five years.
   (2) Equally he shall be punished who takes part in a gathering of at least three persons for the purpose of the commission of the crime under the paragraph 1.
   (3) An offender shall be punished by imprisonment for a term of three to ten years,
      (a) if the act described in the paragraphs 1 or 2 is committed with a weapon, or
      (b) if by such act he injures the health of a public official or of a third person who attempted to protect him, or
      (c) if there is any other aggravating circumstance.

The reader should note that the second paragraph in each section enabled the court to convict any bystander. Also, anyone, whatever his status, who had defended the Establishment was promptly reclassified as a "public official."

The very first trials had a distinct note of kangaroo justice. The defendants were tried in groups of a dozen or so, and the daily norm of imposed servitude exceeded one hundred years. Defense counsels imported by the court from Prague need not have troubled to make the trip. They did next to nothing for their clients. It is interesting to note why the local Plzeň attorneys were disqualified *in toto* from participating. One of their colleagues, Dr. Hegner, appeared as a defendant. The state therefore reasoned that the Plzeň *advokáti*, by virtue of this arrest, forfeited the objectivity indispensable to the conduct of an adequate defense. A strange logic indeed, especially in view of the fact that sharpshooters Tlapák and Fikerle presided over most of these trials. No one questioned the objectivity of the judge toward an accused at whom he previously had emptied his revolver.

The Party-fabricated fable that it was the bourgeoisie who were responsible for the "events" bore no resemblance to the facts. The defendants were not overweight bourgeois parasites nourished by the propaganda of Radio Free Europe and sustained by nostalgic memories of the bygone age of merciless exploitation. Instead, they were the ex-exploited themselves; the true sons and daughters of the victorious proletariat. The judges had to reclassify the culprits; as Marx had dissociated himself from the bourgeoisie and fused with the proletariat, so these workers had gone the other way around.

The most numerous and active among the rioters were young workers from the Škoda plant. Witnessing the trials of these offenders, I strongly felt that their share in the violence directed against the System was not so much the result of a sacred yearning for "democracy," for "freedom"—as some outsiders chose to believe—as the spontaneous release of a host of accumulated frustrations and grievances. These were youngsters burdened by the daily demands of high output norms, the *Gleichschaltung* of their lives, the self-appointed paternalism of Party elders, and the dullness of totalitarian existence in general. They were bored with their lot and would have protested with almost equal vehemence under the banners of the swastika, free trade, nudism or what you will. But there were exceptions. Some of the young demonstrators were politically motivated, and in an extreme way. One might label them as upside-down Stalinists—dogmatic, intolerant advocates of pro-Americanism. With their oversimplified images of black and white, their admiration for the United States was boundless. A number of my acquaintances, too, were of this sort. When, for example, I attempted to temper their unqualified enthusiasm for all things American by referring to such blemishes as racial segregation, unemployment, or the underdeveloped state of social welfare, they would interrupt me with the reminder that I was just another ignorant Communist idiot.

This specimen one might call the total protestor. In short, the person who, in a gathering of people rising to the tunes of the Soviet national anthem, sits down. He had perfected his dedication to the cause of protest to the point of eventually ensuring his own immunity. He was not harmed because he was harmless—he was that obvious. As much as he hated the Party, the Party needed his hatred. He provided the apparatchiki with evidence of the viability and indispensability of the class struggle.

Pro-Americanism could take some peculiar forms, as in the case of the teenage laborer Peklo, a surname which translates as "Hell." He was charged by District Prosecutor Herger with all the crimes of the day, i.e., participation in the protest marches, destruction of Party property, and physical harm inflicted upon public officials. Peklo was much too young to remember the capitalist past, to have become its spiritual captive. Yet here was a proletarian, a product of socialist environment who did not mind revealing to the court his distaste for everything the Party stood for. In the attempt to further blacken Peklo's image before the bench, the Prosecutor ordered him to roll up his sleeve and admonished the judges to examine the evidence: the defendant's forearm was ornamented with numerous tatoos featuring stars and stripes and other assorted emblems of his patriotism for an adopted far-off motherland. The judges concluded that Peklo was a regrettable example of the successful penetration of an alien ideology. The victim of imperialist psychological warfare soon became the additional victim of socialist punishment.[2]

Peklo and those like him were in no sense a desirable catch for the court but an embarrassment and an ideologically confusing nuisance. These defendants were guilty. Clearly they had violated the law. The real sin of the judges was not the conviction of guilty proletarians but of innocent bourgeoisie. The bourgeoisie's defense that only the proximity of their homes, jobs, or other legitimate business had brought them into the neighborhood of the riots carried no weight with the judges. For example, a grey-haired, fragile, retired officer in his late sixties was held to be guilty in advance, owing to the fact that he had worked in military intelligence in the prewar Republic. According to his own plausible account, on the crucial first day of June, in common with thousands of others, he had simply obeyed the official instruction to hand in his old currency to the nearest branch of the State Bank. His branch was located at one corner of the Square of the Republic, and, as it happened, at the opposite end of the Square there was an abundance of anti-state behavior. The defendant pleaded innocent, emphasizing that at no point had he joined the demonstrators. All he had done was what he had been told to do, i.e., to go to the bank. The prosecutor did not bother to challenge the story. The defendant, convicted by his background, was found guilty because, as the court declared, "His presence in the vicinity of the area where the events took place served the purpose of implicit encouragement to those elements actively involved in endangering public order." After this ruling, Assistant Judge Ulč was assigned the task of producing a written opinion which would justify in pious terms of pretended objectivity the guilt and punishment in accordance with Section 154, par. 2 of the Criminal Code.

Assistant Judge Ulč went through even more pain in the case of the Kroupas. Kroupa was a prosperous farmer from a village on the outskirts of Plzeň who, during the campaign against the "rural class enemies," had been labelled a kulak, indicted, and sentenced to a prison term with all property confiscated; his family had been exiled to a State Farm in Northern Moravia. By an unfortunate coincidence, his son and daughter had decided to consult the attorney who had represented their father and had left by train for Plzeň during the weekend of the currency exchange. They arrived at their destination on June 1—and compounded this error by choosing quite the wrong part of town to visit. The attorney's office was located on Sedláčkova Street, just around the corner from the court currently under the demonstrators' attack. The young Kroupas at no time joined them. Nonetheless, the compulsion to uncover hidden wreckers of socialism dictated that the kulak's children be found guilty. No one seemed to be disturbed by the discrepancy in time. How could the Kroupas really have come to Plzeň to join the rioters; how could they have known beforehand about the "events," when they had boarded the train on Saturday and trouble erupted in Plzeň two days later?

In its search for bourgeois culprits, the Establishment left no stone unturned. A certain Zenkl, for example, allegedly a relative of the prominent émigré politician and former Vice-Premier Petr Zenkl, was sentenced to four years in jail. His crime: his name. Some even thought to make the trial of the hapless Zenkl a *cause célèbre,* linking the rebellion with Washington. The Central Committee of the Party, however, ruled out this fantasy. Rather than charge the West with responsibility for the riots and thus inflate its importance, it was preferable to remain silent before the world about the "events."

After a few weeks in attendance at the trials, I found the proceedings increasingly unexciting, though still painful. I waited about two months before I heard a defendant retract a confession made to the police. A sturdy worker in his early thirties addressed the court as follows. "They [the police] beat me and beat me and said they wouldn't stop until I confessed. So I confessed and signed anything they asked me to. I would have confessed to the murder of my own mother."

In those days the police were left free to use violence against the accused, and the extraction of a confession under duress was commonplace. Yet rarely would a victim dare to complain to the court, and I found it rather interesting to observe the reaction of the prosecutor and the judges in the above case. First there was a period of thoughtful silence. Since the Prosecutor seemed in no mood to speak up, presiding Judge Tlapák took the initiative. "Well, well! What an extraordinary fable. It's lucky for you that I am an understanding man; a very lenient one. I shan't treat you the way you deserve, after you have slandered the authorities of our state. I'll give you a very generous chance. Please, prove to us your allegations and give us the name of the police officer who, as you put it, beat you up." Now the secret police are secret, and it is not customary for interrogators to introduce themselves— either under assumed or real names—to their victims. Only anonymous fists break bones and remodel faces. As expected, our defendant was not able to name the police brute, and, according to the court, this failure disproved the charge of maltreatment.[3]

The Party line was to treat the "events" as "non-events." There was nothing in the newspapers. No journalist attended the trials. The proceedings were secret. The most secret of all, and the last in the order of the day, was the trial of Josef Fencl. Fencl operated a newspaper stand in Plzeň on the Square of the Republic and was a well-known figure in the city because of his former anti-Communist activities in the National Socialist Party. Moreover, he had been the chairman of the local chapter of the now-banned Society of American-Czechoslovak Friendship. Well over six feet tall, he was a stocky working-class type. Fencl undeservedly became the hero of the Plzeň revolt. He had distinguished himself among the demonstrators who overran the City Hall by addressing the crowds, and in the most bellicose speech, denouncing Communism. The people had loved it. Subsequently, it was rumored— a rumor that acquired the power of unquestioned truth—that the gallant Fencl had been tortured to death by the vindictive Bolsheviks.

When I met Fencl in court he was very much alive—and his trial furnished some unexpected revelations. It emerged that the accused, besides being an enemy of the state, was also on the payroll of the secret police.

Fencl—who was an essentially weak and compliant character —had signed up with the STB under duress. On June 1, the police had dispatched him to City Hall with orders to mix with the demonstrators, to pretend to be one of them, and to remember as many of their faces as possible. Fencl, however, amidst the destruction of all the Communist artefacts had been carried away and forgetting his assignment, he reached the peak of his revolutionary ardor just as the "events" were about to end.

At the trial, Fencl presented a pitiful picture of a frightened, small man, begging for mercy. Since it was my responsibility to elaborate the written opinion in this case, I decided I had better ask Tlapák for the ideologically correct evaluation of the defendant. Was he an ally, enemy or traitor, a bourgeois or a confused proletarian, a hireling of Wall Street or an ingenious STB undercover agent? How came the secret police to be recruiting former officials of an organization promoting friendship with the United States?

The explanation received from Tlapák offered a valuable insight into the operations of the STB which any of us concerned with our own survival would have done well to learn. Tlapák said, "Obviously, the STB needs informers. Plenty of them. It is not a matter of numbers that counts but the degree of confidence the agent enjoys among the class enemies. There is hardly any one else in Plzeň who has got a more anti-Communist reputation than Fencl. Therefore, we hired him. Of what use would a devoted Party member be to the STB? He wouldn't find out anything of what the people truly feel."

Fencl's sentence, when it came, was rather lenient—imprisonment for seven years. With any qualms over my involvement in this affair dispelled, I worked out the opinion, carefully omitting all allusions to the double-dealing habits of the defendant. Actually, Fencl did not suffer too long in Bolshevik dungeons. Well before my departure from the country in 1959, I saw him again in the streets of Plzeň, a free man and venerated by the public as never before.

Through administrative decisions outside the courts, hundreds of middle class families were evicted from their apartments— sometimes with only eight hours' notice—and exiled to decrepit villages. Many white collar employees lost their jobs and were assigned to manual labor out of town. One of these factories was even dubbed by the public as the "Enterprise of the First of June," since the majority of its workers were those forcibly transferred from the city.

Since 1956, many of the victims have contested the legality of these measures. The road toward remedy, however, was blocked by the resistance of the local apparatchiki. Restitution was, at best, very slow. In 1957, for example, I ran into my former high school teacher, František Lochovský, who was living in exile in one of the most remote villages of the Stříbro district. He complained to me that even President Zápotocký—with whom, some forty years previously, Lochovský had played on a soccer team in Kladno—could do nothing to break the determination of the Party officials in Plzeň to prevent Lochovský and others like him returning home.

The "events" described here provided me with a beneficial lesson on how an angry apparatus treats its disobedient subjects.

1. According to what I think was a rather reliable report, the commanding officer was later tried *in camera* by a military tribunal for violating his orders and withdrawing his unit and was shot. However, I have not had an opportunity to verify this information.

2. In his concluding remarks, Prosecutor Herger derided the defendant, accusing him of having his watch adjusted to "American time." This figure of speech pertinent to Peklo's outlook had to be taken literally with other militant Americanophiles. I knew several youngsters whose watches were set to Eastern Standard Time. They seemed not to mind the constant inconvenience of converting EST to Czechoslovak reality.

3. Judge Tlapák, despite his cat-and-mouse game, was in fact lenient, just as he had promised. Though cynical, he at least did not turn the "provocation" (i.e., the defendant's complaint) into an additional felony, as was common practice with other courts. It suffices to check with the contemporaneous decision (May 31, 1953) of the Supreme Court, published in the *Sbírka*, No. 59, volume 1953, pp. 96-97. A defendant, while on trial for high treason, "falsely accused the state security organs of extorting confession from him by using forbidden and illegal methods." Instead of having the complaint investigated, the Court enlarged the original charge, with the justification that "the accused by this act endangered the confidence of the public in the just and legal execution of public power." It should perhaps be added that this was a secret trial, and the public was barred from the proceedings. Nevertheless, the defendant had managed to endanger the confidence of non-existent spectators.

14 THE ANTI-STATE OFFENSES

Communist reforms simplified both the organizational structure of the courts (e.g., by abolishing the second appeal bench) and the concept of crime itself. With the exception of misdemeanors, which were left to the People's Committees, the judiciary was vested with authority over all felonies (*trestný čin*) as laid down in the second part of the 1950 Criminal Code, referred to as the Specific Part,[1] ranging from Section 78 (high treason) to Section 303 (brutal treatment of POWs). The Specific Part consisted of ten chapters, each dealing with the broad category of offenses, e.g. acts endangering life (Chapter 6), or property (Chapter 8) or military preparedness of the country (Chapter 9). The characteristic common to all felonies listed was the alleged "menace to society" posed by the criminal act. The frequency with which the various sections were violated varied widely, from Section 245, the pilferage of socialist property and by far the most popular crime, to Section 194, par. 1, the damage of submarine cables, an unlikely crime in view of the landlocked fate of Czechoslovakia.

Original jurisdiction over all infractions of the Criminal Code was vested with the District Courts. There were, however, two exceptions to this rule: felonies specified in the Ninth and Tenth Chapters were adjudicated by military courts, and grave political crimes were the sole responsibility of special tribunals. It is with the latter that I will now deal.

Although to a Marxist any crime is, in a way, a political one, the anti-state crimes are interpreted as an attack on the very structure of the State.

The First Chapter of the Specific Part of the Criminal Code, entitled "Crimes against the Republic," enumerated no less than fifty-two different felonies, some of which would make strange reading to Western eyes. For example, among the acts menacing the very foundation of the State were "Voicing Disrespect to the President of the Republic," "Misusing the Religious Office," or "Spreading Rumors." The vast number testifies to the intent of the legislators to cast as wide a net as possible to catch any and all political malcontents.

Though the special tribunals were entitled to adjudicate any of the fifty-two offenses, they usually left the jurisdiction to the District Courts, while securing for themselves the most serious crimes, notably high treason, sabotage and espionage. This revolutionary bench was rather innocuously labelled as the *Státní soud* ("State Court") and the accuser at these trials the *Státní prokurátor* ("State Prosecutor"). The trials were either secret or for selected audiences, or were show trials. The decision to this effect rested with the Party.

It is certainly true that there were more people tried in secret by the State Court and subsequently executed than the government has ever been willing to admit. During my year with the Czechoslovak judiciary I came across a number of cases of defendants who had perished on the gallows without any news of their fate reaching the public.

The second type of proceedings before the State Court—those for selected audiences—were occasionally, though not always, revealed to the public. The rationale behind the decision whether to admit many, few or none of the public to a trial depended on the Party's desire either for secrecy or for the "educational impact of socialist retribution on the toiling masses." The compromise between these two alternatives was the "participation upon invitation," when the exposure was limited to individuals having background, occupation or residence similar to the accused.

The first time I was called upon to attend such a spectacle, I was still a law student at Prague University. The defendants were likewise students, with the exception of their alleged leader.

All were charged, *inter alia*, with compiling a list of names of the Party and Communist Youth activists at the University with the intent to transmit this information to the West. In view of the fact that some of the accused were law school students, the administration arranged for us to attend the trial. The court building, occupied also by the Supreme Court and the Office of the Prosecutor General, is located in the fourteenth district of Prague, called Pankrác, on the Square of Heroes.[2.] Our internal passports were checked and re-checked several times before the stern policemen admitted us to the court room, which was identical, except for its size, with any regular court. We did notice that the prosecutor, to underline the gravity of his mission, was also wearing an official gown, hemmed with dark purple. The judges were robed in their usual black and violet. The defendants appeared separately, and thus, were prevented from hearing each other's testimony. When seated, each of the accused was flanked on both sides by guards to prevent communication among the fellow conspirators. If a defendant attempted to turn his head towards the audience, the presiding judge barked a brisk order preempting this "illegal" move.

Most of the time, the presiding judge posed as an objective umpire, in contrast to the very vituperative prosecutor. The people's assessors were silent. Also silent were the counsels for the defense. They limited their performance to a concluding plea, calling for mercy and generosity towards the confused and misled youth.

The defendants had not been rehearsed in spontaneous self-accusations. Some were even defiant. For example, a former classmate of mine told the court, "I refuse to say anything because it would be meaningless, anyway. This country is not a country of law, and you are not a court but a travesty of justice." To this "provocation"—by itself at least one extra felony—the presiding judge replied: "It is your privilege, defendant, to think whatever you wish. However, since you are a former law student, you ought to appreciate the fact that this court will not hold you in contempt as would be the case in your beloved United States."

This defendant was sentenced to twelve years and the leader to twenty-five; the only acquittal was that of a girl student who, however, was not permitted to continue with her medical studies. Thus ended the affair of compiling a Bolshevik Who's Who. The sentences, though long, were merciful from the defendants' point of view—at least they were not hanged. In those days ten years behind bars was easier to get than a bottle of good brandy. I knew, for example, of a sixteen-year-old girl who, because of her nominal membership in an outlawed scout organization, was incarcerated for twelve years.

The Party ordered the staging of the show trial for both re-education and intimidation. The biggest shows coincided with the Party's campaigns of the day: the assault on the Catholic Church was accompanied by show trials against the leading clergymen; the drive for collectivization of agriculture was underlined by trials such as that of the kulaks accused of killing three Communists in the village of Babice; a propaganda blast at the United States was neatly complemented by the trial of American spies, etc.

During the show trials, the mass communication media, the radio and the press (in the early fifties television was still in its infancy), engaged in a "total campaign" and did a splendid job. The engineered mass hysteria was reflected in endless protest meetings, petitions demanding death penalties, workers' pledges to raise output in return for the scalps of those accused, letters from school children dutifully notifying the Party of their indignation toward the traitors, poems produced for the occasion by distinguished men of letters. One enthusiast, I was told, even started to compose an opera. Lacking inspiration, his protracted undertaking was interrupted by the rehabilitation of the villains.

The top show trial was staged in 1952, this time cutting into the ranks of the Party itself. This auto-da-fe, known in the West as the Slánský trial, was the last in the series of purges that swept Eastern Europe as Stalin's life drew to its close. What had started in Budapest with Rajk, ended in Prague with a record number of casualties. The Secretary General of the Czechoslovak Communist Party, Rudolf Slánský, and a dozen or so unlikely accomplices were accused of highly improbable crimes. All duly confessed, and one of the defendants—André Simone—even insisted on being hanged. The court did not disappoint him.

Among the accused was a prominent economist, Ludvík Frejka. At the time of the trial, the main Party daily *Rudé právo* carried on November 25, 1952, a letter written by the son of the accused, Tomáš Frejka. It read:

To the Chairman of the State Court in Prague:
Dear Comrade:
    I request the most severe punishment for my father—the penalty of death. It is only now that I realize that this creature is not entitled

to be called a human being, because he lacks any feeling and human dignity and has become my biggest and meanest enemy.

I promise to work anywhere and will always work as a devoted Communist. I know that my hatred of all our enemies, of all those who want to destroy our increasingly richer and more joyful life and especially of my father, will always strengthen me in my struggle for the Communist future of our nation.

I request that this letter be made available to my father and that possibly I can tell him of it in person.

The letter received wide publicity, father Frejka was hanged, and the whole story also attracted the attention of the Western press. However, many observers doubted the authenticity of the letter, and it was also rumored that young Frejka, after having been forced to produce the message, committed suicide.

Now might be an appropriate time to set the record straight even at the risk of departing from the main theme of this chapter. One year after the Slánský trial ended—in the fall of 1953—I was drafted into the Czech Army and met Tomáš Frejka, who had been assigned to the same squad. He was a rather shy, withdrawn blond youngster, with a knowledge of English and distinct dislike for manual labor. We were the only two university-trained draftees in the group. Tomáš tried quite hard to become my friend. Naturally, he did not reveal that he was *the* Frejka. This I found out only by chance, while helping to sort documents of the new arrivals at battalion Headquarters. Frejka's file carried a pencilled note: "Father dead. Executed as a traitor."

Several months passed before I made up my mind to have a frank talk with Tomáš. My assumption was that Frejka had written the letter under duress, in which case a discussion about the matter would be of little use. The authorities would have threatened him with dire consequences should be fail to keep silent, and since Frejka had complied in denouncing his own father, he was hardly likely to defy the Establishment by telling me the truth about what had happened in 1952. On the other hand, had he been fanatical enough to genuinely condemn his father, then I might land in serious trouble if I were incautious in my probing.

In the barracks we used to get, free of charge, the Party and the Army newspapers. We were ordered to read them and therefore practically no one did. One day when I was hiding in the lavatory to escape our drill sergeant I spotted quite accidentally an important bit of news. I clipped it out, put it in my pocket, and since it was Saturday, with leave to go downtown, I invited Tomáš to have a drink with me.

In a half-empty, cozy inn on the Bořín Hill, close to the North

Bohemian town of Bílina, after having started on our second bottle of wine, I mentioned to my companion, "Look, I know your father was Ludvík Frejka and that you wrote that hideous letter for the newspaper. Did they force you to do it?"

I could afford to raise this straightforward question. Nobody was sitting close enough to overhear us, and in any case if Tomáš chose to denounce me to the *kontrarozvĕdka* (military STB) I would deny everything. It was hardly likely that the word of a Private and son of a traitor would outweigh that of a Private who was an Assistant Judge.

Apparently there was no need for me to worry. Frejka listened to me and seemed by no means upset. He replied, "Nobody forced me to do anything." Before I was able to digest this surprising news he started to tell his story—about his childhood, the war years spent in England and the relatively luxurious life to which he had been accustomed. "My relationship with my father was always good," he said. "When he was arrested no one in the family knew anything of what had happened. It was only when the trial was broadcast that I again heard my old man's voice. I was then enrolled at the VŠPHV[3.] in Prague. You can imagine that as the son of a prominent personality I had no shortage of friends, but as soon as the trial started I was suddenly alone. I realized that the people around me, and the Party activists in particular, were trying to avoid me. It was suffocating. I had to do something. So I went to the Party organization at the school and told them that I would like to publicly condemn my father's crimes. The comrades were very understanding and they arranged for my contact with the radio and press. As I also wanted to voice my approval of a possible execution of my father at a face-to-face meeting with him, I approached the Ministry of Security. I was not allowed to meet him, but I was promised that I could attend the court on the day the verdict would be passed. Actually they did not keep their word."

Pausing for a while to fortify himself with another drink, Tomáš then continued: "In fact, other disillusionments were in store for me. I was forced to quit the University and go to work in a factory. Originally, when I first thought of making that statement, I must admit that I was anxious to be left free to finish my studies. Yet," he hastened to emphasize, "the main reason for my statement was that, as a convinced Marxist, I had to do it. It was my duty to break with my father and denounce him publicly.

You may dislike my what you might call opportunism—I certainly wanted to stay on at school—but in my opinion it would have been far more immoral if the sentimentality of the son-father relationship had prevailed over the courage to stand up in defense of higher, political values."

Frejka was lying of course. As far as I had been able to judge during the time we had known each other, he was about as much a devoted Communist as I was a practicing cannibal. However, this interesting discussion was not yet at an end. "Now, come on, you weren't born yesterday," I said. "Didn't it occur to you that your father might have been forced to plead guilty and admit to all that phony nonsense? You know as well as I do that they beat people and use scopolamin or whatever those wonder drugs are called."

"Well, one does hear about these things," Tomáš admitted, "but I ruled out that possibility. Father's voice in court, as we heard it over the radio, sounded perfectly natural, and his diction was unchanged. And even if he had been forced to tell the truth, the simple fact that he was guilty still remains, and this fact ultimately justifies what I did."

Now was the right moment to introduce the news clipping I had brought with me. The timing was better than my performance, which in retrospect I find somewhat melodramatic. "Charges against your father were mainly based on his deals with the Western spy Field, weren't they?" He nodded. "Then have a look at this," I exclaimed triumphantly. "They kicked you out of the school anyway. Now you have even lost the flimsy excuse, the guilt of your father. He was innocent. Have a look!" The clipping contained a brief item taken from the Polish press announcing that Field had been released from prison "because the charges of espionage against him appeared to be unsubstantiated."

We did not say anything for a while. Tomáš tried very hard not to appear upset. "Well, let's go back to the barracks," he suggested. "What more is there for me to say?"

Strangely enough, our relationship remained unchanged. In Frejka's opinion I was still his only friend at the unit. After we had been discharged from the Army, I met him only once more, in a Prague night club—still a very lonely figure.

To bring this story to an end: I did not quite comprehend why Frejka, after having taken his stand against his father, had been expelled from the school. This majestic propaganda tool, as I saw it, deserved more friendly treatment. Václav Keltner, a counter-intelligence officer from our battalion, with whom I was on rather cordial terms, supplied me with an explanation, "Man, what makes you think that we could ever fall in love with people like Frejka, who turned against their own parents? Don't you think they would be prepared to betray anybody and anything when the right time came? One may have to use such creatures, but one doesn't have to marry them."

Frejka's strategy in the game for survival had been faulty. Perhaps he had held hopeless cards from the start, but in that case he should not have gambled, but rather accepted the inevitability of guilt through association. By his letter, he violated the rule of proportion referred to in Chapter VIII. In this respect, Frejka reminds us of M. who delivered his brother to the executioner, or of Judge Hluže who was too pale when Stalin died.

It took over ten years before—in August 1963—the victims of the Slansky affair were posthumously rehabilitated. The Party, however, lost its liking for superspectacles of this kind much earlier. With Stalin and Gottwald dead, the State Court and the Office of the State Prosecutor were abolished, and their jurisdiction was transferred to special divisions set up at each of the nineteen provincial courts.

On the whole, however, these were changes in form rather than in substance. The Party Secretariat kept its final say over the conduct and outcome of political trials, the proceedings continued to be secret, and in most of the cases the same judges occupied the bench.

In the Plzeň province the adjudication over these offenses became the monopoly of three ex-proletarians: Chairman of the Regional Court Adam Pittner, his Deputy, Miroslav Tlapák, and, representing the weaker sex, Marie Benková. Benková in particular was a most improbable type to be in charge of liquidating "enemies of the people." In her forties, short and pudgy, she strongly resembled the folksy characters depicted by the cartoonists in the Soviet satirical magazine Krokodil. And yet, this backwoods matron conducted important trials with confidence, handing down death penalties with ease and one might even say, with homeliness. The prosecution before this court was performed by either Ludmila Brožová, who had gained national reputation for her militancy in prominent show trials, or by František Vašek, a tall

Mephistophelian fellow with a brilliant mind, the only university-educated lawyer among the five mentioned.

For the majority of the judiciary, political trials, staged nationally or provincially, remained a *terra incognita*. The files were kept secret from all but a handful of carefully selected, taciturn clerks. One wing of the top floor of the Plzeň court was blocked by iron bars, behind which handleless doors, a system of bells and guards guaranteed against unauthorized entry. In all my years at court I never once succeeded in penetrating this sacred realm, and there were not many who did.

Though we were trusted by the Establishment, we were not trusted enough. The amount and degree of political acceptance the System extended toward us differed, and we were expected to adjust our behavior and expectations to the appropriate level. Trivia such as seating practices in the provincial court cafeteria may illustrate the point. Judges and prosecutors in charge of political trials sat at a separate table, to be joined only by secret police investigators or Party officials: It would never have occurred to the rest of us to drop uninvited into this company. I used to meet Prosecutor Brožová daily. I would always bow and mutter the prescribed greeting "Labor be Honored," but I never expected anyone to introduce me to her. No one did. I am not accusing Brožová of the arrogance so common among political parvenus. It was not rudeness but rather a belief in the propriety of maintaining the hierarchical set up. Prudence cautioned against looking over the fence into the territories of our more privileged colleagues, basking in the sun of the Party's grace.

In Plzeň, the trials of "counter-revolutionaries" were held in a chamber known by the misleading name of Great Jury Hall.[4.] As a judge, I was admitted by the uniformed guard, but I used this privilege only once, and that was more than enough. About a dozen defendants were standing trial, their lives entrusted to the hands of the homely housewife Benková. My feeling of guilt through unwanted association drove me away from the chamber after only a few minutes, never to return.

With the consolidation of the regime during the fifties, there was a noticeable decrease in anti-state criminal behavior. However, Stalinist doctrine on the intensification of class struggle presupposed active enemies, and it was the responsibility of the police, the prosecutors and the courts to prove the veracity of the dogma. Here are a few examples:

The case of S.: S. was one of the executives of the Plzeň brewery who, though a nominal Party member, remained listed with the secret police (STB) as a suspicious bourgeois element. In the mid-fifties a former friend of S., who had once been sentenced *in absentia* for a political offense, sent S. a meaningless letter from abroad. The STB intercepted S.'s acknowledgment and on the basis of this "evidence," a charge was fabricated against S. for having attempted to set up contacts with the enemies of socialism. S. was sentenced to a term of imprisonment despite the embarrassment to one of his relatives, a nationally known scientist.

The case of B.: The STB planted an anti-state leaflet in the mailbox of this former businessman. B. collected the missive and burned it. Twenty-four hours later he was picked up by the STB and charged with failure to report the incident and deliver the leaflet to the proper authorities. A prison term followed.

The case of R.: R., a retired local bureaucrat, was in the habit of meeting a group of friends once a week for a game of chess in a secluded part of the Beseda restaurant in Plzeň. It is difficult to see how the STB could have been attracted to these innocuous senior citizens except for reasons of "production quotas." The police planted monitoring devices under the chess table; once enough evidence of verbal disloyalty had been recorded, the septuagenarians were arrested, tried for incitement and duly sentenced.

A large share of the responsibility for the fabrication of political offenses must go to the *agents provocateurs*. Posing, for example, as members of Western intelligence services, they were dispatched to the households of suspected anti-Communists to ask for nothing more than food and shelter for one night. This hospitality was then rewarded with punishment of from ten to twenty years in jail. These *agents provocateurs* did not testify in person at the trial. The prosecution feared that some defense counsel might be courageous enough to challenge the indictment on the ground that harboring an impostor cannot be interpreted as an act of proven espionage.

The STB was particularly pleased with the services rendered by some double-defectors. The greater the anti-Communist reputation they enjoyed, the better. In this connection I have especially in mind one former employee of Radio Free Europe who rendered sterling service to the STB in Bratislava. A similar *provocateur* was a former member of a Czech guard unit which was established in West Germany after 1948 under the sponsorship of the United

States Army. He was commissioned by the STB to visit the Czech families of his former brothers-in-arms. The STB equipped him with a tape recorder and photo montages showing him in the company of the family's relative, both wearing American uniforms. For added emphasis, the Stars and Stripes made up the background. No wonder the guest appeared as a credible "freedom fighter." Those taken in had several years in which to regret their mistake.

It was not uncommon to keep a person incommunicado for a year or more before he was brought to trial, if he was ever tried at all. I talked to a number of individuals who had been kept in solitary confinement, with no right to receive letters or visitors or to communicate with a lawyer, who, after five hundred days of this ordeal, were released with or without apologies from their captors. Since the fine art of molding the prisoner into the image of his tormentors exceeds the scope of this narrative, I shall limit myself to a few brief points. Defendants selected to appear at the top show trials not surprisingly received most of the attention of the police persuaders. They were beaten, drugged, threatened with reprisals against their families, or encouraged to confess, not as guilty men, but as loyal Communists responding without question to the wishes of the Party.

The elementary instrument in the interrogation of an average suspect was the clenched fist. A common beating was the most frequently used, though not the most effective device. A person's resistance could be broken better by other means, e.g., disorientation in time and place, or imposed solitude. Say, a suspect was arrested in Prague. Charged with nothing, he was blindfolded and transferred to the nearby fortress of Ruzyně. Here, stripped naked, he would be put in a dark cell, with no opportunity to see another living being, served food by an anonymous hand at irregular intervals, and left in this hole for weeks. Candidates for this bruiseless treatment did not know where they were, how long they had been incarcerated, or even whether it was day or night. It was not long before they were no match for an investigator willing to spare his knuckles and wait. As far as I know, the most effective method in extracting a confession was both simple and bloodless: to keep the victim awake and walking. After two weeks of such treatment only a few were still insufficiently intoxicated by fatigue to be unwilling to admit anything they were asked about.

With the investigation completed, the suspect had to confirm by signature that his confession was voluntary, free from duress, and that he would reveal to no one how he had been treated. During the brief period of the thaw in 1956 some of the victims dared to complain. A letter appeared on my desk in which a freed prisoner charged that the police had obtained his confession by unlawful means. He wrote: "I was in custody for over a month. Every night at fifteen minute intervals the guards entered my cell and forced me to do push-ups. Finally, I confessed to the fabricated charge." I sent a copy of the letter to the Ministry of Interior requesting an explanation. In no time at all a mimeographed note bearing an illegible signature came back baldly stating, "These were the investigatory methods considered appropriate during the period under question."

The military justice matched its civilian equivalent in its fervor for substituting imagination for facts and finding crimes against the state where none existed. To illustrate this point: In a remote unit southwest of Prague a group of Army recruits arrived at a somewhat lunatic notion of how to entertain themselves during their spare time. A clandestine outfit was organized along the lines of the ancient Roman legion, with ranks and titles of dubious historical accuracy. Although I did not know personally the Centurion Maximus (a pharmacist by profession), I did know P., one of the lower echelon warriors, who was an alcoholic and an inarticulate fool.[5] Besides riding horses, rented from local farmers, and waving torches on dark nights around Karlštejn Castle — the one-time seat of Charles IV, Emperor of the Holy Roman Empire of the German Nation and founder of my Alma Mater — the boys were pretty harmless. I now ask the reader to guess the crime of which the military court accused the imaginative horsemen. The answer: They were charged with the felony of "Supporting and promoting fascism and similar movements," according to Section 83 of the 1950 Criminal Code — and convicted. P. spent five years in jail, and the commanding pharmacist was awarded a dozen years behind bars.

Similarly, deserters — not infrequent in the Czechoslovak Army — faced stern punishment. It did not seem to matter much to the justices that a lonely farm boy, longing for his sweetheart, had simply run away from his unit for a couple of days, without waiting for that very rare commodity called a furlough, which a soldier without good connections obtained only about once a year, if at all. In the courts' understanding, desertion implied not an attempt to share a bed with the girl friend but a determination to defect abroad to join Wall Street in its sinister schemes of undermining the grandiose Communist future. In a case that occurred in our battalion, the punishment was fifteen years.

The spectrum of circumstances that could be interpreted as a violation of the military code was so wide that its thorough enforcement would have paralyzed the country's military might. When I was about to be discharged I calculated that my record of undetected or tolerated infractions called for a punishment of one hundred and twelve years and eight months. Actually, the only punishment I did not manage to avert was thirty days' confinement to barracks after having "ridiculed a superior officer in front of the assembled unit." However, I hasten to add that I enjoyed fairly preferential treatment in the army. A number of officers profited from my legal advice, and I in turn blackmailed them into leaving me alone. Captain Vodička was struggling with an indemnity charge for a burned down barrack in his Company; Captain Breyer had divorce troubles, and the NCO Vojtěch Pintrava was fighting a discharge order. The Ministry of Defense intended to get rid of this poor man, a milker of cows by training, only because of his having contracted gonorrhoea for the twenty-fifth time, which silver jubilee he disclosed to me blushingly.

Shortly after the February, 1948, coup, the new regime set up special military units consisting of politically inferior draftees. Service in these units implied hard manual labor either in the mines or in the construction industry. Conscripts were not exposed to military training in the real sense of the word. "You don't train your enemies to handle weapons," the Party reasoned. The draft boards selected the candidates for these semi-concentration camps on the basis of recommendations by Local People's Committees, the Party, the police, anonymous letters, or by mistake. Most of them were stained with bourgeois or kulak background, had relatives residing abroad, or were former university students, ex-convicts, Hungarians, Germans or Gypsies. The victims of this interesting example of political prophylaxis were organized in what were euphemistically called "Auxiliary Technical Battalions" (*Pomocné technické prapory*, abbreviated PTP). In 1953 the adjective "Auxiliary" was dropped along with the indefinite duration of the service in these units, and the new TP structure gradually lost most of its punitive character.

Anything relating to the armed forces was held a state secret. Even revelation of one's rank — which a child in kindergarten could read from a uniform shoulder — constituted a crime. In conclusion I should like to permit myself the pleasure of mentioning the location of a dozen of these PTP (PT) "protective camps:" Bílina, Chudeřice, Karviná, Komárno, Libava, Lýně, Mimoň, Nepomuk, Podolinec, Rajhrad, Svatá Dobrotivá and Zdechovice.

Now, with my criminal revelation of state secrets committed, let us return to civilian affairs. As noted earlier, adjudication of less significant political crimes was left to the ordinary district courts. Trials here were especially concerned with misdeeds of the tongue, i.e., verbal offenses. The punitive policy adhered to the Party line to excuse misled proletarians and incarcerate all the rest. Once I attended the trial of two drunks who had exclaimed at midnight in front of the Party Secretariat that under Hitler life had been better. Both defendants were manual laborers. Since it was established, however, that one of them before the war had been temporarily self-employed as a barber, this sufficed to convict him, while his buddy was acquitted. The System was very touchy about political jokes — an established part of Czechoslovak folklore. With the exception of some black humor gems, those jokes that led to trouble were not particularly witty. As far as I could observe the two most popular targets of these "felonies" were the physical dimensions and unsavory past of the First Lady Marta Gottwaldová, and the gigantic size of Antonín Zapotocký's auricles.

Owing to the proximity of the West German frontier, the number of verbal offenses tried in the district courts in the Plzeň province was outstripped by the so-called "Section 95 cases." It is estimated that since 1948, between fifty thousand and a hundred thousand people have illegally fled the country. This high figure discouraged the courts from trying each defector. Instead, *in absentia* proceedings were instituted mainly against those who left considerable property behind — or where, as in my case, political considerations demanded staging a trial.

Such trials were short routine affairs. With no witnesses to be heard, the prosecutor recited the indictment, the *ex officio* counsel for the defense objected meekly that "nothing was known to him about the commission of crime," court ignored the objection, passed the sentence — usually close to five years with confiscation of all property — and Assistant Judge Ulč (when still there) worked out the written opinion. It should be added that the Czechoslovak courts, unlike their Soviet counterparts, did not try the relatives of the defectors unless it could be established that they had aided or were otherwise implicated in the affair.

Occasionally we tried and sentenced phantoms. The responsibility for such mishaps lay not so much with the courts as with the general climate in a totalitarian society. Absence from one's job or apartment put the authorities on the alert. Failure to keep a date could cause a man's friendly neighborhood STB informer to report that the citizen had betrayed the fatherland and joined the French Foreign Legion. The physical unavailability of a suspect sufficed for his indictment. The courts, concerned with production quotas, could not afford to wait until the defector sent from abroad the first postcard. Once I drafted a stiff sentence for a railway employee. At the trial the defense counsel called for acquittal, pointing out that in view of his client's partial lameness, a successful escape across the border was unlikely. Long after the verdict went into imaginary force, the body of the defendant was found in a nearby forest, where he had hanged himself because of marital troubles.

If, in 1948, a would-be defector had more than a fifty-fifty chance of reaching West Germany, with the gradual construction of the "frontier protection devices" the probability of success dwindled, according to reasonable estimates, to about twenty-to-one, at best by 1953. The term "Iron Curtain," nowadays a political cliché, remains a hard reality in the Šumava Mountains of Bohemia. To "get out" means to pass unnoticed through the approximately three-mile strip of "borderland zone" (*pohraniční pásmo*), about a quarter of a mile of the "forbidden zone" (*zakázané pásmo*), barbed wire fence charged with electricity, ploughed no-man's land, mine fields, Border Guard units, watch towers, hidden observation posts, electronic devices, and very nasty dogs. In other words, unless one belongs to the Border Guard and has access to the key to the underground passages built for the commuting spies, it is advisable not to try.[6.]

While the state did not bother to stage *in absentia* trials for all the successful defectors, the same lenience could not apply to those who did not quite make it. Penal Code prescribed equal punishment for an attempted crime and for a crime fully committed. This ruling was of particular significance in cases of the violation of Section 95. Innocent mushroom hunters who inadvertently wandered into the border zone were put on trial with only a minimal chance of persuading the judges that they really did not want to quit socialism. Individual instances of undue judicial leniency were subjected to stern criticism. One judge was publicly castigated by Minister Škoda for a violation of the spirit of socialist legality when he passed a suspended sentence on two sixteen-year-old workers apprehended on their way to Africa to hunt elephants.

The STB, in their fondness for traps, frame-ups and provocations in general, employed particular ingenuity in pursuance of Section 95. Take the case of B., a resident of Karlsbad, the spa of past splendor. A person of some intelligence, he knew that the crossing of the nearby border was something more than an easy afternoon stroll. Fortunately, he chanced to meet a former member of the Czech armed units in exile in Great Britain, a known anti-Communist and, it was rumored, an expert guide over the "zones." The expert promised, for a substantial fee, to get B. across the state line to West Germany. One night B. was marshalled through intricate forest routes until he reached a place where his guide congratulated him on having found freedom — and vanished. In front of the defector was a U.S. Army post, where he was enthusiastically welcomed and offered real American cigarettes and drinks. B. in return gratefully blabbed out all he knew about Czechoslovakia's secrets and emphasized his aversion to Communism. The commanding officer diligently took notes of everything. B. then was directed to proceed in a given direction to the German refugee camp. Back in the woods B. found himself arrested. The whole farce, of course, took place on Czechoslovak soil. The "U.S. soldiers" were STB agents. Only the sentence B. received was authentic.

Reliable guides through the border area were in short supply and, in any case, did not last very long. A number of sinister individuals converted the high demand into a quite profitable business. Contrary to the general opinion at that time, I did not believe that *all* of them were in the employ of the STB, though I cannot substantiate this assertion. My feeling was that the record of some of the guides was too gruesome to be acceptable even to our secret police. Here are two examples: The customers of a former Red Army officer operating in the Karlsbad district, instead of reaching West Germany, ended up as corpses in an abandoned mine shaft. The guide, rich in gold, jewels and Western currency, then disappeared into the unknown. I have never been able to find out whether he was ever apprehended and tried. A second example, about which I have more direct knowledge, involved a certain Hubert Pilčík. Pilčík was an elderly laborer in the Škoda industries who claimed that before the war he had been a sailor on the high seas. He lived with his wife in the village of Senec, near Plzeň. In early 1956, children playing at the Senec pond discovered human remains buried in the sandy shore. Pilčík was quickly arrested, and among other surprises, a pre-teen-age girl was found in his home, in a specially constructed cage, reminiscent of the boxes used by Central Europeans for keeping geese. In this case, Pilčík not only fed but also sexually abused the confined victim. As it turned out Pilčík had for years been conducting a lurid route of no return for those he promised to guide across the border to West Germany. Pointing out the danger of the venture, he always advised his clients to take nothing with them but jewels and hard currency.

The circumstantial evidence of this case places the STB in rather a dim light. Pilčík ran his enterprise for much too long a time not to have become suspect to the STB. Second, Pilčík was arrested with miraculous speed. Third, his customers scheduled for the next trip were also arrested with no delay. Last, but not least, the murderer was not brought to trial, owing to his sudden and very peculiar death. While in custody, Pilčík supposedly committed suicide by strangulation. As the report read, he used his handkerchief as a sort of noose and by self-administered tightening departed from the world of the living. A medical expert might accept the possibility of such a suicide, but a layman would have a hard time understanding how, since one usually loses consciousness before dying, the unconscious Pilčík could have successfully completed the project.

I assume that this last story was macabre enough to facilitate a smooth transition to the next chapter.

1. The First Part of the Criminal Code consists of provisions of a general nature, such as the concept of crime, guilt, negligence, attempt, accessory, legal responsibility, aggravating and mitigating circumstances, etc.
2. *Hrdina* in Czech means both "hero" and "martyr." Inevitably, the Square of the Heroes acquired this double meaning with the public.
3. VŠPHV stands for *Vysoká škola politických a hospodářských věd* (School of Political and Economic Sciences). It should be added that the School was subsequently "purged." The Party dissolved VŠPHV as an alleged "private institute of Rudolf Slánský."
4. This room has been a scene of exercises of questionable legality dating back to the pre-Communist days of 1945. Immediately after the war, the so-called Extraordinary People's Courts (*mimořádné lidové soudy,* known under the abbreviation MLS) were established to settle accounts with the Nazis

and their collaborators. The overall record of MLS was one of revolutionary vengeance. With no pretense at objectivity, the trials were fast and short, verdicts were not subject to appeal, and the penalty of death was always carried out within a few hours. Some of the judges never recovered from the shock of involvement in these kangaroo practices. Dr. Hahn (later a colleague of mine), for instance, was permanently haunted by the ghost of the former teacher Hubert, one of the first people executed in Plzeň. Hahn, who presided over the trial, was outvoted in his protest against the death sentence for Hubert, whose only crime was that he was a harmless pro-Nazi sympathizer. Such excesses were, of course, not limited to Plzeň only. In Prague, a shoemaker from the Krč suburb was summoned to the court as a witness at 10 a.m., and four hours later he was executed. In Klatovy, a defendant from Domažlice pleaded mistaken identity, but Judge D. refused to listen. Only after the execution did the court learn that the wrong man had been hanged.

One rather unusual incident happened in Plzeň in connection with these trials. The law terminated the MLS as of December 31, 1947. On the last Saturday of the year a German was sentenced to die. The execution, however, could not be performed immediately because the local hangman Karas (otherwise, a tax collector) got drunk and failed to arrive at court on time. The court got hold of the intoxicated executioner only after midnight, but Karas refused to function, pointing out that Sunday was the Lord's day. On Monday, alas, it was too late because the law had by then expired. Here then was a man who had to be hanged but was not legally "hangable." After about three months of pondering over what to do, Prague commuted the sentence. During the fifties, the defendant was released and joined his family in West Germany.

5. Actually, it was difficult to determine the true state of his eloquence. P., posing as a Spaniard, pretended to be unable to speak Czech. Since, however, he knew no Spanish (or other foreign language), a conversation with him was a rather trying experience. In a way, P. was a forerunner of some of the characters in Joseph Heller's *Catch 22*.

6. One of the few exceptions to the rule was J. The charming absurdity of his story may excuse its inclusion in this narrative, told to me by O.G., a journalist living in the West. J., faced with multiple alimonies, decided — for political reasons — to leave Czechoslovakia. Not burdened by the complexities of an intellectual mind, he walked straight to the frontier, stepping on nothing and seen by no one. Sneaking through the barracks of the Border Guards — thus avoiding the wire obstacles — he reached the crucial river Morava. Through the darkness he saw the other bank — the Austrian Republic. At this moment J. had to acknowledge the sad fact that he had not learned to swim. So he built a raft, which brought him to freedom, or so he thought for a while. Thanking his Creator, J. disposed of the raft, waiting for morning. The approaching dawn revealed that J. was stranded on a tiny islet, still within Czechoslovak jurisdiction. J. was forced to build a second raft, and he succeeded with his dangerous undertaking despite the proximity of the border guards. On it he finally reached Austria. There he was arrested and kept under lock and key until his unlikely story was verified.

15 MURDERS ORDINARY AND EXTRAORDINARY

So far we have been dealing with acts that could at least loosely qualify as political crimes. In a way, the System welcomed such incidents, as they contributed to the plausibility of "relentless class struggle." They verified the doctrinal assumption that the deposed ruling class would continue to resist the new order. The ideology demanded partial victories but could not permit the announcement of the final triumph. As in the case of the missionary who, after having converted everyone, becomes of no further use, our organs of oppression needed spies, saboteurs and sundry other enemies so badly that any shortage had to be remedied by inventing the wrong-doers. The leadership then determined when and how the public was to be informed — or misinformed — about the developments in class warfare.

The occurrence of common non-political crimes posed an entirely different problem. The need for fabrication was replaced by the art of disguise.

According to the dogma, common criminality was the product of vestiges of a capitalist mentality and of hostile attitudes penetrating from abroad. The poison might affect even an authentic proletarian. However, with the solidification of the new social order and with the ascendancy of the superior morality, violations of the law would steadily decrease until they reached the point of extinction. Theory, once more, outran actuality. The rate of criminality did not conform to expectations. If reality defied the dogma, the Party retaliated by defying the reality. In this case the phenomenon of common crime was relegated to the realm of "non-problem."

According to the Party, "All the News That's Fit to Print" amounted to "constructive messages" promoting the cause of socialism. An item about a drunk laborer who set fire to the office of the Local Soviet did not promote the cause and, therefore, was not to be reported. The results of these selective practices bordered on the metaphysical. For instance, the column *Zprávy ze světa* ("News from the World"), covering events in the capitalist West, consisted solely of disaster messages: airline crashes, hurricanes, earthquakes, mining tragedies, *and* common crimes such as murder, rape and robbery. There was a case of a Czech provincial newspaper that reported the floods in the Ohio Valley while failing to mention the floods which had forced the editors to vacate their desks. This kind of reporting damaged belief not only in the pretense of objectivity, but also in the intrinsic atheism of the Marxist creed. After all, a reader could not help but conclude that some supernatural force was subjecting the world of the exploiters to a multitude of assorted punishments.

A woman reporter — nicknamed *Želva* (Turtle) because she looked like one — once lectured at our court about the political wisdom of this selectivity. To the expressed doubts of her audience concerning the policy of silence with respect to non-political crime, she retorted: "We cannot afford to report such things for several reasons. It would distract the masses from building socialism. It would be misused by our enemies. Finally, as long as we print nothing of that sort, the toiling masses will believe that such things do not happen in our country." To a further comment that some such reporting might conceivably enliven the monotonous, repetitive press, she informed us that for a believer, socialism could never be a dull experience. "Comrades, our job is not to entertain or even to inform. It is to educate."

The Turtle was to some extent correct in assuming that the diet of restrictive information made a non-believer believe or at least confused. During the early fifties, for example, we were supplied with stories, pictures, testimonies, etc., about American G.I.'s "boiling progressive Korean peasants alive and throwing the bodies thus mellowed to wild American dogs." After having seen, read,

and been exposed to the same myth for several years, one became
ready to believe almost anything. Similarly, it became increasingly
difficult for the average man to give credence to the suggestion that
John might choose to strangle Jim for anything other than political
motives.

It was not until the third year at law school that we students
started to learn about what was really going on around us, owing
mainly to our instructor, the VB ("Public Police") Major Němec.
Yet even this competent professional tended to treat common
crimes as regrettable, ideologically embarrassing episodes. For example, he cited a junior police officer in his thirties, a man of proletarian stock with a modest education, four children and an adulterous wife. Unhappily for the reputation of the System, her lover
was not a sinister bourgeois penetrator but an Army officer, also a
proletarian. The husband decided to avenge his humiliation. First,
he shot his wife and children, one after another. During this ghastly
liquidation, which occupied him for a good part of an afternoon, he
composed a sort of running report I subsequently had the opportunity of reading. It was a mixture of guilt, devotion to the ideas
of Communism, and love and hatred for the family — and was
stained with blood. The murderer, while dying from a self-inflicted
bullet wound, continued his incoherent description of how his beloved ones were simultaneously bleeding to death. According to
lecturer Němec, the public was not only to be kept uninformed of
the case, but it was declared an official secret. Disclosure of the
possibility of a murderous policeman would supposedly have endangered the confidence of the toiling masses in the protectors of
public order.

The Penal Code of 1950 dealt with the crime of murder in
Section 216:

> (1) Whoever intentionally kills another person, shall be punished
> by imprisonment for a term of fifteen to twenty-five years.
> (2) An offender shall be punished by life imprisonment or death,
>> (a) if he commits the act described in paragraph 1 against
>> several persons or repeatedly;
>> (b) if he commits such an act during a robbery or in an
>> especially brutal manner; or
>> (c) if other especially aggravating circumstances are pres-
>> ent.[1.]

The fundamental criterion which emerges is that a wrongful act, to
qualify as murder, must involve intent to cause death or reveal an
awareness of this possibility by the offender. That is, if A. did not
want to kill B., but in assaulting him was aware that injury might
result in death and this knowledge did not deter him from attack-

ing B., A. would be charged with murder. It is up to the judges to interpret the circumstances and decide whether murder or manslaughter had been committed.

An offender acting under the influence of alcohol sufficient to incapacitate him from distinguishing between right and wrong would not be convicted of murder, but of "drunkenness," and thus would face imprisonment of no more than five years. This provision, however, did not apply in cases of the so-called *na kuráž* ("for courage") drinking in which the culprit got intoxicated *after* having made up his mind to kill. This, to my mind, reasonable provision remained mainly confined to the books. The courts were very reluctant to try a murderer on a lesser charge, and in cases with any political flavoring, its application was out of the question. Here, "the inherent hostility of a class enemy" always prevailed over the volume of consumed alcohol.

The vast distance between the death penalty and the temporary loss of liberty — a gulf further widened by amnesty or probation or both — put weighty responsibility on the court to decide whether or not the conditions of the "aggravated murder" (paragraph 2 of Section 216) possibly involving the death penalty had been met. The limited specificity of the law and the ineffectual guidance of the Supreme Court on this issue left the burden with the bench — provided, of course, that the decision had not been dictated by the Party Secretariat. As far as I have been able to observe, some of the courts displayed an undue tendency toward reading the crime as "especially brutal" and thus "aggravated."

The predicament involved in punishing culprits who literally were "adult teenagers" may be illustrated by the case of the multiple murderer Šmolík. Šmolík was a youngster living in the village of Křimice near Plzeň. Coming from an unhappy working class home, he was employed as a manual laborer in the Škoda industries, and his record at work was rather unimpressive. Šmolík's reputation as a merited builder of Communism was not better in the village: He was a "good for nothing bum" according to the report of the Local People's Committee. Šmolík spent most of his free time malingering in a cabin with his friends. One afternoon during the course of a card game, Šmolík thought he detected his partner cheating, became incensed, and split his skull with an axe. Before he had time to dispose of the corpse, another friend appeared on the scene, only to meet a similar fate. The culprit fled, avoiding his pursuers for a couple of days, and was finally caught hiding in a hay stack. More revolting than the crime itself was the defiant behavior of the culprit. Both during the police investigation and under questioning by the prosecutor he posed as a hardened cynical criminal. "Why did you do it?" — "The swine asked for it," was his standard reply. He showed no mercy and asked for none.

The presiding judge, Alexander Schindler, a friend of mine, had a hard time in establishing the motive behind the defendant's butchery. The search led nowhere. Šmolík apparently murdered only because he had been in the mood to do so. To his credit Judge Schindler did not attempt to invent an *ex post facto* fairy tale to make the circumstances of the crime appear ideologically palatable. But he was still left with a serious problem. How should the defendant be punished? Šmolík was a multiple murderer and thus, having committed an "aggravated murder," was eligible for the death penalty. In the eyes of the law Šmolík, who was eighteen years and a few months old, had to be treated as an adult — Czechoslovakia had lowered the limit of full criminal responsibility to eighteen years. Now, was it logical and would it have served the concept of justice to send Šmolík to the gallows — a person who might have avoided this ordeal had he been born a hundred or two hundred days later? If the crime had been committed before the defendant's eighteenth birthday, he would have been considered a juvenile delinquent subject to a maximum penalty of fifteen years imprisonment.[2] The court passed, in my opinion, a reasonable decision, sentencing Šmolík to twenty-two years and substantiating the verdict by reference to the mitigating circumstance termed as "age close to the age of minors." Actually in this case it was the only mitigating circumstance applicable.

Not always was the culprit apprehended and made to confess with such ease. Even in a police state the work of the police is not easy. Even in Stalinism the fist of the investigator loses its effectiveness if there is no jaw to strike. Pre-trial investigation of a nonpolitical crime in particular may require diligent, time-consuming research and may well lead to frustration or outright failure.

My first experience of police work from the inside was during Christmas of 1957, when in the village of Víchov a certain Hovorov, a middle-aged bachelor of Bulgarian extraction, was murdered. I then recalled that only a week before, Hovorov had been in my office. I had summoned him and his female neighbor for a conciliatory hearing in a civil law dispute. The session had been very violent and very unsuccessful. Now, Hovorov was dead. I became sufficiently interested in the affair to accept an invitation to participate in the police search for the culprit.

My first surprise in this case was to discover that the investigation was being conducted with a high degree of professional competence. At the Police Headquarters I met a detective, Znamenáček, an old pre-war professional, summoned from Plzeň for the purpose. We drove to Víchov, the scene of the crime. Hovorov had been killed in front of his house by several blows administered with a yard-long stick. The murderer had then dragged the body a distance of about thirty yards, into a barn. Detective Znamenáček inspected the tracks in the melting snow and after a while informed us of the approximate age, weight, size and other characteristics of the culprit. There is no need to go into the technicalities of Znamenáček's diagnosis, except to say that it proved remarkably accurate, and that at that time I refused to believe a word of it. Brains filled with nothing but Marxist formulae were poor substitutes for professional know-how, and it was easy to see why bourgeois leftovers such as Znamenáček were still kept on active duty.

The detective work resulted in the arrest and confession of a certain Oskar Reiser. He was not yet eighteen and thus qualified as a juvenile delinquent, punishable by no more than fifteen years in jail. His trial was presided over by the opportunistic judge Tanzer, who outdid himself. The case was patently apolitical. Both the culprit and the victim were of working class background, with no political affiliations. The apparatchiki, though interested in the outcome of the trial, did not exercise any pressure on the court. The Party Secretary decided to attend, however, and Tanzer had to show what a good Bolshevik he was. He sentenced Reiser to an inexcusably mild term of five years, reasoning: "Though undoubtedly people should not murder other people, one important aspect of this case should be taken into account. Namely, Hovorov was a person who contributed in no significant way to the building of socialism. This finding was not overlooked by the court in its deliberation about the correct punishment of the defendant." Even the Party Secretary was annoyed.

Among the cases of outstanding police performance was one involving a rather grisly murder perpetrated by a group of Gypsies. Later in 1956 I was sent to the Bory prison to obtain some supplementary evidence from them. The crime occurred in the South Slovakian town of Komárno, troubled with a relatively high concentration of Gypsies and a correspondingly high criminality rate.

The police, recruiting informers from all walks of life, also succeeded in penetrating the ranks of the Gypsies. An itinerant Judas reported some incidents of petty theft and pilferage of socialist property — which about exhausted the spectrum of the nefarious activities of these people. Gypsies, with their sense of loyalty, take an act of betrayal far more seriously than would the ordinary Czech citizen. The traitor at Komárno was condemned to a severe and humiliating punishment. A Gypsy girl was used as bait. One summer night she invited the victim designate for a date. In a garden, while the couple was engaged in sexual intercourse, the girl signalled to three appointed avengers, who strangled the man. Then —omitting some unprintable details — the murderers dismembered the body and stuffed the pieces into the carcass of a disemboweled horse, sewed the dead animal together again, and buried the whole thing several feet in the ground. According to the tribal belief, this was the most degrading death of all, descending literally into the grave.

What then happened between the time of the crime and the apprehension of the culprits is worth mentioning. The police discovered the murder but not the murderers. After several years of futile searching, the investigators gave up hope. The three Gypsies were still at large, benefitting from their anonymity, strange language and immunity from the totalitarian control, which in their case the state was not able to enforce. Whereas an ordinary citizen could not make a move without an internal passport and compliance with a variety of registration duties, a Gypsy was *expected* to have his papers in disorder or to possess none at all. The fugitives, devoid of documents, managed to cross the border to Poland where, with the help of local fellow Gypsies, they managed to settle down unnoticed by the authorities. They chose Gdansk (Danzig), selected common-law wives, produced a number of children and lived in tranquility for almost five years. Exactly why and how their nemesis caught up with them I was unable to figure out, either from the court records or through questioning the culprits.

Another rather unusual case was adjudicated in the district of Hradec Králové: A middle-aged man had a secret affair with a teenage mistress. Subsequently, he discovered that the sweetheart had switched her attention to a man of more compatible age. Pretending no hard feelings, the abandoned lover paid her a last visit and, representing himself as an amateur gynecologist, he suggested that he check whether or not the girl was pregnant, so that she could start her new life properly. The girl agreed, and the self-appointed examiner emptied the prepared contents of a syringe into the girl's vagina. Death was instantaneous. The man, unknown in the neighborhood, left the apartment unnoticed. A couple of days later the corpse was discovered, but neither the police investigation nor the autopsy revealed anything of value. The apartment furnished no clue, and the body of the victim bore no signs of violence or poisoning. The case was closed unsolved.

Some time afterwards, our man happened to be investigated under the suspicion of having performed illegal abortions. At this point the story becomes unclear. Was it an accident, or the work of an informer, or a sign of the investigator's genius, or perhaps, the impact of his blows? At any rate, the suspected abortionist confessed to the killing of the girl — a crime utterly unrelated to the investigation. He also allegedly divulged the formula of the poison which had left no post mortem traces. The defendant was sentenced to a long prison term that, in view of his age, was the equivalent of life imprisonment.

Probably the greatest, longest, and most expensive manhunt of any single criminal in Czechoslovak history took place under the code name "Action Bronislava" — the first name of the first victim. In the early fifties, over half a dozen women were murdered in the Chomutov-Jiříkov area of the northwestern borderland. The criminal pattern developed: a bicyclist, a pistol shot, sexual abuse of the corpse. Besides these murders it was widely — and correctly, as it later turned out — believed that the culprit was also responsible for numerous robberies and sexually motivated assaults.

The main reason for the government's concern with the activities of this Czech Jack the Ripper was, believe it or not, the fulfillment of the Five Year Plan. The industrialized area of Chomutov, namely, depended to a large extent on a female work force.[3] After the first murders, the weaker sex, fearing for their safety, did not turn up for the afternoon and night shifts. Production was in jeopardy, and the state had to act. A special police force was set up and dispatched to Chomutov. Despite their efforts, similar murders continued for three or four years. The investigators were able to decipher from the traces of the sperm of the attacker his blood group, and from his footprints, his approximate height and weight. With the help of the police residence registry, a list of about twenty thousand suspects was painstakingly compiled. The next step required the assistance of the reserve draft boards. Its district offices summoned under various pretexts all the suspects for a blood test, thus reducing the list of potential murderers accordingly. While the police search continued, Mr. X.'s death toll also grew. Actually it only emerged after the apprehension of the culprit that, though his name had been included on the original list of suspects, it had later been dropped, for reasons no one was able to explain.

The initial ineptitude of the police was exculpated by a lucky break and the praiseworthy imagination of one investigator. About three years after the last Chomutov murder, in the Kladno district west of Prague, a miner suffered an injury, left the shaft, and while going to change his clothes spotted a maintenance man breaking into the locker of a co-worker. The thief's name was Mrázek. The miner reported the case, the police picked up Mrázek and went to search his home. It was during this search that the enterprising investigator came up with his highly improbable idea. Among Mrázek's possessions he noticed an old-fashioned barber's hair clipper. A similar tool, the policeman recalled, was missing from a house where, several years before, a woman had been raped and murdered in front of a four-year-old child, who in turn had been sexually molested. Though this case differed from the Chomutov killings both in location and in criminal pattern, it was decided to investigate the possibility of a link. A more thorough search of Mrázek's home was ordered. In the cellar under the heap of coal a pistol was found; it was sent to Prague for ballistic examination. The impatiently awaited news finally arrived. "This is the weapon that killed all the victims of Mr. X. in the Chomutov area." Mrázek was told nothing of this, and the police chief ordered a sumptuous dinner for two in Mrázek's cell. During the feast, the host asked quite casually, "Did you kill those girls in Chomutov?" and Mrázek, gnawing a bone, nodded.

Mrázek was a slightly-built laborer in his early thirties, a taciturn, unassuming loner who, as often happens in such cases, enjoyed a good reputation in the community. His record at work was also favorable. He had never been married, although he used to share his household with an occasional common-law wife. Mrázek's education was modest and his social background was working class. His upbringing and family record offered nothing unusual. The culprit was moderately active politically, not in the Party but in the ancillary organizations.

The investigators were, naturally, most interested in the motive behind his annihilation program. Mrázek supplied a very

simple explanation. He was sexually over-endowed. Normal intercourse brought him no satisfaction; he had to settle for coitus
accompanied by violence to meet his erotic drives. This was also
the reason why he deserted his mistresses when he became fond
of them, because he did not want to harm them. Perfect pleasure
had to be found with strangers. So on his bicycle he would hunt
for hours until he came across a lonely woman. Conditions per-
mitting—Mrázek was a very cautious murderer—he shot the
victim, and the visual experience of death led to his immediate
orgasm. Then he sexually abused the corpse "for a second time."
Since the sight of blood disturbed him, he either covered the wound
or washed away the traces.

The court-appointed psychiatrists concurred with this elaboration, though other experts, I was told, were not quite satisfied
with the version. It may account for the murders, the attacks,
committed or only attempted, and the dozens of assaults of minors,
but it does not seem to explain the almost one hundred cases of
robbery and theft. In view of the murders, these attacks on
property were, of course, of only marginal importance.

At the trial Mrázek pleaded guilty but begged for clemency,
promising rehabilitation and his full share in the debt which he
owed to the construction of socialism. The judges were not impressed by this belated penitence. Mrázek was condemned to death
and executed. On this occasion, our invariably silent press carried
a brief notice about the verdict and the execution. The limited
publicity given to the case does not refute the rule mentioned at
the outset of the chapter. Though the crime was not political, its
consequences were. Once more, the female factory workers in the
northwest borderland could go to the afternoon and night shifts
in peace to fulfill the production plan.[4.]

Contrary to the dogma, non-political murders were committed
in the era of People's Democracy and continue to be committed
in the era of full-blooded socialism. Official silence about these
happenings nourished public ignorance but did not change the
reality. During the sixties, however, the press has become less
inhibited, apparently realizing that a life violently taken is not
necessarily the deed of a villain in the pay of American imperialism.

---

1. The new 1961 Criminal Code is less explicit. It merely states in Section

219 that "Whoever intentionally kills another person, shall be punished by imprisonment for a term of ten to fifteen years or by death."

2. The law recognized juveniles as those between the ages of fifteen and eighteen. Their culpability and responsibility before the law was restricted. A person who had not attained fifteen years of age at the time of the crime was not regarded as legally liable.

3. The environment of just such a small town with its surplus of factory girls is well depicted in the successful Czech movie *Lásky jedné plavovlásky* ("Loves of a Blond"). The picture was made available for commercial distribution in the United States in 1966.

4. More explicit about the affair than the daily press was the *Knižnice kriminalistiky*, a journal published by the Ministry of the Interior and available only to the police, prosecutors and judges. One entire issue was devoted to Mrázek. Save for the investigators who finally caught Mrázek, the rest of the police force fared badly. The criticism of the large force of investigators which for years had futilely roamed the Chomutov area centered on two points: first, the failure to deploy police dogs, and, second, lack of attention paid to the fact that the culprit was also a bicyclist.

16 WRONG SEXUAL VENTURES

While the expropriation of capitalist property in Czechoslovakia did not lead to the extinction of common murders, it did not generate their increase either. The new political order did, nevertheless, father some new categories of deviant behavior, notably the pilferage of socialist property, and what was termed verbal offenses. This was not an altogether unexpected development; the growth in state ownership increased the temptation to steal, and the policies of the Party disturbed enough people for whom grumbling was a natural release. Given the nature of the regime, neither of these practices could remain unpunished.

There was no such explanation, however, for the increase in sexual crimes under socialism. Why should these particular violations of the law become more popular at the very time when we were supposed to be bending all of our energies towards the building of a classless society? Did these felonies mushroom because or in spite of socialism? We who were in charge of condemning the wrongdoers were not quite sure. The public, as usual, was kept uninformed about such matters.

The 1950 Criminal Code listed under the heading "Crimes against Human Dignity" only rape, sexual abuse, homosexuality, incest, "traffic in women," and the endangering of public morals

159

(e.g., pornography). The maximum penalties varied from one year of imprisonment for homosexual acts between consenting adults to life imprisonment (twenty-five years) for rape which resulted in the death of the victim. Unlike the prurient American statutes, the law mentioned neither adultery nor fornication, neither prostitution nor sodomy. These omissions are not so much attributable to the magnanimity of the present government as to the fact that the country was never exposed to the sour grip of the Puritan tradition. However, the law might have included at least one rather broad provision for a variety of sexually oriented misdeeds. Considering the limitless inventiveness of sensual man, the law could have come much closer than it did to filling this gap.

As law students, we questioned our professor of criminal law as to why, for example, the legislators had chosen to disregard the crime of sodomy. The teacher offered this explanation: "What is a crime [*trestný čin*]? A crime is an act that, first, was caused by a wrongdoer, either intentionally or through negligence; second, is specified in the Code; and finally and most importantly, constitutes a menace to society. Sodomy, owing to its rare occurrence, does not qualify as a social menace. In addition, the record shows that the mental horizon of such culprits is so narrow as to preclude their culpability."

Prostitution certainly was not—and is not—rare. In this case, the lawmaker offered a partial reproach, advising that the practitioners of the oldest trade could be prosecuted for a "violation of the rules of socialist community life," in an administrative proceeding before a District People's Committee. The Committees were also entitled to try adulterers on the same charge and impose fines. However, I never heard of a single case when a transgressor of marital fidelity had to suffer this hardship.

Occasionally the court, wrestling with a legally unidentifiable offense, chose refuge in a ruling of insanity. According to the Code, a person who was unable, at the time of the crime, to recognize its danger to society or to control his action, because of mental disorder (but not alcohol or narcotics), was not to be regarded as criminally responsible. An example of the usefulness of this clause follows: an employee at the railway station in K. developed a peculiar habit. He was wont to spend his spare time *under* the ladies' room—more a primitive latrine than a toilet of this modern age—in order to indulge in the visual delights therein. His entertainment continued for several seasons until he was spotted by a startled occupant. What should be done with such a connoisseur? Or, again, to cite another example, how should the court regard a truckdriver who fell in love with his truck (type V 3 S) and penetrated the exhaust pipe? The court ordered psychiatric examinations in both cases. Though the medical reports were far from conclusive, the judges decreed confinement in a mental institution rather than trying to accommodate the misdeeds to some ill-fitting provision of the law.

Among the numerous amendments that belatedly attempted to ameliorate the inadequacies of the Code was the provision referring to "gross indecency." The question remained open as to whether behavior confined to strict privacy could endanger public morals. The courts answered the question both ways. For example, a policeman on night duty in the town of O., attracted by sounds of merry-making emanating from a villa, decided to enter the premises and investigate the disturbers of the peace. He discovered a group of undressed blindfolded ladies, who, bending forward, were engaged in a competition to identify the male penetrators of their private parts. The guardian of public order joined the party. His decision raised the level of communal joy. The blindfolded panel, puzzled by the mystery guest, became even more clamorous, and the male participants, thankful for the aid, threw the policeman's cap, belt, and pistol out of the window in their desire to make him feel at ease. As luck would have it, a colleague happened to be passing by. He also entered the house, but did not join the fun. The jolly crowd was arrested and found guilty of gross indecency endangering public morals.

In another case the judiciary interpreted the law rather differently. One Saturday afternoon at the District People's Committee in B., the local nobility, plus some assorted female employees, were enjoying their weekly party. The beverages served were financed out of the so-called *Rudý Koutek* ("Red Corner") fund, an expense account reserved for cultural activities. Before the adjournment, a standard procedure took place. The ladies stayed in one room and the gentlemen retired outside. There, each selected a different-colored ribbon, which he attached to his penis. This decorated item was then inserted through a large keyhole in the door of the room occupied by the fair sex. Each lady selected a ribbon. The door was opened and the "strings attached" determined who would cohabitate with whom in this comradely environment of orchestrated togetherness. Tradition demanded that the participant whose virility outclassed the rest of the male performers be declared "king of the week." Habit does not seem to coexist with caution; the beneficiaries of the "red corner" account failed, one crucial afternoon, to pull down the venetian blinds. Across the street was a hotel, and one of its guests happened to be enjoying the view from his window. Moreover, he was an official from—of all things—the Ministry of State Control. His camera immortalized the grand finale of the party, and the near-perfect prints were handed over to appropriate authorities. Though the cases in O. and B. were rather similar, the prosecutor in B. declined to indict the participants—not even for improper use of socialist funds.[1.]

Though homosexuality was specified among the crimes against human dignity, the state rarely prosecuted these offenders. The police knew about most of them, kept their names on an "active list," but generally left them in peace. This magnanimity was certainly not due to any difficulty in obtaining incriminating evidence. Since our law enforcement officers managed to beat confessions out of the innocent, they had no trouble with the guilty. According to some statistics I had the opportunity to examine, homosexuality in Czechoslovakia, though far less popular than in some of the Western countries, was by no means negligible. Among artists in particular, including some well-known names from the stage and screen, its incidence was rather high.

Homosexual life was unharassed, with some minor exceptions. Checking upon homosexuals was a part of police routine in investigating more serious crimes. A few detectives confessed to me that among the most difficult of all crimes to solve were murders among homosexuals. Save for some who were "going steady," fidelity was not particularly esteemed. The switching of partners was rather common; so were the jealousies that occasionally led to killing. Since typical locations for the murders were obscure places such as cellars, attics, abandoned shacks, etc., it usually took quite a while before the body was discovered, leaving the police with little evidence on which to build a case.

Fraternization of plainclothesmen with homosexuals facilitated access to the Prague semi-underworld of part-time pimps, prostitutes, pickpockets and black marketeers. Among the notorious places in Prague where homosexuals made their contacts were the Koruna public bath and the public toilet in the park at the main railway station (formerly Woodrow Wilson Station). The police knew that out-of-town deviants looked for partners at this lavatory —dubbed by the initiated as *Rudý d'ábel* (Red Devil)—and kept the Devil under surveillance.

A partial explanation of why the rate of prosecution did not match the rate of committed sexual crimes known to the authorities may be found in the difficulties the police encountered in recruiting their informers. The insufficient network of volunteers had to be complemented by offenders prepared to trade cooperation for immunity. Persons implicated in sexual crimes were among the most frequent candidates for such deals. Despite—or, rather, because of—the fact that the Czechs are far from prudish people and would probably qualify as libertines by American standards, the sexual crimes were considered among the least permissible infractions of the social code. If I were punished for stealing from the state, my friends would not ostracize me. If I were caught molesting little girls, I would be stigmatized for life, and thus all the more eager to accept a deal with the police.

Rapists never constituted a social menace. The case of murderer Mrázek ("Action Bronislava") was an exception to the rule that a Czech woman, alone in a dark street, would probably never need to feel uneasiness. She would be hard put to understand the fear of her counterpart in, say, New York City. Czechoslovakia is a country hospitable to carnal adventures, and the ease and frequency of extra-marital affairs makes the use of force rather superfluous. During my career in the judiciary I came across only a handful of convictions on rape charges. Often the accused were acquitted. The courts also ruled that a woman was not a victim of rape unless "she did not want to be raped." A woman claiming she was raped would hardly be believed unless she could prove there was more than one attacker, or in the case of only one man, that he was a giant subduing a tiny, fragile bird, or, with no Hercules around, that she had been incapacitated—whether by blows or alcohol. To add a point of interest: according to the opinion of the Supreme Court, a husband could be charged with the rape of his own wife if the unwilling partner was subjected to the use or threat of force, or taken advantage of while defenseless (sleeping, or intoxicated). The judiciary also held that a "woman rapist" was a contradiction in terms.[2.]

The sexual abuse of minors, once a rather rare felony, developed into a phenomenon of dangerous proportions during the fifties. The traumatic effect on the victims was all the worse because a typical offender, before he was apprehended, caused a great deal of harm to large numbers of children. This was an area where the Party's self-imposed silence about common crime was especially unfortunate. The communications media did not warn parents about the dangers of friendly strangers. While praising ourselves for our superior work in crime prevention, we remained mute when we ought to have roared. The System chose to advertise only those cases that fitted the formula of the "class struggle." What could better promote atheism and discredit the Church than a trumpeted charge against a Catholic priest for sexually abusing an innocent student? Several priests were singled out for this treatment and their trials, of course, received more than adequate publicity.

The commission of this crime was *not* conditioned by the use of violence. The cardinal element of the felony was the age of one of the participants. Physical contact with a person who had not yet reached the age of fifteen was a crime no matter how enthusiastic the young person's response. A number of men got into serious trouble because, misled by the physical endowments of their young friends, they failed to check their birth certificates. Actually, not all prosecutors were willing to bring charges in these cases. In my capacity as a civil law judge I uncovered numerous incidents of girls with very colorful pasts—or pregnancies. Though I reported everything to the prosecutor, he merely summoned the lovers, reproved them and sent them home.

These were not the kinds of offenders the state was after. It was the seedy retired gentleman, roaming parks and hanging around playgrounds, who was the culprit. The teaching profession also seemed to attract men of such persuasions. Such an offender, once caught, could purchase immunity only by selling himself as a police informer—provided that a deal was available. Otherwise he would be charged with the crime even if he had not actually cohabitated. The clause "whoever sexually abuses such a person in any other manner" could mean anything, and the courts chose to read it as any contact with any part of the body with lewd intent. I knew of one music teacher who was sentenced only because his fingers had wandered over the sweater of a pupil to whom he had been giving a flute lesson.

In my opinion, this interpretation often led to grave injustice. If, in the absence of other evidence, the court ruled only on the basis of "her word against his" and found the defendant guilty, it could well encourage a child to fabricate a charge just to avenge

a bad grade or to assuage any number of real or imagined grievances. It should be added that the reference to the abuse of "the
dependence of a person" applied not only to teachers but also to
step-parents, guardians, employers, or any adults in position of
power and influence over a juvenile. Criminal liability extended
until the eighteenth birthday of the dependent.

Following the Soviet example, since the end of the fifties the
Czechoslovak Criminal Code has been enriched with some novel
provisions. Prostitution is now punishable under the label of
parasitism, as are the nonconformist poets. Only sodomy remains
off the books. But even a molester of animals does not escape if
the beast is under socialist ownership. The next chapter will tell
us more.

---

1. Since a number of high Czech Army officers were implicated in the
latter affair, after my defection to the West I mentioned it to U.S. Intelligence. The moral indignation on the part of my interrogators was profound,
judging from the fact that they questioned me at great length several times,
with a meticulous concern for the most minute details of the case.

2. Some of my friends who during the war fought with the guerillas in
Slovakia knew otherwise. They told me about frequent incidents concerning
female members of the Soviet Army whose approaches consisted of a submachine gun pointed in the direction of their chosen lovers.

17 "HE WHO DOES NOT STEAL FROM THE STATE . . .

. . . steals from his family." In pre-Communist days, this witticism would hardly have been understood. Since then, however, it has acquired the power of proverbial wisdom, indicating a major ailment of Czechoslovak society and a persistent headache of the leadership. The pilferage of socialist property is the most popular crime in the country. Never before has so much been stolen by so many, the Party bewails. The statistics on national economic losses as a result of pilferage vary, according to time, to the willingness of the leadership to reveal honest figures, and to the nature of the audience. At our closed judicial meetings, we were told that "privatization" of public wealth retarded planned economic development by roughly twenty per cent. I cannot quite visualize just what that involved, but I certainly do know that the section on pilferage in the Criminal Code represented the bulkiest segment of Czechoslovak adjudication and grew steadily despite all efforts to prevent, punish, and educate.

Traditionally, the Czechs were not a nation of thieves. Whatever their flaws, an endemic dishonesty was not among them. But values changed with the times. The corrosion of public respect for some one else's possessions was largely the Party's own doing. First the System taught that the sanctity of private property was a bourgeois device, a devious trick to keep the toiling masses under the yoke of economic oppression. Accordingly, the state expropriated fortunes, and the have-nots applauded. Somewhere along the way, however, the swollen ranks of the have-nots lost any feelings of respect for any property, whoever might be the owner. As it turned out, the only landlord left in the national edifice was the Party.

The expropriators' appetites exceeded their digestive capacity. It would have been impressive and very revolutionary if the sky had been the limit for nationalization. But at some stage the voracious state should have realized that it had become the owner of more wealth than it could possibly protect. No matter how numerous the army of full-time guardians, they would never be equal to the task of controlling, checking, and re-checking the rest of the population with access to socialist factories, socialist fields, and socialist services. The volume and unpredictability of the public inventory had become an open temptation, and man was easily tempted.

If my toilet plumbing leaked several courses were open to me: I could place an order for the repair with the appropriate municipal enterprise. With luck, in about a year the defect would be remedied. But, if, having become accustomed to the convenience of a flushing toilet, I had no wish to wait four seasons, I might take the risk of committing the crime of "complicity in parasitism" and hire a craftsman who operated without a license, for profit. But in all probability, because of the expense of such a plumber, I would decide to repair the toilet myself. For this I would need materials, and the state retail stores carried none. So I would choose to steal ("de-nationalize") the material from the factory where I worked. If I could not get hold of the necessary pipes, a friend would. In return, I would agree to provide him with valuables he needed that I had access to. Whether I was a waiter, a store manager or a diamond cutter, I would feel, justly or not, underpaid and so seek a way to supplement my income through illegal, though in my opinion not unjustified, means. My frustration with the political status quo and my inability to change it could be mitigated by a furtive project of petty theft, which in my own eyes would be both daring—I would be a *practicing* anti-Communist!—and highly utilitarian. To blow up President Novotný along with the entire Hradčany Castle would make little sense to someone simply in need of a sack of garlic. All the valiant

efforts of the Party to exhort the masses to protect *posvátné*
("sacred") socialist property were no match for the attitudes of
the alienated men who easily became stealing men.

The public condoned incidents of "de-nationalization," provided the appetite of the pilferer was not boundless, and/or the
crime harmed no one but the state. Pilferage often advanced to
the level of art, as exemplified by the case of Prague chimney-
sweeps. Some members of this sooty craft worked out a bizarre,
Chaplinesque, and very successful scheme to raise their living
standards. First, they made a deal with a group of employees at
the Prague slaughter house. Then, they signed a *socialistický*
závazek ("socialist endeavor pledge") to clean the chimneys in
the classless fatherland, day and night—especially during the
night and in particular at the premises of the slaughter house.
While their accomplices produced salami inside the building, the
shockworkers on the roof fished for the products, in keeping with
their calling, down the chimneys. Ludicrous as it may sound, this
project lasted for a long time and proved very profitable. The
average reaction to this enterprise was one of amusement rather
than indignation or desire for revenge.

The ingenuity of these plotters was by no means atypical.
Many showed remarkable imagination in securing more than their
assigned shares of the socialist pie. As a rule, however, being a
successful pilferer did not require a mastermind. The average
offender could operate undetected because of the seemingly irre-
mediable deficiency in the control system. The State's eagerness to
supervise each and every aspect of economic life was submerged in
a deluge of conflicting regulations, and often the only outcome was
confusion. Take, for example, the case of an aging though not
maturing lady, the head accountant in charge of paychecks at the
Plzeň papermill. She happened to be very much enamoured of K.,
the Prague Opera star who even at the time of this writing in-
fatuates his female audiences. The lady's organizational talent
was accompanied by an extraordinary generosity. She bought her
hero sets of silk pajamas and paid outrageous sums for taxi trips
from Prague half across Bohemia to Karlsbad and, of course, also
to Plzeň. The prosecutor later submitted scores of enraptured letters written by the defendant to K., and the court file was rather
interesting to read. The justices, drowning in these lyrical incanta-
tions, could not avoid noticing several points which seemed to have
escaped everyone else. How had it been possible, in an environment

in which spying had become second nature, for a person to lead a
life of such ostentatious affluence, far in excess of her legitimate
means, and still remain undetected? More importantly, how had
the defendant managed for years to add scores of non-existent
employees to the payroll and pocket the salaries for her own use?
The total sum embezzled amounted to the monetary value of ten
years' work by the average salaried employee. The defendant was
sentenced to a term of ten years. Nothing at all happened to the
officials supposedly responsible for the overall control and supervision at the papermill.

This example of improper auditing was by no means exceptional. In Plzeň we had a department store, *Obchodní Domy,*
where a floor manager was indicted on the suspicion of having
pilfered state property. A lengthy trial ended in his acquittal.
Despite the loads of paper work with which the employees had
to wrestle, it was impossible either to get any picture of the store's
business transactions, or to figure out upon which floor the losses,
if any, had occurred. The prosecutor was so furious that he contemplated indicting the senior executive for gross negligence in the
administration of entrusted state funds. Before such an action
could be initiated, however, the Provincial Party Secretariat conceived of a better idea. The Secretary thought of a way to promote
this incompetent bungler to a more responsible and more demanding position with the Ministry of Domestic Trade in Prague.

The manifold endeavors of the populace to disencumber the
state of its many possessions came under the heading of the
notorious Section 245 of the 1950 Penal Code:

(1) Whoever pilfers property which is in national or cooperative
ownership by
    (a) appropriating an article of such property by taking
        possession of it,
    (b) appropriating an article of such property which was en-
        trusted to him, or
    (c) enriching himself to the detriment of such property, shall
        be punished by imprisonment for a term of up to five
        years.
(2) Equally shall be punished he who intentionally damages
national or cooperative property, especially by destroying, damaging
or rendering useless the articles of such property.
(3) An offender shall be punished by imprisonment for a term of
five to ten years,
    (a) if he commits such act described in paragraph 1 for gain,
    (b) if by such act described in paragraph 1 or 2 causes con-
        siderable damage, or
    (c) if other especially serious consequence is present.
(4) The offender shall be punished by imprisonment for a term
of ten to twenty years if by the act described in paragraph 1 or 2

he by misusing his position as public official, causes considerable
damage.[1.]

The weakest spot of the provision was Section 1, lit. c, calling
for the punishment of a person "who enriches himself to the detriment of such property." Around this vague formula revolved a
maze of sophistry and juridicial pseudoargumentation. For example, consider this charge: A number of state restaurant managers
worked out a profitable deal with the meat suppliers from the
municipal slaughter house. They upgraded inferior merchandise
—including some meat condemned by the veterinarian as a health
hazard—to top quality meat. This was then served to customers.
Common sense would presumably have concluded that the only
losers were the customers. Only their stomachs suffered, and only
their pockets had been cheated. The courts knew otherwise. The
fraud was interpreted as pilferage of socialist property. By the
same token, if I bought a lollipop in a state retail store for double
the proper price, the excess which I paid would be considered
"pilferage of socialist property." The state suffered the damage,
not I. Therefore, I would be left with no legal claim to recover
the loss.

This quaint reasoning could be traced back to the concept of
management of entrusted socialist property. This concept held the
manager liable—criminally and/or materially—for all losses but
did not entitle him to keep any surpluses. Surplus, irrespective of
the way it had been acquired, belonged to the state. This strange
logic was hardly likely to promote honesty among the sales personnel. Let us suppose I was the manager of a candy store with
two sales girls helping me to sweeten the life of the toiling masses.
I suspected one of the girls of stealing. Probably both were doing
so—and needed to, in view of their low wages. Yet, according to
the terms of the "contract of material responsibility," I as manager
would be solely liable for the losses. Something had to be done to
compensate for the money that vanished from the cash register,
and for the merchandise which disappeared from the shelves. The
customers also stole, and so did I, because I, too, felt underpaid.
In order that I might not be on the losing side on Tuesday, Monday would be the right time to cheat the lollipop buyer. The surplus would be stowed away in an emergency fund for the lean days
ahead.

Pilferers came in all sizes. The mastermind behind the largest
affair in all the years of the Plzeň people's democratic existence

was a man of the poetic surname Konvalinka—"Lily of the Valley" in English. Mr. Konvalinka was employed by the state monopoly Benzina as a supervisor and repairman of the metering system for all the filling stations in Western Bohemia. The job turned into a bonanza. The supervisor conspired with a vast number of station attendants to adjust the gas pumps to indicate more fuel than actually had been received by the customers. The difference was then sold and the profit split between the dealer and Konvalinka. No one but the customer suffered under Konvalinka's scheme, but again, when the affair came into the open, the culprits were tried and sentenced to stiff terms for having pilfered socialist property, and all compensation was paid to the state.

The algebra of the cited Section might read as follows: wrong-doer A. who defrauds citizen B. is punished because of damaging the State C. The State emerges from the trial as the only bene-ficiary, with sole title to compensation for damages.

I would like to give one more example in this connection—an absurd story involving phonograph records. The totalitarian state applies political criteria to nearly everything. Thus, in the case of phonograph records, prices started from a low of five crowns for speeches of the leaders, anthems and revolutionary songs, to a ceiling price of over thirty crowns for a jazz disk. One Sunday, during a fair, a truck arrived in town bearing the name of an un-known national enterprise. This in itself provoked no suspicion, because if anything abounded in Czechoslovakia, it was obscurely titled socialist undertakings. The employees of the mysterious outfit drew a large crowd by broadcasting the feeble-minded hit of the season, *A hloupý Honza se jen smál* ("Silly Johnny did not stop laughing"). The high price of thirty crowns did not deter the customers, who soon bought out the supply. The truck left for an unknown destination. A rather annoying discovery awaited the buyer, at home. When they played the record, they discovered that only the label was genuine—they had bought a rendering of the national anthem of the Union of Soviet Socialist Republics, avail-able in unlimited supply in local stores for a paltry five crowns. The vanished entrepreneurs had made a handsome profit of twenty-five crowns per record. The enraged customers reported the nefarious trick to the police, who prepared "a case against the unknown culprit." When the story came to our attention at the court, we were anxious to meet the practitioners of such mercurial ingenuity. Our wish remained unfulfilled; the offenders were never apprehended. Yet another case against "pilferers of socialist property" had to be closed.

Even when the state succeeded in apprehending a culprit, arrest and punishment were one thing; the recovery of—or compensation for—the stolen property was another. The punitive hand of the System was busy while the economic hand was reaching into an empty pocket. The prosecutors and the criminal law judges, piling up their achievements in socialist competition and production quotas, cared about the penalty but hardly at all about the indemnity. The recovery of losses was left to our civil law bench, which I shall discuss in the third part of this book. Thousands of managers were convicted and sentenced without the state ever collecting one cent from them. What could be done about an ex-housewife who, after having brought a grocery store to bankruptcy and served her term in jail, returned to the household? There were no means of recovering losses from a propertyless and unemployed wife and mother.

Let us now assume it is winter, with ice everywhere and slippery roads. You are driving your own car and cause a collision. If the other car involved in the accident is privately owned, the incident is reported to the state insurance company, which will settle the bill. If, however, you happened to ram a socialist automobile, you become subject to criminal prosecution according to Section 246 of the Penal Code. This provision reads: "Whoever causes through negligence a not insignificant amount of damage to national or cooperative property, shall be punished by imprisonment for a term up to one year." The 1955 volume of the "Collection of Decisions of Czechoslovak Courts," for example, listed under Number 20 a verdict of the District Court in Kraslice. Two drivers—one employed by the Party District Secretariat, the other by the District People's Committee—were tried and sentenced under Section 246 on the grounds that they "should have known that both cars were a part of national property." Apparently the drivers, fortified by this knowledge, would have found the roads less slippery.

This provision linking negligent damage to property with criminal liability constitutes a dangerous departure from the rudimentary concept of justice. I do not believe that this deterrent formula saved much socialist property. It certainly did not save those who, with no intent to harm the cause of socialism, found themselves regarded and treated as criminals.

The application of Section 246 also bordered on the ridiculous. At the end of the preceding chapter I promised to cite a case against a sodomist who, though not liable for sodomy, was held criminally liable anyway. This is what happened: In 1958 the Stříbro police investigated a young man who had indulged in sexual intercourse with cows. Contrary to the assumption regarding such culprits, this offender was of sound mind, with above-average education. He simply enjoyed bovine love. The simpleton cops wrestled with this unusual case along lines reminiscent of a rape charge. The police questionnaire read: Question: "What was the response of the object of your lust during the intercourse?" Answer: "The object of my lust seemed to be rather impassive during the intercourse." A number of other gems followed. But the apotheosis of the nonsense was yet to come. Criminal law Judge Lev Tanzer, to whom I never fail to be unfriendly in this narrative, was tormented by a dilemma. He had to reconcile the facts that on the one hand sodomy was not a crime, while on the other, socialist property, including socialist cows, had to be protected. This was his brilliant solution: "The defendant X.Y. is guilty and shall be sentenced according to Section 246 of the Penal Code for the felony of damaging socialist property through negligence, with respect to the cows in cooperative ownership. The private owners of cows molested are hereby advised to initiate a civil law suit for damages." This leads us to the moral: He who is the victim of an irrepressible desire to fornicate with cows should inquire about their ownership status first and fornicate later. As far as I can recall, the court of appeals upheld Tanzer's verdict.

With fresh exhortation toward class warfare, we introduced in 1956 two felonies so vague and general that they could mean anything or nothing. The much-heralded new crimes were parasitism and speculation. Example: An aged private cobbler—one of the last of this dying craft—went to the state hardware store *Řemeslnické potřeby* and bought a supply of nails, pegs and other articles, the names of which I know neither in English nor in Czech. Notwithstanding the legitimacy of the purchase, the cobbler was indicted and charged with "speculation." In the court's reasoning, the merchandise qualified under "scarce goods," thus indicating the man's implicit intention to harm the economy and torpedo socialist construction. He was sentenced with appropriate severity. With whom, against whom, with what and how he was supposed to speculate, it was hard to say. Any profit could be read as speculation, any thought of profit—or, at times, any thought at all —as parasitism, depending greatly on the socio-political classification of the person in question.

Compared with misdeeds against socialist ownership, those against private property were treated far less severely. While the pilferers from the state were frequently punished by a term of ten years, the maximum sentence for larceny of private possessions was two years. If private property was less protected, it was also less threatened.

Despite the severity of the sanctions, the offender generally preferred to leave unmolested his equally non-affluent fellow-citizen, and steal from the distended coffers of the state. By and large, pickpockets became relics of a nostalgic past. It is true that some stubborn adherents still practiced this obsolete trade, but the politically up-to-date courts did not take them too seriously. In the days of hectic campaigns against pilferers and assorted wreckers of socialist construction, it was inappropriate to be too concerned with an old-fashioned thief. Once I witnessed the trial of a gentle grandfather. It was his golden anniversary—the fiftieth time in his long career he was facing the bench for petty theft. The defendant seemed so hopelessly behind the times that the court did not even bother with any token political verbiage about class struggle, world peace, etc.; the quaintly relaxed atmosphere of the proceedings was undisturbed.

The new 1961 Criminal Code remedied some of the inadequacies of the old law. However, low respect for the "sacred socialist ownership" continues to be one of the major concerns of the government. The Czechoslovak press has begun to admit the widespread popularity of pilfering, and there is even talk of a revival of larceny and other threats to personal property.

---

1. This is the original version of the law. Section 245 was amended several times.

8 PRISON

Czechoslovak punitive policies were a mixture of barbarism and enlightenment. The law stipulated that incorrigible offenders, convicted for the gravest crimes, be executed; the rest were to be rehabilitated, through hard work, into worthwhile citizens of the socialist state. To emphasize its concern with rehabilitation, the government searched for a fitting euphemism for the bourgeois terms *vězení* and *žalář* (prison and jail). At the time of my association with the Czechoslovak judiciary, the label NPT—*Nápravne pracovni tábory* ("Camps of Corrective Labor") was in force.

The title was fairly appropriate in some instances and grossly misleading in others. NPT included both the reasonably tolerable life at the Nedražice prison farm and incarceration in the murky dungeons of the former monastery at Kartouzy. A stay in a Czechoslovak jail could carry overtones of both the Twentieth Century and the Middle Ages. Most like a concentration camp was the large complex in the northwestern borderland near Jáchymov (Joachimsthal) with its barbed wire, watch towers and rows of barracks. Rich deposits of uranium ore nearby—the existence of which had been known to Pierre and Marie Curie—were the reason for this largest concentration of convicts in Czechoslovakia. A labor force of many thousands extracted the raw material; the Soviet

175

Union was the sole customer. By the end of the fifties, however, the Jáchymov uranium deposits—once estimated as the richest in the entire Communist orbit—had dwindled to zero and had forced the inmates and the Soviet "advisors" to move to the new site of another radioactive bonanza at Příbram, south of Prague.

A score of other places earned their bad reputations with the public. Mírov, Leopoldov, Ilava, Pankrác, Bory, and the modern fortress at Ruzyně (where prominent political prisoners were stored for mellowing before trial) were among the best known. Members of the armed forces were certainly familiar with a place called Bochov; the female population had heard of Řepy; the teen-age boys knew of Zámrsek, and the girls, Kostomlaty.

I was never able to distinguish any systematic pattern in the Ministry of the Interior's policy of separating political offenders from common criminals. While some NPT units catered predominantly—or exclusively—to one group or the other, some units spared no efforts in attempting to integrate "politicals" with "commons." The only consistent policy was the segregation of first offenders from habitual criminals, especially if the novice was a young person. This policy was, however, only introduced in the late fifties, and even then it was not always followed by individual authorities.

Despite the transfer of jurisdiction over the prison system from the Ministry of Justice to the Ministry of the Interior, we still retained some knowledge of conditions in NPT establishments. This was so because of our access to files, the testimonies of inmates and ex-convicts, and the principles of economy. A citizen from district A. serving a prison term in B. and being sued for divorce by his wife would not be summoned to appear in court at home in A., except in the unlikely event that he was both able and willing to pay the transportation costs for himself and an escort. Instead, the court in A. would approach its counterpart in B. to act as a sort of proxy. The court in B. could not decline; it would send one of its judges to the imprisoned husband to prepare the necessary papers, furnish legal assistance and function as both court and counsel. In this way a judge was exposed to convicts from many areas of the country.

If no one volunteered, the unwanted job went to the most junior member. During my stay at the court in Plzeň, this procedure resulted in my visiting the local jail on official business once or twice a week. This was the prison fortress of rather odd architectural design in the suburb of Bory. In addition, the visiting junior judge delivered indictments to suspects held in custody or to convicts charged with supplementary crimes. Thus, inmates were interrogated either as defendants, litigants or witnesses.

With an average of ten files in my briefcase, I would take the streetcar across the city and walk from the terminal through a lovely municipal park for some fifteen minutes before reaching the enormous prison gate. A special pass, rich with stamps and signatures, was the prerequisite of entry. The guard would telephone from the gate to the main office to have my clients assembled, and another guard would accompany me through a further set of gates to a room provided for the investigations.

The hundreds of inmates I dealt with at Bory provided me with no grounds for generalizations about the typical prisoner or his attitudes. All manner of men were represented: the frightened and the relaxed, the servile and the dignified, the admirable and the repulsive, short-termers and those condemned to death, petty thieves and multiple murderers, slimy sex offenders and idealists whose principles had driven them to commit grave political crimes. However, the absolute majority were not victims of totalitarianism but genuine violators of law, misfits which any society must protect itself against. The occasional "freedom fighter" was almost invisible in the crowd of deviants and *déclassé* elements.

Bail was something unknown in Czechoslovakia. The suspect was either set free or kept under arrest. The law ordered custody for any person suspected of a grave crime (i.e., one with a minimum punishment of at least ten years). In addition to this mandatory rule, the suspect could be held in custody, irrespective of the nature of the felony, if there was danger that he might escape, repeat the crime, influence the witnesses, or otherwise "obstruct the ascertainment of material truth." The police and the prosecutors on occasions interpreted these provisions rather extensively, keeping under lock and key defendants who did not qualify. Despite these violations, as far as I was able to observe most of the accused came to their trial at the district court as free men. Also, a great number of those found guilty left the court room equally free, only to be notified later by the prosecutor about the commencement of their terms. Immediate arrest followed only after the imposition of a penalty of at least one year (since 1957, two years). The date could be postponed, mainly on the grounds of ill health or pregnancy. The prosecutor, however, would not grant deferment to a petitioner who claimed he was a family man whose imprisonment would cause material hardship to the dependents. The state reasoned that the convict would be put to work and his wages mailed by the authorities to the family. Actually, I came across a number of letters to the prosecutor or to the courts from wives worried that their husbands might be paroled. "Please, keep him where he is," was the plea. "When he is behind bars at least I get some money for my children. If you let him go, he won't take care of us and we shall starve again."

Convicts were expected to expiate their guilt towards society through hard work. Such labor could, on occasions, be dangerous. The aforementioned uranium mines were short of civilian workers, despite the lure of the highest wages paid in Czechoslovakia. I knew of a few cases where the Party did not call for the death penalty for a prominent political offender, but instead ordered him to work in the uranium mines, where he subsequently would perish because of exposure to radiation.

Some prisons could not furnish enough opportunities for productive work within their own confines and had to solicit jobs from national enterprises in order to employ their idle manpower. In such instances, the NPT signed a contract with a plant, "renting" the inmates. The prisoner would be paid according to the wage scale of the civilian employees, and the management was enjoined not to discriminate against the convicts. An inmate was entitled to full earnings, minus, alas, the following deductions kept by the NPT: expenses for board, lodging and "service" (i.e., "protection" furnished by the jailers) and some additional taxation. What remained belonged to the convict. In the majority of cases this amount was negligible, though some of the miners of uranium ore managed to earn up to 2,000 Kčs a month — a sum exceeding the average salary of a judge. The NPT deposited the income of the inmate in a frozen savings account, which was returned to him on his release. If the prisoner was burdened with alimony obligations, the NPT forwarded the better part of his earnings to the dependents, and the remainder went into savings. In addition, the convict was permitted — depending on his performance at work and overall behavior — to draw small amounts from his account for purchases of items such as soap and cigarettes from the prison canteen. Alcohol was prohibited.

The prison work program was far from perfect, and the prosecutors often criticized the NPT administration for keeping idle able-bodied prisoners whose families were in dire need of support. On other occasions, the chief warden assigned work to persons who were sick or otherwise unfit. In general, the inmates preferred work to inactivity, a trifling income to the boredom of four walls. Work meant a change in one's physical environment, even if only for eight hours a day. Secondly, gainful labor brought not only an income, but also other advantages, such as the right to receive packages and visitors. Seeing one's beloved once a month rather than once a year made quite a difference. Finally, an opportunity to work also meant a chance to work very hard — the speediest way to secure a probationary release.

As far as I was able to observe, the medical attention the convicts received in Czechoslovak prisons was adequate and, in the case of Bory, perhaps even superior to that in civilian life. This should not be attributed to an excessive concern for the well-being of the violators of the law, however. The prisoners benefited because of an administrative dichotomy. While the civilian hospitals fell under the Ministry of Health, NPT medical facilities operated under the authority of the Ministry of the Interior, and it was the latter which, because of its intelligence service operations, contacts abroad, and relative autonomy in foreign currency deals, had access to Western-made drugs. Once, for example, the head of the section of pulmonary diseases at the civilian hospital in Plzeň asked me whether, through my contacts with the NPT, I could obtain for him certain drugs which were available only in the Bory prison. The prison hospitals were particularly well-equipped to fight the epidemics that from time to time struck their premises. Also, the doctor-patient ratio was probably more favorable within rather than outside the prison walls, and the NPT authorities made good use of any incarcerated members of the medical profession.

Any rehabilitation of a prisoner through hard work had to be supplemented by the transformation of his socio-political outlook. Both political and common criminals were not only permitted but encouraged to read "progressive literature" in their spare time. The barely literate wardens themselves were not avid readers, and this was probably the reason why the prison libraries included, in addition to Stalinist trash, such worthwhile items as books by Karel Čapek, who could hardly pass for a protagonist of socialist realism.

The convicts also attended political indoctrination lectures and were urged to debate domestic and foreign policy issues (e.g., the deterioration of the living standards of the proletariat in the

United States of America over the last hundred years.) The response of each individual was carefully recorded on a "performance sheet," but since the sheet was one of the avenues to parole, one's activism expressed during political debates was a poor indicator of genuine conversion. The load of indoctrination varied. While very intensive in some of the camps at Jáchymov, it was nominal or non-existent in other places.

The "bedside manner" approach to the supposedly sick mind of the wrongdoer under the auspices of a magnanimous state left very much to be desired. The guards were the least probable healers one could imagine. They treated the prisoner with contempt when he arrived and with suspicion when he was released. To them, the prisoner was a pariah, a rascal, an *enemy*, and not a fellow citizen who had erred and now was in need of help and understanding. Primitivism prevented the guards from grasping the psychology of their charges, and their political temperament ruled out benevolence.

A fairly successful device for converting infidels to the socialist creed was the granting of a leave of absence from the prison. The law allowed for the interruption of a prison term when a convict suffered from a grave ailment. The length of the leave depended on the success of the cure. In addition, an inmate could be granted up to fifteen days leave as a reward for good performance at work, or for "pressing family reasons." These two-week holidays were counted as part of the term and did not affect the date of the prisoner's final release. J.H., an acquaintance of mine, was granted a furlough to straighten up his marital affairs, endangered by a divorce petition and the surprise pregnancy of his wife. J.H. visited me at court and we had a lengthy talk. He seemed to be genuinely grateful to the Establishment for its generosity: "The chief warden called me to his office and told me he knew that I was distressed by my wife's fooling around. Then he said he would prove to me the superiority of the socialist system by letting me — a bourgeois — go home for a while. And he did. If it had been a capitalist prison nobody would have bothered about my worries." The overwhelmed J.H. failed to notice that under the capitalist regime he would not have been in jail in the first place. He had been sentenced to a long prison term for some imprudent remarks about the Soviet intervention in Hungary in 1956.

The law stipulated that a prisoner, after having served half his term, was entitled to petition for parole. A special parole tribunal was set up at each provincial court. Its proceedings were rather short, and the outcome was determined by two pieces of evidence: the statement of the prisoner's Local People's Committee and the affidavit submitted by the commanding NPT officer. As long as the Committee informed the bench that "the toiling masses did not object to the release of the prisoner," and the NPT stated that "the applicant, through hard work and indoctrination, promises to become a useful member of our society marching to Communism," the petitioner was a free man.

The adjudication of this agenda was characterized by a considerable timidity. The judges were voluntary slaves of the letters of recommendation, even when the messages were narrow-minded and capricious. In one case, the petitioner lost only because of this statement from the prison commander: "I do not consider the petitioner qualified for parole because five years ago he was spotted playing cards." In general, however, negative responses of the local People's Committees constituted the main road blocks. I do not recall having seen a single truly sympathetic endorsement of an application by a local Soviet. In contrast, the prison authorities on some occasions not only favored parole in many cases, but even initiated the proceedings.

The prisoner's best hope for freedom, regardless of any recommendations, was a presidential amnesty. There was an amnesty in 1953 when Zápotocký became President, one in 1955 at the tenth anniversary of the country's liberation, one in 1956 as a tribute to de-Stalinization, and one in 1957, with Novotný's assumption to the office of Head of State. All of them opened, more or less, the prison gates.

The record of the punitive policies of the regime shows both excessive severity and unpredictable magnanimity, revolutionary zeal and, almost simultaneously, mitigation of its consequences. In line with the stick and carrot approach, the courts rendered harsh verdicts, and the President freed the condemned. This seeming inconsistency was not so much the result of misunderstanding as of a need to keep up with dialectics — the law of perpetual change. Inflexibility might have deposited in the same cell — to cite the ancient anecdote — citizen A., incarcerated because of his criticism of Slánský, citizen B., a supporter of Slánský, and citizen C., Slánský himself. The erratic policy shifts, the high mortality rate of official values, necessitated an accelerated turnover in NPT establishments. It should be added, though, that this was mainly a matter of selective generosity, favoring the common criminal and bypassing serious political offenders.

In addition to parole and amnesty, freedom could descend on the wings of "higher state interest." Physician Dr. K., a handsome, sociable and multilingual *bon vivant*, was sentenced to a seven-year term for having performed illegal abortions. Despite the unavailability of an amnesty and his ineligibility for parole, Dr. K. was released after only two years and was issued a passport in order "to restore his health abroad." The doctor suddenly popped up in West Germany, posing as a political refugee. He settled in Cologne where, thanks to his personal charm, he became a great social success. Having fulfilled the "spy-refugee" mission, Dr. K., in due course, returned to Czechoslovakia. The state, in appreciation of his services, rescinded the remainder of the sentence and as a bonus renewed his license to practice medicine.

STB was likely to offer "liberation through cooperation" to a prisoner sentenced for a political crime. The more profound the aura of anti-Communist martyrdom surrounding an individual, the better his chances for such liberation. A former employee of the U.S. Embassy in Prague, for example, had easy access to the class enemies and to their confidence, which was the most essential qualification for the *agent provocateur*, as we saw in an earlier chapter.

Let us now turn from the inmates returning to civilian life to those subjected to additional disciplinary punishment for infraction of prison regulations. This form of punishment was called *korekce*. The whims of NPT officials influenced their interpretation of the behavior of convicts as a violation of discipline and their selection from a variety of punitive measures. For example, during the Christmas of 1952, a group of prisoners in one of the Jáchymov camps performed an improvised Mass commemorating the death of a comrade killed while attempting to escape. The participants were punished with *korekce* of two weeks solitary confinement in concrete bunkers measuring one cubic meter. Without blankets, and in the beastly cold, not all of them survived. I happened to talk to two who did, and their health had been permanently damaged. Another form of *korekce* consisted of wearing chains and heavy iron balls.

It was not necessary to inconvenience the errant convict with medieval paraphernalia; feathers sufficed. The ordeal of "cleaning feathers" — i.e., manually stripping each individual feather of its down — mellowed the most defiant. Failure to meet the well-nigh impossible quota of some 90 dkg (about two pounds) of clean

feathers per day meant a cut in food rations and invited further
punitive measures. The convicts assured me that "feathers" was
one of the worst assignments one could be exposed to in a Czechoslovak prison. It meant bleeding finger tips, unbreathable air, and
the idiocy of monotonous, never-ending task. Feathers, as we know,
are feather-weight.

Though it was regarded as a form of *korekce*, some convicts
were singled out for this work without having violated prison rules.
Similarly, even a compliant inmate was not safe from the danger of
solitary confinement. For instance, a certain Z., who had been
found guilty of a very improbable spy charge, was put in solitary
in 1949. Ten years later, at the time of my leaving the country, his
lot remained unchanged. Imposed solitude caused mental damage
to some, but not to all, and a few even learned to enjoy it — or, to
be more accurate, they learned to prefer loneliness to companion-
ship. When prisoners, after experiencing several years in solitary
confinement, were switched to regular cells, they often complained
that the adjustment to the proximity of other human beings was
very difficult, especially if three inmates had to share a room. "Three
is the worst combination," I was told. "It always ends in two con-
spiring against the third, or so the third — and each of the three
could imagine himself to be the third — was prone to think. Two
or four together makes life easier." The aversion to a trio sharing a
cell was also voiced by inmates who had not experienced solitary
confinement.

The courts' sense of justice was not at its best when considering NPT intramural infractions of the law. In Leopoldov, the ill-
famed prison fortress in Slovakia, a political prisoner attempted to
escape and was apprehended. Undeterred, he tried again. This
time he seized a truck, breaking through all but the very last gate.
The prosecutor indicted him for the attempted murder of the guard
at the gate. The culprit had meant and done no harm to the guard.
All he had attempted was to get out. Yet, contrary to all the evidence, the bench found him guilty as charged, and he was condemned to death and executed.

According to the law, in peace time executions were performed
by hanging. Except for sporadic common murderers, death row was
the preserve for those found guilty of high treason, sabotage, or
espionage. Only the judges entrusted with political adjudication
were informed about these macabre spectacles. The rest of us knew
almost as little as the public, and, typically, we had no desire to

learn more. The closest I ever came to judicial execution was reading the notices in inheritance files issued by the Office of the Prosecutor General — with a bill for the cost of the hanging attached. These notices were usually signed by Jan Tolar, a noted Czechoslovak jurist and writer.

The law stipulated that the judge who condemned the defendant to death had to attend the execution. However, during the economy drive in the fifties, provincial executions were centralized in Prague, and the local judges were no longer required to be present. In Prague hangings were performed in the courtyard of the Pankrac prison, situated in the shadow of the Supreme Court. Supreme Court Justices, notably those from the civil law bench, were the most distressed to attend the executions, substituting for the colleagues from the countryside. In order to make the procedure more palatable, a partial remedy was found by administering drugs to the condemned before he reached the scaffold. This measure designed for the comfort of the witnesses spared the semi-conscious victim from being fully aware of his destruction.

The System was not noted for being excessively humanitarian toward its enemies. In 1956 at the Bory prison I spent a good part of the day talking to a Slovak, a former businessman of about forty, calm, composed, and intelligent. His story was as follows: in one of the provincial show trials he had been sentenced to death as an American spy. After the court of appeals had upheld the decision, he was transferred to the prison in the Moravian town of Jihlava. There he was put in death row — the so-called *provázkáři* ("stringers," "ropers," "noosers" in English) section. The cell was brightly-lit day and night, and he was surrounded by guards around the clock. In the interest of their physical and mental health, the prisoners had to walk in circles in the courtyard for a couple of minutes each day. In the outer circle promenaded the ordinary convicts, while the inner circle was reserved for the candidates for death — all in chains. The number of the condemned walkers changed from day to day; some vanished, never to return, and their places were taken by newcomers. My informant walked in the inner circle for more than six months, surviving several sets of comrades, until, for inexplicable reasons, his sentence was commuted to life imprisonment.

The whereabouts of executions were — as with so many other and far more trivial affairs — clouded in official secrecy, except for occasional terse press releases about "the death penalty having been carried out." Executions were not public; they were accessible only to the most select audience. The hour for hanging was shortly before dawn, and as far as I know the relatives of the victim were not allowed to claim the body. Instead of receiving a family burial, the body served a utilitarian and truly post mortem role as a training ground for medical students. The remains were buried in an unmarked grave in a prison cemetery.

PART THREE. ESSENTIALLY NON-PUNITIVE MATTERS

19 BUCOLICA IURIDICA: A STUDY IN SADNESS

Czechoslovak society experienced under Communist management a significant political, social, and economic metamorphosis. While the change affected the scope and sort of criminality and the punitive responses of the state, the imprint of change in the sphere of civil law was even more profound. The average citizen is more likely to become involved in a civil litigation than a criminal procedure. The range of penal jurisdiction is circumscribed by the list of specified misdeeds, while civil law is concerned with a multitude of situations in which a person figures as employee, tenant, buyer, husband, parent, or beneficiary of an inheritance. A trivial divorce might turn into a political affair almost as burning as the trial of the arsonist of the Presidential Castle. The politicization of civil adjudication, though more subtle than that of criminal law, was nonetheless profound.

As pointed out in the second part of this book, the transformation of the country after 1948 generated a change in the criminal court calendar: for example, people started to steal from the state rather than from each other. The nature of civil litigations also underwent a change: contractual and property disputes between private parties declined considerably in comparison with prewar figures. A buyer would hardly sue a merchant when the state virtually monopolized all marketing.

The Communist Party rejoiced over the statistical decline of civil litigations in some sub-fields, claiming this trend as evidence of increasing social harmony in particular and of the superiority of the new political order in general. The elation was ill-founded in view of numerous new wounds, self-inflicted by the System, that we in the judiciary were called upon to cure. Certain dwarfs withered away only to have their places taken by surprising new giants. Among the latter, the very formidable were "agricultural affairs," the topic of this chapter, which is focused predominantly on the Sudeten border regions.

To begin the story: In 1956 the Regional Court Administration in Plzeň informed me, to my considerable displeasure, that I had just volunteered for a transfer to the District Court at Stříbro, as of January 1, 1957. The reasons behind my exile to the agricultural world were rather bizarre. The Stříbro court had become burdened by an influx of civil litigations involving the peasantry, and the judge there, Josef Hluže, was not up to the task. Prematurely old and sclerotic, my rural colleague had become slightly mad — a development, to quote a pompous local official, "which had penetrated into the consciousness of the toiling masses." The masses noticed, for instance, when Hluže, dressed in judicial gown, went searching in broad daylight through the town for his secretary, who had abandoned her official duties and joined the crowd eager to purchase a luxury item called oranges, two per customer. Hluže's escapades were many, both in and out of court, and so I had to replace him. "It will be a grand experience for you," the bosses in Plzeň assured me. "This will be the test of your Marxist convictions."

My religious fervor could not be tested, because I was possessed by none, but agricultural affairs came to occupy most of my time to cause me considerable frustration. In order to understand the complexity of that environment, one must look back to 1945.

Our age seems to me one of selective indignation. Bombs were dropped on Hiroshima and Nagasaki, and we are unlikely ever to recover from our guilt. The awareness that the two bombs shortened the war and thus perhaps saved more lives than the atomic blast destroyed does little to assuage our pangs of conscience. The 1945 air raid on Dresden, which shortened nothing, set one of the grand records in mass killing. In the absence of a convincing military justification, the thousands of children in Dresden were apparently roasted for the sake of roasting. Yet no tears were shed, and the world's conscience was not moved. After all, the victims were only German children. We are upset, wave picket signs and practice self-immolation because of Caucasian aggressions. Nonwhite exercises in genocide, whether of the Watusi, Ibo or Sudanese variety, do not count.[1]

I shall hardly endear myself to Czech patriots by bringing up the case of the three million Sudeten Germans expelled from the country after 1945. Admittedly, the years of the Nazi occupation were bad; we endured them. The victims of Lidice and the thousands who perished in concentration camps were heroes; I bow to their memory. Yet, to be honest with myself, I must state that the representative attitude of the man-in-the-street during the war was closer to collaboration with the Nazis than to resistance. The belated post-May, 1945, vengeance against the Germans, by then safely defeated by others, does not, in my view, improve the record. We, the Slavic doves, recaptured the Sudetenland with our RG units ("Revolutionary Guards," better known as "Robbing Guards") and in the process occupied, plundered, molested and also murdered. Again, not all violence is equal.

All sermonizing apart, the Germans were expelled from the country, some dead, most of them still alive. Moving to a fatherland they had never seen, they left behind an Eldorado of empty villages, ghost towns, villas and palaces. The abandoned fortunes also attracted the adventurous and greedy. The average farmer, attached to inherited land, had no good reason to move to *Sudety* and "steal." The candidates for easy countryside ownership were mainly the farm laborers, holders of inadequate and infertile acreage, and re-emigrants. Among the re-emigrants, the most numerous were the so-called *Volynští Češi* ("Volyn Czechs"). These were descendants of Czechs who had settled in the Ukraine in the Nineteenth Century; they had received permission from the Soviet government to leave the country after World War II.

Above everything else, what the settlers lacked was direct experience of independent farming. It was not only the lazy ones who fared poorly. An appetite for hard work was an inadequate substitute for managerial skills, for an ability to count, to invest and to husband sensibly — in short, "to farm." As long as the former German owners remained, they supplied the new landlords with both labor and know-how. By 1947, however, with the exodus of the Teutons almost complete, conditions in the Sudetenland went from bad to worse. Gone were such displays of misconceived opulence as that in Těchlovice village, where the merry Slavic pioneers danced in a truckload of cakes to celebrate the advent of a carefree era of riches.

Communist policies, whether in Albania or Zanzibar, consist essentially of two phases: the phase of giving and the phase of taking away. First, distribution of land; second, collectivization. In Czechoslovakia, especially prior to the 1946 election, Communist Minister of Agriculture Julius Ďuriš personally presided over well-engineered festivities during which ownership titles to the Sudetenland property were distributed. In the pervading whirlwind of acquisitive instincts, the hard fact was overlooked or forgotten that one day the happy owners would have to pay for their possessions. More than ten years later, it became one of my duties in Stříbro to solve this misunderstanding.

The settlers missed the chance to dispose of their debts while currency was inflated and available. By June 1, 1953 — the day of the monetary reform — it was too late. They also failed to notice that the debts for German property were subject to an annual interest of five per cent. Neglecting to pay as they did, after several years they ended up in the red for almost double the original amount! Add to this a decade's unpaid taxes and compulsory insurance premiums and one could easily conclude that the neo-Sudetenland population was bankrupt.

As pointed out before, they were not really farmers in the true sense of the term. Their preference for the immediate gratification of material needs left no room for concern with tomorrow, for planning and responsibility. I was puzzled mainly by the *degree* of their inertia, the total insensitivity toward their immediate environment. It did not always occur to them to fix a leaking roof or replace a door that was falling to pieces. To drive from Plzeň to Marienbad, one had to pass through the village of Těchlovice. There, close to a sharp curve, stood an inhabited house with a broken window. The hole was filled by a huge radio set, undoubtedly confiscated from a dispossessed German. I first noticed the broken window in 1951. After that, I drove over the route quite often. By 1959, the damage had still not been repaired. Should the reader happen to travel to Czechoslovakia and visit the spas of West Bohemia, he is likely to take this highway. He might care to see whether or not the frame is still unglazed.[2.]

This lethargy was usually blamed on enforced collectivization, which made the people indifferent to almost everything; or on the alienation of the settler, who failed to regard *Sudety* as his home. I am not quite convinced by either of these excuses. Though to some of the colonists the borderland remained a strange place, to others it was as much their home as any place else. Similarly, in the mid-forties, *kolkhozy* were but a remote threat.

The state opened its crusade for the recovering of the lost millions not only without lawyers but also without an adequate substantiation of the claims. The local accountant from the bank simply presented to the court, with his Power of Attorney, a mimeographed stereotype statement, charging the defendant with mismanagement of Sudetenland property, resulting in the loss of an amount X. The eventual victory for the plaintiff was preconditioned by the presentation of two documents: the inventory and monetary evaluation of the property the defendant took over in 1945, and that of the one he later left behind. In practice this evidence was either unavailable or inadequate, lacking the defendant's signature certifying the accuracy of the findings. Even if the State had bothered to look after the abandoned property, the lapse of time spoke in favor of the accused. Let us take a hypothetical yet typical example: The defendant settled in Sudetenland in 1945, and five years later he had had enough of this experience. The date of his departure did not coincide with the date of the Commission's finding of what was left of the devastated farm. If he departed in 1950, and the Commission did not manage to get to his property until 1952, the court had to give credit to the defendant's objection that he could not be held liable for the losses that had occurred during the interim period. Since there was no way to ascertain the value of the property as of 1950, the claim of the state was lost.

It will never be known how much money went down the drain because of the greed and incompetent husbandry of the settlers, their fraudulent and negligent inventory procedure, the State's ill-thought-out reorganization of the administrative units, and its inept representation in the courts. The state was bled white. The few defendants who were sentenced to pay damages failed to honor the judgment because of insolvency.

In Stříbro I became acquainted with a remarkable civil servant, Eduard Kratochvíl. Though already a septuagenarian, he was one of the most efficient members of the district administration. A rare exception to the rule of high turnover among borderland officials, he had been with the Department of Agriculture of the District People's Committee since 1945. Endowed with an encyclopedic memory, Kratochvíl could recount in great detail the individual histories of plundering in the district; he was the greatest living reference source on roguery I have ever come across. His knowledge made him a much hated man, not least by people with established Party standing. Yet the Party did not press for the dismissal of the evidently indispensable Kratochvíl. Through him I learned about the real background of the damages, their extent, and the legitimacy of the claims which the state had lost because of its sloppy homework.

The Czech Communists were certainly not timid in meting out punishments; yet neither Kratochvíl nor anyone else was able to explain to me the Party's strange inconsistency toward certain misfits who were not even Communists, but on whom they turned a blind eye. Take the case of a certain Chvátal, a well-known figure in Stříbro. This empty-headed chatterbox had proved incompetent in all the fields of human endeavour he had tried — and these were many. More of such Chvátals would bring to bankruptcy states more affluent than Czechoslovakia. First, he "secured" (*zajistiti* — a favorite euphemism of those days) a prosperous farm in the village of Holostřevy. This instant peasant succeeded as long as the family of the original German owner remained to do the work. After their expulsion from the country, Chvátal stayed on at the farm for some time. When he finally notified the authorities that he was quitting, the fields had turned into deserts, and the emaciated livestock had literally to be carried away and destroyed. After this and other equally inept ventures, Chvátal became the head of the municipal enterprise *Domovní správa* in charge of publicly owned housing properties. No one could possibly have brought it to a worse condition than Chvátal did — again, with impunity. Others born under less auspicious stars would have ended in jail, guilty of sabotage. The last time I saw Chvátal he was boasting about his merits in building up the District Construction Enterprise in Stříbro. A remarkable chap, indeed.

By 1950, the bountiful era of "giving" was coming to the end. There were no more land reforms, festivities and deed distributions; now collectivization was the order of the day. Since the process of forced collectivization is fairly well-known, I shall be rather brief and stress only a few significant points. First of all, it should be emphasized that the Party misinterpreted entirely the intentions of the settlers. The apparatchiki had anticipated that the introduction of kolkhozy into the borderlands, where the colonists had not had time to develop emotional ties to their new homes, would encounter far less opposition than elsewhere in the country. They were wrong. The settlers resisted, in particular the re-emigrants, because of their previous experience with kolkhozy. "We did not leave the Soviet Union only to be dragged into collectives for the second time," they would tell me. Because of this unexpected resistance, the Party had to employ the same methods of force as in the rest of Czechoslovakia: the reluctant were harassed, subjected to capricious fines and prohibitive taxation, barred from purchases of farm supplies, or labelled kulaks and thrown into jail, their property confiscated and their families evicted.

Logic posed no limits to the recruitment practices. The villagers in Očín, for example, complained to me: "Comrade Šafránek from *okres* [literally "District," a term commonly used to denote the local power structure] and his gang summoned us, distributed the applications for membership and ordered that the kolkhoz was to be established that very moment. Šafránek warned us that anyone who refused to sign would be considered an enemy of collectivization. Anyone opposing collectivization was also against world peace and such a warmonger would be reported to the prosecutor and punished. So we signed—voluntarily, you know."

Save for a few exceptions, the settlers were hostile to the idea of farming in a kolkhoz. The only case I know of where the cooperative was born through "the spontaneous enthusiasm of the rural masses" occurred in the village of Telice. During the May Day celebration some ill-tempered peasants beat up a Communist in the local inn and tore the Party emblem from his jacket, thus desecrating the most sacrosanct among the symbols of secular divinity. The misdeed would ordinarily have constituted a relatively minor felony, but in the tense nervous period of collectivization, it could well have passed for high treason. The assailants did not need to be lawyers to recognize their danger. To neutralize the threat they came upon a brilliant idea: to establish a kolkhoz on the spot in the village. As anticipated, this evidence of active repentance contributing to the socialization of the countryside encouraged the authorities to ignore the incident.

It has been said that kolkhozy were an excellent idea except for two minor points: they did not work, and people did not want them. The poor performance of the first kolkhozy did not discourage our apparatchiki. Restiveness in the villages, bad management and worse morale at work, failure to meet production quotas, all this was accounted for with the magic formula of *obtíže růstu* ("difficulties of growth"). Despite the growing difficulties of growth, the Party continued to press for more collectives.

The better part of the country's agriculture was already socialized when Stalin and Gottwald died in 1953. Antonín Zápotocký, the new President, was rather popular. A former Social Democrat, this jovial old-timer was dubbed "Anthony the Benevolent" (his successor Novotný was known as "Anthony the Terrible"), enjoyed mixing with the people, and was known for his incautious remarks—to one of which I attribute my transfer to Stříbro.

Shortly after his ascendancy to office, Zápotocký delivered a speech at the Klíčava dam where he alluded to "Voices being heard that some farmers were forced to join the cooperative," and pledged that "membership was voluntary and those who did not like socialized farming, were free to quit." There were so many quitters in the spontaneous cooperative in Telice that soon no one was left. The kolkhoz collapsed, as did many others. The total number of defectors was never made public. A highly placed official in the Ministry of Justice, however, disclosed to me that more than ten thousand families were involved in the exodus.

The farmers deserted the kolkhozy in 1953, and the Party could not make up its mind on how best to cope with this setback to socialism. In almost three years the decision makers managed to decide nothing; meanwhile the defectors were left alone—except, of course, for local harassment and pressures. Finally the Party decided to settle the affair "the legal way" and instructed the District People's Committees to initiate civil law suits against the recalcitrant peasants. The Party calculated that the indemnity claims, if sufficiently inflated, would be an effective spur to incite the loners to change their minds about the advantages of private farming. Thus, as of December 31, 1956, the courts were flooded with a deluge of litigations.

Compared with the previous group of indemnity claims against negligent settlers, the suits were even more complex and politically far more significant. Though the Party was concerned about the individual instances in 1945 when pioneers had ruined the farms, the defection from the kolkhozy constituted an issue of top

priority for the apparatchiki. Their interference into the work of
the court expanded accordingly.

The former members were charged with financial co-responsibility for the debt of the cooperative. Invariably, when a new
kolkhoz was born the State Bank supplied it with a substantial
amount of money. Though officially termed a loan, both the
recipient and the state considered it a grant. The Party had
anticipated (wrongly) that generous financial backing of the cooperatives would lead the still hesitant rural communities down
the path of socialization. After the total or partial breakdown of
individual kolkhozy, the gift turned into a loan, and enrichment
into indebtedness. This became the main item in the litigations,
along with claims for payments for seeds, fertilizers, etc., and
services performed by the Tractor Station.

We at the bench despaired. The Civil Code—enacted in 1950
when socialization of the countryside was still in its infancy—did
not specifically cover kolkhoz affairs, and the general guidance
available proved to be of little assistance. Emergency legislation
following the breakdown of the cooperatives was either non-
existent or inadequate and very confusing. No better basis for
adjudication was found than the numerously amended "Model
Charter of the Cooperative," more of a political manifesto than a
legal document. The "Charter" was a modified replica of the
Soviet model enacted in the thirties.

The kolkhozy in Czechoslovakia were known under the
abbreviation "JZD" which stands for *Jednotné zemědělské
družstvo* ("Uniform Agricultural Cooperative"). Like his Soviet
counterpart, the Czech farmer, when he became a member of a
cooperative, pooled all his property except for articles of personal
and household use. Both received a private lot (*záhumenek*) and
a specified number of domestic animals. The Czech system departed from the Soviet model mainly on the question of the ownership of the pooled land. While in the USSR all the land was
nationalized, the farmer in Czechoslovakia retained legal title to
the real estate once he had joined the JZD, though not the "title
of disposition."

The Charter specified the conditions of membership, proprietary rights, labor obligations and remuneration. This document
allowed for the termination of individual membership, but not for
the termination of the JZD as the legal entity. JZD was immune—
legally "immortal"—vis-a-vis all attempts at dissolution by its

members. Only the state could strike the cooperative out of existence and order re-settlement of the villagers, whether for political, economic or military reasons.

Disregarding for the moment the inadequacy of the evidence offered by participants in these suits, the courts had to wrestle with three cardinal questions. The first centered on the extent of the liability of individual defendants. Let us assume that kolkhoz X. received a loan of 500,000 Kčs (old currency). The money was spent, and the JZD became inoperative. The Charter offered no guidance on whether or not the individuals could be held liable for the debt. The general rules of the Civil Code seemed to exculpate the defendants on this count, as the JZD was regarded a *socialistická právnická osoba* ("socialist legal person"). According to the Code, a member—present or former—was not liable for the contractual responsibilities the "socialist legal person" entered into. The bank granted the loan to the JZD as a legal entity and not to a consortium of individual, identifiable members. Hence, honoring the spirit of the law, the defendants seemed to be off the hook.

The most vocal protest against this interpretation came from the Ministry of Finance. Their position was subsequently supported by the Office of the Prosecutor General, but not by the judiciary. While the first two groups demanded that the defendants take full financial responsibility, we argued for the distinction between the liability of a member (e.g., kolkhoznik Mr. Novák killed a horse) and of the cooperative per se (e.g., a bad harvest or an epidemic killed the horses). To our surprise, the Ministry of Justice did not force us to abandon this moderate interpretation.

The second fundamental problem was not caused by the lack of legal clarity but the lack of the defendants' willingness to accept the letter of the Charter relating to the so-called "indivisible fund." According to the Charter, a member, should he withdraw from the JZD, was entitled to the full recovery of his possessions *minus* twenty per cent of their value, which he was obliged to surrender to the indivisible fund. Where the JZD survived he could pay in kind, and in the cases of a "de-activated" JZD, the custodian demanded monetary indemnification.

To illustrate the farmers' resentment: in village T., it was decided after Zápotocký's speech to dissolve the JZD. The chairman drove his motorcycle to the District People's Committee, where he handed over the keys, seal, stationary and the rest of the bureaucratic paraphernalia, with the words "we are through." The peasants recovered their property and reverted to private farming, forgetting among other things the "twenty per cent." Four years later, a representative farmer from T. appeared in my courtroom. When he had joined the JZD, he had brought in ten cows. Because of the prevailing neglect and inexperience with communal farming, forty per cent of the livestock had perished (in other villages the casualties were even greater). Thus, our defendant had recovered only six of his animals. Blaming the expired JZD for his losses (i.e., 4 cows) he then found himself called upon to pay the price of two cows for the indivisible fund. He failed to understand the arithmetic: "I brought in ten cows, I got back only six cows. Now, *they* want two more from me. I would like to know why I should owe *them* anything. *They* owe me," was the standard argument of the somewhat alienated member of the rural toiling masses.

The third and last fundamental issue was also the most disputed one. It involved the pecuniary renumeration of the members of the JZD—what the Russians call *trudoden* and the Czechs *pracovní jednotka* ("labor unit"), P.J. A kolkhoznik was a combination of a wage earner and profit sharer. His income was computed on the basis of the "PJ," i.e. labor units. The units were the measure of his daily performance at work, and increased according to the difficulty of the labor and the skill required. For example, one day in the life of a shepherd equaled, say, 0.8 PJ; that of a harvester of wheat, 1.2 PJ; and of the operator of the harvesting machine, 2.0 PJ. The collective farmer had a good idea of his total of earned labor units, but he did not know until the end of the year what each was worth. The monetary value of the PJ depended upon the overall economic annual performance of the collective.

At the beginning of each year the JZD prepared the budget and the annual production plan. The final figure of expected profit was projected against the number of labor units needed for the fulfillment of the plan. For example, a JZD might anticipate that the effort of its fifty members, with an average annual output of 400 PJ—altogether 20,000 PJ— would lead to the fulfillment of the plan and a net profit of 200,000 Kčs. The profit, divided by the total amount of PJ, would give a value of 10 Kčs to 1 PJ. The plan would subsequently be approved by the District People's Committee. The JZD would have to wait until the end of the economic year for its earnings, but the members, in the meantime, could not be left without cash. Therefore, on the basis of its approved production plan, the JZD would apply for and receive from the bank a loan to pay advances (so-called *záloha*) of 50 per cent of planned PJ value per month, in this case 5 Kčs, for work performed. If, by the end of the year, the profit jumped from 200,000 Kčs to 400,000 Kčs, the value of a PJ would increase accordingly, i.e. from 10 Kčs to 20 Kčs. In practice, however, profits frequently fell behind the plan and the reverse happened. In this hypothetical JZD, the actual value of a PJ—planned at 10 Kčs, and paid in advance through the loan at 5 Kčs—dropped to 3 Kčs. This meant that at the end of the year the kolkhozniki, instead of receiving *dobírka* (the lump sum payment of the second half of anticipated earnings), had to return excess payments, i.e. the difference between 5 Kčs per 1 PJ loaned by the bank and 3 Kčs of the real value of 1 PJ. The State insisted on the return of these overpayments. The result was that the harder a man worked the more he received on an advance payment and the more he had to pay back. Meanwhile, the lazy kolkhozniki who precipitated the economic loss of the JZD had to return far less, if anything at all. Naturally, many defendants protested. When we brought this manifestly anti-socialist contradiction to the attention of the Ministry of Justice and the Supreme Court, they had no advice for us, simply suggesting that we seek the guidance of the Ordinance of the Ministry of Agriculture, No. 10 of 1954. That guidance proved totally unhelpful.

For a state given to disgorging acts, decrees and ordinances with the energy of a cement mixer, this legislative inertia was rather strange. It can probably best be explained by the Party's expectation that the dissident farmers sooner or later would renew their ties with the kolkhozy and that the political purpose of the trials would be fulfilled if they started but did not end. Litigation was supposed to discourage the defendants from further pursuit of private farming, not to solidify it through a final verdict. In the long run, the Party's tactics proved successful, but before the deterrent became effective and the defendants gave up, it was agony for us on the bench. Again, the same story: complex claims backed by no evidence; no inventory records, no accounts reached the court. Moreover, what testimony was heard was of questionable value. The solidarity of the defendants did not extend beyond their dislike of collective farming. Their mutual animosities, accumulated over the years of their twisted social experience, ran very high. On the one hand a judge was responsible for just socialist adjudication; on the other, he had his production quotas to meet. How the pursuit of conscientious decision-making without any legal basis or evidence was to be reconciled with our production deadlines, I really did not know.

Let us choose as an example one defendant, and from his case select only one very minor item—geese. The defendant had brought to the JZD twenty geese. During the three years of the kolkhoz's existence, the birds multiplied; some were consumed by the community, including the former owners, some perished or were stolen, and some were sold on the free market; all were fed from the supplies of the JZD, and occasionally from private provender. Question: How many geese is the defendant entitled to recover? How big is the slice of the "indivisible fund?" A standard civil law procedure could not easily cope with such a conundrum.

The reader may recall the villagers in Telice who desecrated the Party emblems and in order to expiate the incident promptly founded a JZD. This JZD was also one of the first to collapse, and subsequently all the former members appeared before my bench. The only evidence the state managed to muster were the minutes of the meetings of the defunct collective—a remarkable piece of evidence, indeed! The minutes consisted of a handwritten narrative produced by the secretary of the JZD, who was not quite accustomed to the demands of literacy. He recorded the doomsday of the JZD in Telice in roughly these words: "Today there was a meeting. We had to elect a new chairman of the JZD. Fourteen members were present. The first candidate for the chairmanship was comrade A., but he was rejected. Everybody knew that A. was an old thief. Then, comrade B. was under consideration. He did not make it because he is never sober. He drinks too much." The minutes continued until they reached the final result: "All the members were rejected for one reason or another, we don't have a chairman and without a chairman we can't have a JZD. It was generally agreed that this was the end of our kolkhoz."

With this document from Telice—written in a wonderfully inept Czech—in my possession, I adjourned the proceedings "for further study." I wrapped the precious evidence and sent it registered to Minister of Justice Václav Škoda, requesting advice on how to adjudicate in the true spirit of socialist justice on the basis of this single masterpiece. The Minister did not bother to respond. However, I happened to meet Škoda shortly afterwards at one of the interdepartmental meetings. "So, you are Ulč," he said. "Well, I got your letter and I didn't forget it. You asked me a peculiar question, comrade. I have thought about it. Do you know what? I'll tell you. You should persuade the defendants to re-join the cooperative, and that will take care of the problem."

This we were doing, anyway. Prior to scheduling the first court hearing, we were obliged to go on a conciliatory mission into the villages, to threaten and cajole the obstinate peasants, and persuade them to rejoin their JZD, because it was common knowledge that such a union meant happiness, prosperity, and also world peace. I took part in dozens of such expeditions. Prior to each the participants—the judge, the prosecutor, someone from the Party Secretariat and from the District People's Committee, and occasionally also the chief of police and a member of the Attorney's Office—held a meeting to "unlock the specific problematics of the village." No matter what the specifics, the strategy of the visitors inevitably ended up as promises and intimidations: either collectivize or face the prospect of permanent impoverishment.

Most of the ex-kolkhozniki were prepared to talk to us or, at least, to listen. One of the rather surprising findings was the heterogeneity of the problems, grievances and expectations. While in one place the peasants requested their transfer to a State Farm, in others their strong preference was for private farming. The people at Břetislav conveyed an impression of backwardness reminiscent of the Russian *muzhik* of the Nineteenth Century. At Světec—only a couple of miles distant—the residents were clear-thinking farmers, well-read and imaginative. For example, they boosted their standard of living mightily by falsifying their acreage data. More land tilled than reported meant a lower quota of crops to be sold at official prices. The surplus fetched a handsome profit on the free market. The political system was responsible for regenerating many, though not all, of the miseries of the area. Some wounds were self-inflicted, such as in the case of the village with the improbable name of Sviňomazy (literally "Swine-greasing"), where the peasants, instead of harvesting their flax, set it on fire.

All the defendants—whether hard-working or tardy, sophisticated or illiterate—shared a common dislike for collective farming. Let us illustrate this attitude with the case of the one-time prosperous farmers at Vranov. Our group arrived in the early morning to address the peasants summoned to the office of the Chairman of the Local People's Committee. Mindful of the presence of the District Party Secretary, who had come with us to Vranov, I made sure that my speech placed due emphasis on the advantages of socialist farming and its bountiful future. Then, having descended from the outer space of prescribed political vistas, I put a straightforward question to those present. "Tell me, *sousedé* ["neighbors," a compromise between the bourgeois *pan*, "Mister" and the somewhat inappropriate *soudruh*, "Comrade"] how is it possible that when you ran your farms privately you were among the richest in the district, and now, having decided [*sic!*] to set up a cooperative, you have ended in bankruptcy? Neighbors, tell me why."

The neighbors responded through the chairman of the local Soviet. "Look, judge, and the rest of you. When we farmed on our own I was up and in the fields plowing by three in the morning. And even then my friend probably had an hour's start on me. After we had been pushed into the kolkhoz, during the harvest time it could be noon and we still had not stopped quarrelling as to who would do what sort of job. Don't forget that the moment you become collectivized your first thought is to make sure that you don't work one minute more for 'the common cause' than the next fellow. So, to make sure we were even we did practically nothing and our glorious JZD came to a standstill."

No amount of pamphleteering and exhortation could destroy the essential veracity of the Vranov Chairman's explanation. The economic laws of socialism did not quite work out the way the Party had anticipated; their dedication to the aged dogma failed to reckon with the peasants' psychology. Imposed "voluntarism" demolished instead of promoting the solidarity of the villagers. Instead of enthusiasm for collectivization, one found hostility or, at best, apathy. This is not to argue that the notion of agricultural cooperatives per se was diabolical and unworkable. I do not champion tiny private holdings tied to a low yield and the farmer's drudgery, the labor of his children substituting for the tractor he cannot afford to buy. The Israel kibbutzim must be judged successful, and, some of the collectives in the United States, too, have members who can work together. However, if performance is the proper test of a theory, we must conclude that in Czechoslovakia in the fifties the theory was very wrong.

Most of the defendants did not fail to recognize that their

interests largely coincided with ours—to dispose of the claims and thus save time and expenses for everyone. In some cases the litigants agreed upon "de-activation" of the suit, in others they signed a settlement to repay in modest installments at least a part of the debt. To my knowledge, however, none honored the obligation, not because of defiance of the authorities, but owing to insolvency.

The Party's policy to force defectors back to the collective farms the "legal way" was not a success. These civil litigations more angered than frightened the defendants. The Party recognized that nothing could match the old reliable method of "administrative pressure." Zapotocký died in 1957, and with Novotný as undisputed master, the farmers once again were subjected to intensive "persuasion campaigns"—threats, discrimination, and even the occasional show trial. By 1958 the renegades of socialist farming were safely back in "their" kolkhozy.

In rural areas the Party's energies were centered on the consolidation of the kolkhozy and on preventing the flow of manpower from agriculture. Though the entire country was affected by this trend, the attraction of *Sudety* as a promised land faded at double-quick speed. A change of residence or employment without state permission was contrary to regulations. Notwithstanding this obstacle, the exodus did not stop. Escapees from Sudetenland chose various methods. The most impatient abandoned the farm summarily, only to run into conflict with the criminal courts. The more sophisticated burned the farm to the grounds, claiming it was an accident. Arson was very popular in Klatovy—a district only partly considered a borderland—and one could not help but wonder at how fast values were transformed. After the war a farm had meant security and prosperity; within a decade the peasant sought refuge in its ashes.

Another device for fleeing the land that involved the civil law judges was the phony divorce. The pattern of these cases was identical: First, the wife would move out of the district, leaving behind the husband, the children and the collectivization. Then the abandoned husband would charge his spouse with desertion and win a divorce. Next, the plaintiff would apply for permission to leave the village, claiming he could not be all things—a good father, cook, nurse and kolkhoznik. With permission granted, father and children would depart, the parents would remarry and, finally, move to a place of their own choice.

Forcible transfer of offspring living in the cities back to the parental home in the countryside was twentieth century feudalism at its height. After 1948, the government had chased the better part of the young rural population into city factories. Ten years later, in order to rejuvenate the kolkhozniki stratum, whose average age was more than fifty, the same government decreed that established city dwellers terminate their way of life, abandon their jobs, forget their skills and return "home." This would proceed as follows:

1. A letter from the JZD to the District People's Committee complaining about the shortage of manpower in general and of young people in particular and requesting assistance in "securing" the return of the son of kolkhoznik X.

2. A letter from the District People's Committee—endorsed by the District Party Secretariat—to young X.'s employer calling for his dismissal.

3. A reply from the reluctant management requesting permission to retain X. on the grounds that he is indispensable to the fulfillment of the plan.

4. The District People's Committee accuses the management of anti-Bolshevik attitudes.

5. The management summons X. and attempts to persuade him to volunteer for his parents' collective farm.

6. The friendly persuasion does not work.

7. The enterprise terminates X.'s employment, and he thus becomes unemployable except by the suppliant JZD.

8. X. either gives up or, continuing to resist, runs the risk of criminal prosecution for parasitism ("because he does not want to work").

9. The result: the JZD gains another young volunteer.

Manpower for agriculture was the top issue of the day. Appropriately, the Party Secretary from Tachov reported that after a long battle an obscure JZD in his district had won a manpower case against none other than the "HPS"—the "Main Political Administration of the Ministry of Defense." The HPS was forced to discharge a political officer who, understandably, was not eager to exchange his fancy uniform for the attire of a common kolkhoznik.

JZD requests penetrated into all walks of life, not excluding the ranks of the professionals. A number of teachers, for example, had to go. Their years of hard study—at state expense—were no valid excuse. I knew of only one case when the designate victim was ultimately left to pursue the career of her choice. A.K., a talented surgeon and an acquaintance of mine, was—after a long fight—permitted to operate on people rather than to clean the stables in her parents' village.

The snatching of unwilling kolkhozniki at the request of an individual JZD was a makeshift remedy that could not really cure the ailing condition of agriculture. The government, recognizing the limited impact of forcible recruitment, decided to launch a program to attract genuine volunteers. This became known as the so-called *dosídlenecká akce* ("late settlement action").

As in other walks of totalitarian life, "persuasion" was substituted for spontaneity. I should like to recount a not uncommon episode illustrating the ill-effects of this pseudo-voluntarism. One ugly icy morning District Prosecutor Josef Stehlík asked me to accompany him to the village of Úterý, where he was scheduled to represent the Establishment at the annual meeting of the local kolkhoz. "It will help your political growth," he remarked in his characteristic way, making it difficult to separate the message from the irony of this non-intellectual but intelligent ex-proletarian. Since the lack of central heating in the court building and the cold stove in my office promised a day at least as unpleasant as a visit to the kolkhozniki, I agreed to go.

Úterý is located in a romantic valley, and it is occasionally selected by Czech movie makers as a setting. However, no director has ever chosen to portray the socialist reality of its local kolkhoz. This would have made for a rather nihilistic opus. The cooperative was poor and the morale of the workers low. The Party Secretariat had demanded an improvement, and this accounted for our visit.

After the standard homily on the virtues of socialist farming, we carried out our instructions to demote the chairman of the JZD, a former boy scout leader, a Marxist and a homosexual. In his place we submitted the recent settler and newcomer Kabourek, a stocky, inarticulate and very unpleasant chap. The thoroughly apathetic audience raised no objection to the candidate and approved the nomination with the customary unanimity.

Some three months later, Prosecutor Stehlík dropped into my office. He informed me, with his usual grin, that worthy Comrade Kabourek had been arrested. The galaxy of crimes he was charged with ranged from petty theft and fraud to pilferage of cooperative property on a grand scale. Stehlík pointed out that this development ought to come as no surprise since this favorite son—as we belatedly learned—was a habitual criminal who had already served a dozen terms for assorted infractions of the law. "What happened to our Bolshevik vigilance?" I gasped. "What happened to our Bolshevik future?" retorted the prosecutor.

No one in his right mind could reproach either Stehlík or me for Kabourek's investiture at Úterý. We had installed the chairman on instructions; we had not selected him. Selections like this and scores of others almost as bad were severely damaging to the "late settlement" campaign. The districts and industrial enterprises had to fill quotas of recruits for the kolkhozy. As usual, in the absence of authentic volunteers, someone had to be "volunteered," and, not surprisingly, the management chose from among the most expendable personnel. A worker caught stealing socialist property, instead of being sent to the police, would be offered a deal to sign up for the Sudetenland. This, in fact, was how we had acquired Kabourek.

The migration of unsavory characters to the Sudetenland considerably boosted the volume of my court calendar. The new settlers were soon followed by a collection of bulky files charging them with a variety of misdeeds. In the cases involving the court's supervision of minors I encountered the most despicable *déclassé* elements. A transfusion of this sort of new blood would have harmed a patient enjoying more vigorous health than did our Czech agriculture. The settlers of 1945, who themselves could by no means have qualified for sainthood, found it hard to coexist with this human refuse. However, the tensions between the old and new settlers only rarely reached the courtroom.

In addition to damage suits against negligent and defecting settlers from the kolkhozy, numerous litigations were initiated by the STS—the *Strojní traktorová stanice* ("Machine Tractor Station"). A replica of the Soviet MTS, the Czech STS were set up in every district and operated along the same lines as other industrial enterprises. Their purpose was essentially functional. I cannot agree with those Western writers who have asserted that the STS in Czechoslovakia served as an effective instrument for state and Party control over the peasantry. They were never intended for that. The tractor stations, by virtue of their monopoly over agricultural machinery, exerted considerable *economic* pressure, but that was about all. The STS employees were not equipped for indoctrination or for forcing unwilling peasants into kolkhozy. For this task, the Party, the District People's Committees and even the courts were more suitable. STS employees were not political agitators, but tractor drivers, young lads who cared for big wages, not Communism. The only display of revolutionary zeal I encountered among these men was from the STS legal representative, Comrade Kopeček. While other good comrades used to address the judge with *Čest práci* ("Labor be Honored"), in his understanding this greeting was deficient in militance and optimism. He preferred the crushing salutation *Se Sovětským Svazem na věčné časy* ("With the Soviet Union Forever") to which the only fitting response was a nod.

The bulk of the STS litigations revolved around the failure of the farmer to pay for services rendered. The defendants were either agricultural cooperatives or individuals—private farmers or members of the JZD who were being sued for services rendered prior to their entry into the cooperative. The main argument of the accused was an objection to the poor quality of STS work. If, for example, the STS was hired to plough a cornfield, and instead ploughed a meadow, the defendant felt that it was up to the STS to pay for damages, rather than vice versa. It was often difficult for the court to secure satisfactory evidence in such cases.

Space does not allow for elaborations on litigations where the STS invariably ended as a loser. The Tractor Station did, however, score a victory in one set of very dubious claims. The history of this suit is relatively complex, and I ask the reader to pay attention to the dates as they appear. In February, 1948, the Communists took control in Czechoslovakia. In no time, a law was promulgated calling for "the compulsory sale of privately owned heavy agricultural machinery to the state." The state "purchased" tractors, harvesting machines, etc., without paying a cent to the farmers—the law in fact decreed not purchase, but confiscation without compensation. The nationwide program for the removal of agricultural machinery from private ownership, and its pooling in the STS enterprises could not be completed overnight. It was not uncommon for three, even six months to pass before the state deprived the farmer of his tractor. By the end of 1948, the economic self-sufficiency of the peasantry had been broken. Five years later—in 1953—the farmers, along with everybody else, lost their savings under the "Currency Reform Act." Having thus surrendered their money to the state and their property to the kolkhoz or State Farm, there was little left for the farmers to rejoice about. Then, beginning in 1956, the STS

launched civil law suits against the peasants—private or collectivized—demanding indemnity for "the illegal use of duly purchased machinery for the period between the promulgation of the
law in early 1948 and the actual take over of the machinery later
the same year."

"Illegal use of duly purchased machinery!" In the face of
this claim, I had to take a stand of judicial impartiality and listen
to a defendant: "Look, your honor. I had a farm. One day the
Communists came and stole my tractor. Later they told us our
savings were worthless. Then they forced me in the kolkhoz. Now,
when I have nothing left, they want me to pay for having used
my own property. If this is socialism, keep it. I don't want to be
part of this fraud. Your honor, please, try to convince me that I
am wrong."

What could I tell him? Attempt to sweeten his lot with
promises of paradise for his grandchildren? Yet, according to the
law, the defendant was wrong and had to lose. The state had
"purchased" the tractor; the farmer had used the tractor; the
farmer now had to pay. I cannot think of any other instances in
my career that made me feel more ashamed. These litigations were
not only immoral—they were utterly useless. The state could not
possibly benefit from its victories, because of the defendants' insolvency. The farmers did not honor the court's decision, and all
the state achieved was the further alienation of the peasantry.
When I wrote to Prague about these nonsensical proceedings, the
only response to my complaints was a phone call from the Ministry
of Justice. I was told that they had decided to be benevolent and
forget I had ever written "such immature, politically shortsighted
folly."

Sometimes it was difficult if not impossible to break the code of
the decision-makers' strange logic. Fortunes were wasted in the
Sudetenland with no effective measures undertaken to recover the
losses. Rather than holding the real culprits responsible, wrong
victims were singled out for wrong causes. Messages like the one
received from the Ministry of Justice reminded me of Lenin's
explanation of socialist stupidity: either the act of a loyal fool or
of a clever enemy. With the Ministry the latter alternative was
highly implausible. True, there were numerous misfits among the
settlers, but many of the farmers were honest, hard-working, worn-
out, unhappy souls who had come to the *Sudety* in search of a piece
of land and peace of mind. My letter to the Ministry was not

motivated by concern for the tarnished image of the Party. All I
cared about was my shame at having to preside over these cases
and about the Kafkaesque ordeal to which the defendants were
subjected. Though insolvency saved them from honoring the judgment, they could ill afford the expense of traveling to the court and
did not deserve the humiliation that met them there. Many of the
accused seemed on the brink of despair. "Hang me now, and fast.
How much more do you think I can stand after all these years?"
one asked, and I believe this was not a display of a hysterical
bravado. I sat there, supposed to comfort him with a sermon about
historical inevitability. Yet, we had been taught at the university
that Marxism-Leninism was *věda všech věd a umění všech umění*
("science of all sciences and art of all arts"). Anyone who doubted
that was both an intellectual and a moral degenerate.

Our strength as dialecticians lay in our flexibility. Permit me
to illustrate. The collectivization of Soviet agriculture in the
thirties was accompanied by the liquidation of those rich farmers
called "kulaks." Two decades later, our Communists followed this
blueprint. But if there were any genuine rural capitalists in
Czechoslovakia, *Sudety* was the wrong place to look for them. The
borderlands were essentially a haven for the have-nots. In 1945 no
settler was allotted more than thirty-two acres of land; no one could
obtain, let alone afford, hired help. There was no time to develop
exploitative instincts, since ownership decrees were soon replaced by
applications for kolkhoz membership. Yet kulaks had to be found,
and the apparatchiki continued to adhere to this article of faith
with the insistence of medieval theologians. Each District Party
Secretary kept a "kulak register"—a haphazard collection of names
of the most improbable capitalist vampires. Gossip, denunciations,
or disfavor with the village People's Committee were the avenues
leading to the blacklist. The kulaks-designate were as authentic
as play money. The air of unreality was evident to all but the
apparatchiki. The only concession to reason was the mitigation of
oppressive measures. These "kulaks" were seldom subjected to the
ordeal of a show trial. Criminal proceedings were largely replaced
by civil law suits, administrative harassment, and public ostracism.
The Sudeten "kulak" did not reach the scaffold. But neither did his
child qualify for college education. The victim was viewed as a
sort of socio-political leper, whom it was advisable to avoid in every
instance. A dutiful socialist would not share a kulak's table in a
restaurant or ask his daughter for a date.

As I said, the Sudetenland was the least suitable place to hunt for class enemies. Various unsavory types lived there, and also devout anti-Communists, but certainly not exploiters and textbook kulaks. Therefore, it seemed rather odd to me that the "kulak register" did not include the name of one very interesting gentleman with whom I became acquainted through an insignificant civil case. He was a retired resident of one of the most remote villages in the district. Though a great Czech patriot who had his children baptized with cumbersome names taken from Bohemian mythology, he was married to an English woman—the only Anglo-Saxon in the area, and, by implication, the fomentor of nuclear holocaust. This was only a minor sin compared to his past exploits—a former professional hunter of big game in Africa, a veteran of the Boer War on the side of the British, and the acquaintance of a fellow named Winston Churchill, whom he had met in the POW camp. He showed me a picture from the camp—"Winston and I"—autographed by Churchill. Yet this Czech stooge of colonialism managed to avoid the attention of our apparatchiki.

Contrary to occasional reports in the Western press, the persistent and successful opposition of the Czech rural strata to collectivization is a myth. By the time I left the country, some obstinate peasants still retained private ownership of their holdings, largely decrepit, decaying farms. These peasants were scattered, atomized, bitter, lonely wolves; misanthropes rather than champions of a virtuous cause. The Party does not seem to care about them any longer.

The government used to remind the citizenry that the problems of agriculture were everybody's concern. In 1959 the judges, prosecutors and notaries were obliged to submit a report analyzing the ailments of agriculture and suggesting suitable remedies. My report was almost as long as this chapter; in fact, the contents were not very different. In the careful protective language of "constructive criticism" I depicted the manifold self-defeating stupidities, the unnecessary oppression and the overwhelming waste. Our messages brought about little change, judging from the Czech press of subsequent years.

---

1. An explanatory footnote may be in order: It was quite late in my adult life that I met peoples of different races. And then I got married to a person who is not entirely white. I do not share the masochistic feeling of an Ameri-

can white liberal penitent. I am not guilt-ridden and refuse to apologize for my type of pigmentation.

2. However, I would not be surprised if the Party, after reading this book, has rebuilt the house into a stately mansion, just to prove me a liar.

20 TERMINATING THE MARITAL YOKE

During the late fifties, the majority of civil litigations at Stříbro concerned agricultural affairs. This was also true with other predominantly rural districts during the same period. On the nation-wide scale, however, the most frequent cases were those petitioning for divorce. This reflected the economic emancipation of women, fading religious influences, and socio-political transformations generally. This trend also explained the high percentage of female lay assessors, since the Ministry of Justice required at least one woman to share the bench for litigations involving family matters.

One of the first important decisions of post-1948 Czech jurisprudence was the exclusion from the civil code of legal matters concerning the family. An autonomous new legal discipline, "family law," was established, and a special Family Code promulgated. According to the new code, marriage was no longer viewed as a contract, but as a voluntary union of a man and a woman based solely on emotional, non-material values.

This Code was not copied from the Soviets — who had little if anything to offer by way of guidance. Its language was comprehensible to a layman, and the prerequisites for a simplified, speedy, and inexpensive trial were laid down. Money could not purchase

an exit visa from matrimonial bondage. Equally, the host of big-
otries and double standards common to other legal systems were
absent. All legal distinctions between children born in or out of
wedlock were eliminated. The birth certificate no longer indicated
the "sinful" origin of the illegitimate child, and such a baby could
not be discriminated against during probate. Dark-haired or olive-
skinned applicants could adopt a blond orphan. Only political pigmentation mattered. Even a single person could qualify as an
adoptive parent. In the case of the death of a child's father, the
widow was vested with all parental authority. The anachronism of
the court-appointed male guardian to the half-orphaned minor was
dropped. The Family Code changed the principle of equality between the sexes from a meaningless pronouncement into a workable
set of rules. As we shall see later, divorce proceedings were not contests in which the husband traded his liberty for impoverishment.
The divorcee was entitled to resume her maiden name, but not to
become a parasitic recipient of a fat alimony.

An engaged couple faced their first encounter with the principle of equality between the sexes at the People's Committee —
the setting for their wedding ceremony. There the couple was given
the option of retaining their respective surnames or jointly adopting
the surname of either partner — whether of the bride or the groom.
For example, the last name of my law school colleague was Krásná,
which means, according to the Procházka's Czech-English Diction-
ary "beautiful, lovely, fair, excellent." The husband adopted her
name, thus becoming Mr. Beautiful.

According to the standard interpretation of the principle of
equality, either of the spouses was entitled to remain in the household. Our law school teachers referred to the male housewife as a
species unusual yet acceptable, in socialism. However, political and
economic pressures almost ruled out such an arrangement. In all
the years of my Czechoslovak existence I met only one family with
this sort of division of labor: the wife — a physician — practiced
her profession, and her less talented husband took care of the cook-
ing and the diapers of their four offspring.

The law declared, "In the married state husband and wife enjoy the same rights and have the same duties. It is their duty to
live together, to be faithful to each other and mutually to help each
other" (Section 15). Both had to satisfy the needs of the family
founded by their marriage (Section 19). These provisions require
some explanation. The scope of marital responsibilities was nar-

rowed in comparison to the classic formula of *obligatio mensae et thori*. Sexual cohabitation was no longer a duty, but a matter of choice. Thus the woman's dignity was protected — or so we were told at law school. In Chapter XVII I referred to the prevalent legal opinion which held that a husband could be charged with the rape of his own wife if she had been subjected to the use or threat of force, or had been taken advantage of while defenseless. I also confessed that I had never heard of anyone's having been prosecuted on this charge. The law, of course, was not intended to promote physical abstinence. While an over-zealous athlete might find himself before the criminal bench, on the other hand, he might also have grounds for a divorce owing to his partner's lack of sexual responsiveness. All the legislators and the judiciary had in mind was to uphold the bedroom as a place of mutual, voluntary demonstrations of affection, rather than a forced labor camp.

It was not the State the Moralist, but the State the Economist which was bent on emphasizing the equality of the sexes. One of the foremost tasks of the post-1948 government was to eject the wife from the kitchen onto the assembly line. At the time of this writing, Czechoslovak women represent almost a half of the country's labor force. The economic motivation of equality of the sexes becomes apparent if one examines the courts' interpretation of the marital duty "to live together." It was held that choice of employment — and of residence for that matter — should not be based on the consent of one's spouse. Husbands were free to leave their families and move, say, to top priority areas of socialist construction such as the industrial complex of Ostrava. Should the distressed wife seek a remedy at court she would get none. Again, this freedom to leave was open to both sexes. When I was at the University, a student complained to me that his wife, the mother of two, had surprised him with the news that she had joined the secret police. His protests were in vain, ran contrary to the spirit of the Family Code, and invoked the wrath of the Party cell at the school. The apparatchiki summoned the distressed comrade for an ordeal of criticism and self-criticism — and condemned him for nurturing feudal tendencies to incarcerate his progressive wife in the bondage of domesticity.

Those spouses who expected Czech Communists to emulate the ultra-liberal divorce policy of the Russian Bolsheviks after 1917 were disappoined. Our revolution did not sanction unilateral termination of matrimony — the so-called postcard divorces. While dissolution of a marriage became a less troublesome and far less expensive affair, it was almost never degraded into a meaningless routine. As a rule, litigants had to work hard to obtain a favorable ruling, and even then many were denied.

The Family Code required only five short articles (Sections 30-34) to cover the entire field of divorce. Among the old provisions dropped was the concept of legal separation. In most cases the husband and wife still shared the same abode at the time of the trial. The retention of a common residence was a matter of necessity. This is as good a time as any to stress the fact that the tight housing market in Czechoslovakia was — and remains — one of the main causes of marital breakdown. Besides adultery, the unavailability of the couple's own apartment destroyed more marriages than any other single factor, and also helped to poison life after the divorce. I knew of a number of former couples who for years were stranded in the same apartment after they had each chosen new spouses — two new families sharing two rooms. Their chances of succeeding at the second attempt were hardly improved.

The conditions which would authorize the judge to grant a divorce were broadly formulated: "If for grave reasons a profound and permanent rift has arisen between husband and wife, either spouse may apply for dissolution of the marriage by divorce." The marriage, however, could not be dissolved if divorce would be detrimental to the interests of the couple's children who were still minors. As a rule, Communist law shuns specificity in favor of broad, rather vague wording, supplemented by qualifying clauses. Concrete formulae handicap the "class interpretations" that often aim beyond and against the obvious meaning of the law. In this case, however, I am inclined to accept as genuine the official stand that life was too complex for rigid categories of marital maladies. "Let the judge be the arbiter of the crises and not a passive interpreter and agent of the printed word," we were told.

The general terms of the cited provision ruled out the need for retaining the traditional escape clause of "unsurmountable aversion" (*nepřekonatelný odpor*), an equivalent to the ridiculous Anglo-Saxon "mental cruelty." Perhaps my criticism of the latter is too sweeping, but I am not likely to recant until someone convinces me that mental cruelty is compatible with holding an office of responsibility such as that of Governor or Supreme Court Justice of the United States. As I see it, these individuals are not what the court declares them to be — and in that case the court is guilty of bad justice. If the court has not erred, such despicable characters should withdraw from public life.

The judges were advised to avoid the extremes of undue permissiveness and inflexibility. On the one hand it was not right to force the petitioners to live together if their marriage was beyond repair and of no further use to society. On the other hand, we were supposed to guard against the irresponsible notion that it should be as easy to terminate a marriage as to obtain a marriage license. By the same token, the law forbade the court to rule in favor of a plaintiff should the dissolution of the marriage adversely affect the interests of any minor children. Prague told us that the child of divorced parents was always a loser — the inheritor of half a home or none at all. The Supreme Court supported this view — but also added that the children's interests could be just as badly served when they were exposed to the fights, abuse and vulgarities of parents who, having been denied a divorce, were forced to live together.

The directives issued by the Supreme Court and the Ministry of Justice varied from season to season, depending upon which aspect of the statistical reports Prague found most disturbing. If Prague was worried by the number of denied divorces and unsalvaged marriages, we were castigated and advised to be more lenient. If the rate of petitions granted exceeded the anticipated figures, we were criticized for wrecking the institution of the socialist family. The *aurea via media* did not seem to be within our reach. Whatever we did, we were wrong.

To repeat, a judge could grant a divorce if the legal death of the marriage could be established by the presence of these factors: the rift had to be deep, permanent, and the product of grave reasons. The freedom from any binding precedents enabled the judge to apply fresh criteria to each new case as he saw fit; an act of adultery in one case shattered conjugal life beyond repair, while in another case resulted in only a slight hangover. Throughout the years, however, a set of tentative rules developed: with some exceptions, we did not consider the rift permanent and profound unless the spouses had avoided intimate contact for at least six months prior to the trial. Similarly, desertion, the commission of a crime, adultery, and physical maltreatment were regarded as grave indications of marital crisis.

The mounting divorce rate during the fifties led the government to experiment with the delaying tactics practiced in the postwar years by the Soviet courts. We were ordered to attempt man-

datory reconciliations. We experimented with summoning the
spouses to the judge's office for an informal talk to probe into the
depths of their marital discord. We expected that the parties, removed from the rigidity of the court room, would be more responsive to our efforts at reconciliation. The results were meager.
Often the informality of the pre-trial session opened the gate to a
flood of accusations and vilifications. If each spouse viewed the
other with an unfriendly eye when they entered our offices, by the
time they left, their mood was one of hardened hostility. The emotional climate of such interviews often led the spouses to abandon
the restraint customarily maintained when dealing with the authorities. A person who under less exacting circumstances, would have
acceded to anything totalitarianism demanded, here became incensed enough to tell the judge who was urging reconciliation to
go to hell.

In the Soviet Union the court fee served as an ancillary regu-
lator of the divorce rate, and, according to all indications, some
deterrent effect has been established. This was not true of Czechoslovakia; throughout my stay with the judiciary, divorce remained
an inexpensive undertaking. The state demanded a fee of only
400 Kčs — an amount slightly exceeding the average weekly income
— subject to partial or full recovery if the court deemed it appropriate. Moreover, with less affluent plaintiffs, a waiver of the
fee was issued.

Divorce could become a costly affair for a party choosing to be
represented by an attorney. Approximately one third of those
seeking a divorce did so. Their money was not wasted. An attorney
was no guarantee of victory, but invariably was of more assistance
here than in a criminal trial. His value was not in dominating the
court room — which he could not do — but in preparing his client
for the match. The counsel familiarized him with the personality
of the presiding judge, his outlook, temperament and idiosyncrasies;
instructed him on proper court room behavior, how to avoid irritating the chairman of the bench, and how to solicit the sympathy of
the people's assessors. The attorney also helped to tailor the claim
to satisfy the requirements of the Family Code. The client learned
about the kind of traps the court was likely to prepare for him, and
how to elude them, even at the price of an unabashed lie. I should
like to illustrate this last point. As we already know, the petitioner
had to convince the court that his marriage was dead. Yet it was
the habit of many Czech would-be divorcees to engage in a farewell

coitus the night before the trial. During the proceeding, the judge usually managed to catch an unwary do-it-yourself litigant by employing a set of well-timed and seemingly innocent questions referring to the couple's separation. Once he — or she, or both — confessed, the case was lost.

Couples who appeared in court unattended by an attorney often exhibited a surprising degree of ignorance of the most rudimentary legal matters. Probably the most frequent misconception was the belief that divorce was solely a matter of mutual consent, immune from the interference of the state. Words from the bench that the conclusion but not the termination of a marriage was left up to the spouses left them unconvinced.

Another very popular myth concerned the number of divorces to which a citizen was entitled during his life. The lay estimates varied from four to seven. When I told the couples that the number was unlimited and that they might try as often as they pleased, this information was received with astonishment. For the lack of a more plausible explanation, the origin of this myth can perhaps be ascribed to the universal socialist preoccupation with quotas and targets.

The number of hearings in a trial ranged from a single court session to five or more, all depending upon the complexity of the case, the merits of the arguments, the availability and persuasiveness of the evidence, the couple's consensus regarding the termination of the marriage, and, very important, whether or not the litigants were the parents of minors. On the average, a childless couple was summoned for two hearings, while the existence of young offspring extended the trial to three or perhaps four sessions. The period of time between the sessions was usually not less than a week and not more than a month. The smoothest release from matrimonial bondage was available to childless litigants whose claim was substantiated by the gross guilt of one or both. Besides those meaningless petitions satisfying none of the legal prerequisites, the person with the rockiest road was the exclusively guilty plaintiff whose opponent insisted upon the preservation of the marriage. To sum up this introductory survey of divorce, I might venture the tentative estimate that during the fifties more than half of all petitioned-for divorces in Czechoslovakia were granted.

The divorce trial consisted predominantly of the gathering and evaluation of oral evidence. On occasions, a litigant offered a written document in evidence, such as an intercepted letter from a lover or a medical report on injuries sustained by the adulterous spouse. For the most part, however, we had to content ourselves with what we heard from the witness stand. Responsible adjudication was to some extent obstructed by frequent violations of the oath, and by the state's seeming reluctance to prosecute perjurers. Witnesses, mostly friends or relatives of the litigants, often presented a deliberately deceptive or, at least a subjective, emotionally-charged story. Some of my colleagues regarded the hearing of testimony from litigants' children (provided they were over eighteen) as a beneficial contribution to "the ascertainment of material truth." I tried it once and the witness' evident embarrassment and pain dissuaded me from ever repeating such an experiment.

The very nature of marriage, which is, after all, an intimate experience, rendered the judgment of an outsider only marginally relevant, and of doubtful accuracy. A totalitarian country, with its legions of police spies, leaves little hidden from the ever-present official eye. However, it is the state, and not the subjects, who are supposed to be knowledgeable. A suspicious spouse could not hire a detective to spy on his sweetheart.

In this context I would like to mention a rather extraordinary incident that provided the court with a piece of unshakable evidence. In one division of the Škoda Industries, a female crane-operator invited a fellow worker to the cabin of her crane, high under the roof of the factory structure during the lunch hour. The two—both married, though not to each other—engaged in sexual intercourse, profiting from the perfect seclusion of the suspended cabin. The operator, however, contracted a spasm, leading to the disaster known as *penis captivus*. When the factory personnel resumed work, the crane remained inactive. A volunteer climbed up to investigate, and lost no time in trumpeting out his findings. An ambulance had to be sent over to facilitate the descent of the inseparable duo. This exercise in Alpinism was tensely followed by the assembled toiling masses. In this case the court was not short of reliable witnesses.

Litigation based on gross guilt of the defendant was a quick affair. Once the court had established that the violation of the marital code was grave enough to justify the innocent party's unwillingness to maintain the conjugal union, the proceedings were reduced to verification of the guilt.

An affirmative judgment was easiest to obtain against a defendant serving a long term for a commission of a crime—preferably

a political one. The typical attitude toward these culprits was
articulated by the Regional Court at Ostrava:

There is no doubt that the anti-state activity itself, proving
the defendant to be an enemy of the People's Democracy, who
joined the rank of the enemies of the working class, must have
caused disdain and disgust on part of his wife, loyal to the
People's Democracy, and destroyed all her emotions for the
defendant, provided that such emotions are still left.[1]

Trials of this sort were speedy even if the litigants were not
childless, and the defendant was serving his term in a distant district. In the latter case, the judge submitted the file to the court
where the defendant was imprisoned, with a request to hear him
and record his argument. It was, however, immaterial whether or
not he consented to the petition. As a rule, convicts neither objected to the divorce nor insisted upon being escorted to the trial.

Short of murder, the fastest way out of marriage was to have
one's spouse defect to the West. The trial then shrank into a mere
formality, the purpose of which was merely to establish the defendant's physical absence from the country.

A person wishing for a smooth divorce, and married neither
to a jailbird or a defector, did well to be childless, with an un-
embittered spouse who shared a desire for the termination of the
marriage, and was intelligent enough to comprehend the advantages
of the "abbreviated formula" offered by the law. The Family Code
stipulated that upon the application of both litigants to dispense
with the decision, concerning guilt, the court, by omitting the
search for the villain, limits the trial to the ascertainment of the
rift—its length, depth, and the gravity of the cause. The bench's
obligation to find out whether or not the marriage in question could
still be saved for society remained unchanged. The courts welcomed this abridged alternative, protecting both the judges and
the litigants from troublesome quarrels about who was responsible
for the marital mishap. Typical applicants for the short version
of the trial were of rather sophisticated stock—usually college
graduates—with no liking for a courtroom battle. This sort of trial
I experienced about a hundred times as a presiding judge, and once
as a party.

The court was powerless to impose the guiltless rule on the
parties if they did not explicitly request it—and most of them did
not. The typical litigant expected something more from the court
than just a smooth settlement of his marital crisis. He felt that he

was both a petitioner for an exit visa and the prosecutor of his estranged spouse. The courtroom seemed the most suitable place to air accumulated grievances and proclaim his own judgment of moral indignation, under the auspices of state authority.

A court decision finding one's partner exclusively guilty of the marriage rift, besides providing emotional and largely symbolic satisfaction, also brought with it permanent immunity from eventual financial obligations. According to the law, an exclusively guilty party—male or female—forfeited the right to alimony. As we shall see later, however, a divorcee, guilty or not, had only a slim chance of securing material assistance from the former spouse.

The law furnished no precise analysis of the concept of guilt (vina). In terms of the law and the court's interpretation, a vina was a deliberate willful act causing substantial damage to matrimonial harmony, in which the offending spouse was aware—within reason—of the harmful consequences of such behavior. A marriage could perish with perhaps equal ease from other "objective" causes, with neither spouse intentionally responsible. In that case, the vina ruling was precluded. Usually there was not one contestant who was all to blame and another aglow with angelic virtues. The question the court had to decide was not "who" but "how much by each?" Varying degrees of co-responsibility were commonplace. The judge had to ask himself whether or not the blame referred only to the prime cause of the crisis. Who had thrown the first stone? Was, for example, Mrs. Synčáková[2], an emotionally disturbed postal employee, solely guilty because she deserted her husband? Mr. Synčák was faithful, did not drink and treated his wife well. The fact that he was an ex-convict could not be held against him. Yet the motive behind the desertion was not negligible: the plaintiff had found out that her husband had been suspected of murdering three of his former wives and told me, "three was already enough." Even though her argument could not stand up in the light of available evidence, the desertion lost the stigma of the unexcusably capricious act.

Even if the court succeeded in identifying the prime sinner, the law offered no clear-cut guidance on how to judge subsequent infractions committed by the injured party. Say a husband committed adultery and failed to conceal the secret from his wife. Convinced that marital happiness was irreparably shattered, she, too, embarked upon a voyage of infidelity. Finally the couple resorted to the court for final settlement. Could the bench accept the wife's plea of innocence, based on the argument that her act of adultery was blameless and could cause no further damage to a marriage already destroyed by the concupiscence of her husband? "It's like saying that today I damaged a car which yesterday my husband smashed to pieces," a litigant told me once. "How could I wreck a wreck" was the cornerstone of the plea. In such situations, the judge tended to display a kind of moralistic inflexibility. They maintained that violation of one's responsibilities as a spouse constituted guilt irrespective of the state of mutual alienation at the time the act was committed. On two occasions I deviated from this practice—in effect, condoning adultery—and both times the appeal court threw out my verdict.

Age difference of the spouses, impotence, sterility, or sexual incompatibility were viewed as "objective causes" rather than "willful acts." On the whole, luke-warm lovers fared better than zealous ones. In one case the wife charged that during the seven years of her marriage the husband had made love to her only twice —both times resulting in pregnancy. The defendant concurred, adding that in his opinion "the frequency of the exercise of marital responsibilities was pretty adequate." The divorce was granted, with guilt being attributed to no one. On the other hand, I held Mr. M. guilty. His never-ceasing sexual appetite had driven his wife to seek the help of the court, claiming, *inter alia*, that the physical exertion handicapped her in fulfilling the production quota in the Škoda factory.[3]

The most common valid causes of guilt were adultery, desertion, alcoholism and maltreatment. Those of us judges stationed in Sudetenland had to cope with the heterogeneity of values the settlers brought with them, which to a large extent they had preserved, despite the pressures of the socialist melting pot. We tried to detect the symptoms of cultural specificity without, however, granting allowances for behavior that was perhaps legitimate within the minority group but not with the rest of us. For example, the Czech, Moravian and, to a lesser degree, the Slovak cultures do not condone wife-beating. The repatriates from Russia, however, thought otherwise and were very upset by the intransigent judges. Once I even presided over a case of a wife who complained that her husband did not love her any more, judging from his sudden failure to administer the customary blows.

When parents of dependent children applied for divorce, they had to fight harder to convince the court about the merits of the case. A divorce petition could only be granted after a final settlement had been made concerning the future of the children. At the larger courts, one or more judges specialized in this agenda, but at places like Stříbro I had to preside over both the divorce trial and the proceedings establishing custody and the *alimenty*[4.] for the minors.

Let us illustrate the supplementary trial procedure by using a typical example: the divorce petition of a couple who are both gainfully employed and have one child—a boy five years old. After the unsuccessful mandatory conciliation attempt, the first hearing, and the accumulation of some evidence, I adjourn the trial resolving that "no further action can be undertaken until the matter of the custody and material support of the minor X. has been decided." As the next step I appoint the ÚOM ("Youth Protection Office") as the child's legal representative. The social worker from the ÚOM then automatically opens an investigation of the parents' residence to ascertain their living conditions and their respective abilities to take care of the boy. Meanwhile, I dispatch letters to the Local People's Committee—on occasions also to the police— inquiring about the same matters, and to the parents' employers about their incomes. Within some three weeks I have received all the evidence I need: the litigants are members of the working class and, though politically inactive, they are presumed to be loyal to the System. Nothing is known that would detract from their fitness as parents. I then summon the parties to the court. Both demand custody of their son. Acting on the ÚOM recommendation, I entrust the child to the mother and go on to rule that the father shall support the boy to the extent of 200 Kčs out of his income of 1,200 Kčs a month. Both parents are unhappy with the decision —the father wants the child and the mother wants more money. They appeal to the higher court, but the verdict is upheld. With the decision in force, a copy is attached to the divorce file, and the original trial can now be resumed.

A public myth existed which held that the courts, in deciding the custody of more than one child in a family, left the boys with the mother and the daughters with the father. This was, of course, unsubstantiated nonsense. We at the bench regarded the minors of divorced couples as losers anyway, and did not want to aggravate their lot by separating them only to satisfy the parents' selfish preferences. Judges passed such decisions in truly exceptional cases, and personally I never did so. The public was, however, quite

correct in assuming that the mother had a better chance of securing the guardianship of a child—provided "the moral and political
profile" of both the litigants was found to be about even. It was
at this point that custody disputes turned into acrimonious political
battles, accusations, denunciations, interventions by the Party, and
an overall explosive situation which the judge had to handle with
care and a great deal of luck.

Under the masquerade of pious concern with the optimal conditions necessary to make a good Communist of their child lay the
parents' financial self-interest. The exercise of custody was less
expensive than the *alimenty* payments. Let us assume that I was
in the shoes of the father in the cited example: my monthly income was 1,200 Kčs, out of which I would have to pay 200 Kčs to
support one child. This salary would have been inadequate enough
as it was, and with one sixth deducted, I could barely provide myself
with essentials. Should I have fathered two children and be requested to pay 400 Kčs, such an onerous obligation would almost
certainly have prohibited me from re-marrying. No woman in her
right mind would consent to a proposal from a man earning only
800 Kčs. My only recourse, therefore, would be to fight to gain
custody. Were I to win, not only would I save my 400 Kčs, but I
would receive about the same amount from my former wife. In
addition, I would pay less income tax and receive a children's allow-
ance from the state. With all these gains duly collected, I would
then leave the child in the care of my parents. *Babička* (grand-
mother) looks after everything, as the Czechs nowadays say. But
in order for my shrewd scheme to succeed, I would have to prove
to the court that I was better qualified both as citizen and as
educator than my ex-wife. In view of my non-existent merits, my
only recourse would be a smearing campaign. Thus, I would tell
the court that my wife believed in God, or that her cousin defected
to Australia ten years ago, or that her father's brother was, in my
opinion, a latent stooge of Wall Street. If the court threw out my
case, and I also lost the appeal, I would still fight. The brother-
in-law of my mistress knew someone in the Central Committee of
the Party. Should he be willing and able to solicit the support of
an important comrade, the Supreme Court could yet annul the
verdicts of the lower courts. All in all, not a very edifying business.

A fantasy? Hardly. On April 29, 1958, the Supreme Court
passed a verdict under the file number Cz 71/58—later published
in the "Collection of Decisions of Czechoslovak Courts," No. 97,

volume 1958, pp. 211-212—involving a custody case. Both parents were members of the working class, and no objections were raised to their political attitudes. They were divorced. Their one child had been brought up by the incurably ill mother; the court did not identify the disease, merely indicating that her handicap was of a mental rather than a physical nature. Each summer the child was allowed a prolonged vacation with the father, during which time the minor prospered both physically and mentally. The father then petitioned for a transfer of custody and won. The decision of the Regional Court went into force only to be annulled by the Supreme Court on the pretext of its having violated the spirit of socialist legality. The Supreme Court offered the following biased reasoning:

> The mother of the child is sick. According to expert testimony her illness is virtually incurable. However, at present it is on the decrease so that there is nothing to prove that the mother is unfit to exercise due care of the child. The civic and moral behavior of the mother is absolutely in order. The mother lives with the child at her parents' home. Her father is the chairman of the Uniform Agricultural Cooperative in his place of residence and the chairman of the local cell of the Communist Party of Czechoslovakia. This educational environment guarantees the righteous education of the child in becoming a politically loyal member of our society.

The Supreme Court, subsequently, rejected as irrelevant the weight gain of the child during the time spent with the father and the loss in weight after the return to the mother, both confirmed by an expert witness. Finally, to consummate the persuasiveness of their decision, the supreme judicial authority in the country referred to a passage in the Communist Party weekly, *Tvorba*, No. 37 of 1957, on the importance of politicization from cradle to grave.

The issue of financial support for divorced wives can be disposed of in a brief paragraph. While the child retains an unrestricted claim on his parents' pockets until the day he can take care of himself (including the college years when he is already of legal age), the divorced party is not so fortunate. She (or he as the case may be) *may* file a claim for financial support only if the court had exonerated her from blame for the break-up of the marriage and was satisfied that she could not reasonably be expected to provide for herself. In effect, only the seriously ill, or mothers of small babies with no opportunity of leaving them in a state nursery, could qualify.

We regarded alimony for a divorcee as an emergency measure, a last resort, and not an act of standard settlement or a payoff in exchange for personal freedom. A claimant's stereotyped plea that she gave her ex-husband the best years of her life and now the thankless rascal refused to pay may move an American adjudicator to tears. We were less impressed: "So did he. He, too, sacrificed the best years." Our attitude was based both on consistency in applying the principle of equality of the sexes, and, more importantly, on the raw economic reality. Ours was a society in which a maintainance of a more or less decent standard of living demanded the employment of both spouses. How, then, could a single individual be expected to support two households? Because of the economic reality, a successful plaintiff in these litigations was left with the laurels of a token victory. Often, a plaintiff was not so much concerned with enrichment as with pestering the former spouse—the only kind of vengeance left. A lump sum settlement was out of the question: the court could award alimony only in the form of monthly payments, subject to termination when the children had reached school age and/or when the beneficiary had recovered from some disability. It should also be added that by re-marrying, a plaintiff forfeited all claims and titles against the former spouse.

Friends used to tease me by saying how lucky I was to be paid for an activity that was more like fun than a real job, since that which other mortals could only find in rare volumes of pre-war pornography, I presided over in the splendor of a judicial gown. In a way, they were right. Had I been a bureaucrat with the municipal waterworks, it would have been most unlikely for Mrs. R. to enter my office, lift her skirt, and submit in evidence bruises allegedly inflicted on her posterior by her husband. On another occasion, a very agitated bride, still in her wedding gown, rushed in to tell this story: An hour before, the marital vows had been completed. The wedding party journeyed home in a number of carriages, and since the bride loved to command horses, she took over the reins, while her husband and her mother occupied the rear seat. During the exhilarating ride through the woods, at one point the bride turned around only to see her passengers engaged in sexual intercourse. So, here she was, demanding that I do something.

Although after a time the fare tended to pall out of sheer repetition, life at the bench could be colorful—and dangerous. One could, I suppose, have been mildly amused by a wife's complaint that her husband forced her to sexually manipulate him under the table in a room packed with five hundred people; but not if the husband happened to be one of the provincial potentates, in this case a trade union official in charge of cultural activities. Marital affairs were of too much interest to the Party for us to be left alone. There were judges who, because of their resistance to certain apparatchiki's wishes, ended up neatly framed in jail.

As law students we were told that "under the surface disorder in a marriage, class struggle phenomena of paramount importance can be detected." To the bench's role of producers and quota-chasers was added that of "detectors." To reduce marital crisis to a conflict between an infidel and a believer in the System was more than common sense would allow. Czech people usually did not marry across political lines, and those who did, or who began to disagree on matters of faith after marriage, prudently kept silent, aware that such charges might backfire. Admittedly, we presided over a number of "bourgeois divorces," and discovered that the litigants had married with material gain in mind, an attitude which the arrival of the lean years of socialization had forced them to reconsider. For example, in Plzeň a twenty-year-old girl married a well-known impotent simpleton who for the previous three decades had harbored the delusion that he was Western Bohemia's Don Juan. With his business nationalized and the hidden money spent, divorce was an obvious solution for the girl. Yet, on the other hand, litigants of proletarian stock did not seem to be any less greedy. And so the doctrinal differences between bourgeois and proletarian crises were hard to detect.

The judge often learned too late that an inconspicuous litigant had access to those in power. Our fears of behind-the-scenes vendettas were real, although, on reflection, perhaps just a little exaggerated. The political climate of the fifties obliterated distinctions between imaginary, potential and real dangers, and we, to be on the safe side and to avoid being caught unprepared, anticipated the worst. The diversions of our litigants' sexual histories were not enough to compensate for our anxieties.

An unsuccessful petitioner often grew angry when the judge applied the Family Code provision that a spouse solely guilty of the rift could not be granted a divorce against the wish of the innocent party. Our laws were characterized by their flexibility, but the cited clause was clear, unequivocal, not allowing for exceptions or mutilating re-interpretations under the pretext of "the spirit of socialist justice." In the long run, this provision became a stumbling block of considerable significance.

For the explanation of this development we have to look back to the year 1948. The February coup was a signal for heavy social traffic in both directions—up and down. Many beneficiaries of this mobility were ambitious proletarians whose loyalty to the Party was their only qualification for taking over positions of importance ranging from the so-called "proletarian executives" (*dělnický ředitel*) to seats in the cabinet. From small towns and forgotten villages they moved to Prague or other cities, often leaving their families behind. The initial pressures of revolutionary change, that perhaps permitted no thought of marital reunion, were often followed by the recognition that, though the new housing was commensurate to the new status, the wives were not. Yesterday's nobody was aware that his humble background provided for a short-cut on the road toward prominence. Though no doubt grateful for the august accident of proletarian birth, as far as I could see he was very rarely proud of it. Working class origin, a negligible education, lack of exposure to the amenities of "bourgeois" life brought political but not emotional security. Parvenus in chauffeur-driven cars and in generals' uniforms could—as long as they kept silent— pass themselves off for "something better," but the moment a wife appeared on the scene, the camouflage crumbled. There she was —worn out, ugly, fat, and clumsy—a nagging reminder of the husband's own insecurity in his role in high society. Divorce, therefore, seemed to be the only logical solution.

A number of these protagonists of proletarian virtues, in search for more adequate partners—usually from among their secretaries —settled for mistresses of ex-bourgeois coinage, the irony of their choice perhaps eluding most of them. With a pretty, neat helpmeet secured, the divorce petition was then filed. But the abandoned spouses, with typically unsophisticated reasoning ("He ruined my life so I'll ruin his"), refused to join the petition. Because of the husbands' exclusive guilt (i.e., adultery), their chances of obtaining a divorce were nil, and many political proteges were forced to lead a rather unsettled private life. In return, a section of the informed public questioned whether or not these politically mature comrades were quite qualified to preach about the new socialist morality.

This was the background for the inconveniences caused by the stern clause of the Family Code. A good, efficient socialist law must be vague and capable of adaptation to the needs of the day. With no way to re-interpret the formula out of its meaning, the Family Code had to be amended in 1955 to the effect that in exceptional cases involving the public interest a divorce could be granted to an exclusively guilty spouse irrespective of the attitude of the innocent party. As can be seen, this amendment was formulated very vaguely, with "public interest" to be read as the "interest of the Party." The provision was tailored for the sake of the troubled political elite, and as I was told confidentially by an official of the Ministry of Justice, after these divorces had been settled, the amendment—a textbook example in political expediency—would be "de-activated."

With no magic yardstick to fathom the "rift" and the "guilt," we were bound to err. I am sure that on occasions we tried to patch together a hopeless wreck, while elsewhere we performed an autopsy on a body that was not yet quite dead. One of my colleagues had to live with a fine legal conundrum. This is what happened: A wife — her name, I believe was Mrs. Nováková — filed a divorce petition against her husband, who at the time was residing at Ostrov u Karlových Varů, P.O.B. 100, the address of the concentration camp attached to the Jáchymov uranium mines. The economizing judge did not summon the defendant to Plzeň, but requested a hearing at the branch of the Karlsbad court at Ostrov. The file was returned with Mr. Novák's testimony, admitting his guilt and contesting nothing. The divorce was granted. Some years later, Mr. Novák was released; he returned home, only to discover that his wife had remarried. Accused of bigamy, she displayed a divorce decree. Mr. Novák claimed total ignorance. Perplexed, he went to see the prosecutor. An investigation revealed that the prison authorities had sent the judge at Ostrov the wrong Mr. Novák. The impostor must have been something of a practical joker, and the judge an idiot. The following questions arose: Was Mrs. Nováková a bigamist even though she had contracted a second marriage in good faith? If she was not a bigamist, and her second marriage remained valid, what was the legal status of her first husband? If the wrong Mr. Novák could be identified (he could not) what charge would be brought against him? Could the judge at Ostrov be held liable for something? Unless I am mistaken, the problem solved itself peacefully—either Mr. or Mrs. Novák suddenly passed away.

Any law is essentially a crude, inadequate instrument in the light of the complexities of real life. The reader fond of legalistic riddles may also appreciate the following example. In 1956, I shared an office at the Plzeň court with Judge Jan Kašpar. Among his pending cases was a divorce petition which we debated for hours. In a nutshell, it involved a woman who could not get married because she was not divorced, and could not obtain a divorce because she could not prove that she was married. She was a Sudeten German who, in order to cover up her record as an active Nazi, had contracted a marriage of convenience with a Czech in Prague in May, 1945, one of the last days of the war. Notwithstanding this, the court sentenced her to a long term, of which she had served a full ten years. In 1955, released from prison, she found employment with a State Farm, the Mecca of political outcasts. There she also became pregnant. Though anxious to marry the father of her expected child, she unwisely disclosed to the Local People's Committee her nominal marrige of 1945, and the fact that she had not heard of her husband since. The Committee, of course, had to decline the issuance of the marriage license, advising her to get divorced first. The law provided for the eventuality of a claim against a litigant of unknown residence, but failed to anticipate a situation in which the marriage certificate was also missing. A search in Prague for the document led nowhere; the Town Hall had burned down in 1945, and the witnesses to the nuptials had been two unknown German soldiers picked up in the street. After thorough deliberation, Judge Kašpar decided to undertake a seemingly Quixotic struggle with the socialist bureaucracy and, to the surprise of all concerned, he won. Communicating back and forth with the Ministry of Justice, the Ministry of Interior, and the Prague city fathers, the municipal government finally consented to issue a bona fide substitute marriage certificate. With the acquisition of this document, the rest of the story became mere routine.[5.]

Our overall policy toward divorce carried distinct preventive and even punitive overtones, notably with respect to young couples. It was estimated that about fifty per cent of all the divorces in the country affected marriages of less than five years' duration. The government followed this increasing trend with grave concern, admonishing us to be strict with the irresponsible youth. The abortion reform law of 1957 reduced the number of marriages of necessity, but did not significantly improve the general picture of marital harmony of this group.

If anyone had to be blamed it was the Establishment—for neglecting housing development and condemning young couples to live either separated or with in-laws. Homelessness and lack of privacy were the most general causes of rifts among the newlyweds, even surpassing that very popular Czech habit, adultery. Mr. and Mrs. S. were typical casualties of this frustration. Both white collar employees with the Škoda Industries and childless, they had been married for three years. For all this time they had been forced to stay with the wife's parents and two pre-adolescent brothers, sharing an apartment consisting of a kitchen and two rooms. The young couple's room had served as "a passage-way" between the other room, where the rest of the family slept, and the kitchen and bathroom. The embarrassing surprises, commencing with the honeymoon, can well be imagined. Frustration developed into tensions between the old and the young, then between the young themselves, followed by maltreatment, adultery and divorce. Once again, when filling out the statistical sheet for the Ministry, I had to single out the housing problem as the prime cause of the divorce.

A search for an apartment in Czechoslovakia serves as a reminder that we are in the country of Franz Kafka. A man is advised not to get married unless he has secured a place to live, but he cannot obtain such a place unless he is married. The state issues "tenancy decrees," but somehow there is no decree for him. Should the improbable happen, and he finds a room on his own, the state will not let him move in.

The representatives of the toiling masses did not appear upset by the plight of the applicants. Once I accompanied a friend to the Office of the President of the Republic, to inquire about the fate of a petition he had submitted. This poor man, in despair at having to live with his wife and two children in a one-room attic, begged comrade President for help. As might have been expected, our trip was futile. On our way out of the Castle we ran into comrade Jankovcová, a Social Democrat turned Communist and a member of the cabinet. My friend saw her as his last straw and recited at speed the circumstances of his sorrow. Madam Jankovcová did not let him finish, interrupting him with this remarkable statement: "You, comrade, must be a very special case indeed, because as far as I know, all the young people in our state have a decent place to live."

Let Kafka now be our tourist guide through the premises of the Municipal Dwelling Space Distribution Office of the People's Committee of the City of Plzeň, where I peddled my cause in 1953, the year I got married. Whenever I came there, no matter how early in the morning, the corridors were packed with applicants. When there were fewer than this, they were waiting in vain, because on that day the office was closed. Despite the respectability of my profession and that of my wife, who was a physician, and despite the fact that I only desired to move into a tiny apartment in a house nominally owned by my father, I felt as uneasy as if I were soliciting an outrageously undeserved favor. Finally, one day, I reached the bureaucrat in charge. "How many children have you got?" the weary official asked. "I just got married a few weeks ago," was my response. He: "Answer the question. I am not interested in your marriage but in the number of kids." I: "Well, as a matter of fact, we haven't got any, and she, that is, my wife, is not pregnant." "Bad, very bad," the bureaucrat muttered. "But, perhaps, there is some hope," he continued. "Perhaps you or your wife suffer from T.B." Alas, our suffering lay elsewhere. When I asked him what I should do or might expect, he furnished me with the following friendly advice: "Well, comrade, come again and ask. In about five years. Or, to be on the safe side, let's make it seven years. This would be about the right time." In seven years I was happily divorced and out of the country.

The reader will perhaps wonder if my personal experience made me magnify the corrosive effect of the housing problem on marital stability. I ask doubters to try to imagine themselves with no place to stay and no privacy, always "sharing." You try, and the result is only failure. The years pass by, and you still do not have anywhere to call your own. To this very day I have not stopped blessing America for the possibility of renting a few square feet and staying, undisturbed, as long as I am on time with my rent. Of all the things America has to offer, it is perhaps this apartment that my Czech friends envy most.

Adultery, either as the prime cause of the rift, or as the consequence of another crisis (e.g., lack of an apartment), was the most frequently cited reason for seeking a way out of marriage in the courts. Marital infidelity appeared in all age groups, and equally with men and women—though, according to our findings, the latter seemed to hold a slight lead. The Communists, of course, did not invent these sins. The Czechs have never been puritans, and our post-war generation was highly promiscuous. But, to repeat, the present fulltime employment of married women led to their emotional as well as economic emancipation. How much togetherness could be left between two tired, irritated individuals when, say, the husband worked the morning shift and the wife the afternoon shift? They would rarely meet, spending most of their time with fellow employees in the factory or the office. The factory became a synonym for the Sodom of socialist sin. The government was realistic enough to discard the eventuality of extirpating adultery, but decided, nevertheless, to combat the rising trend. In the absence of criminal prosecution of the adulterers, (adultery was not crime), the remedy called for was social pressure. The "Comradely Courts"—the lay tribunals established in factories in the late fifties to try petty infractions of the law—frequently tried such offenders in public hearings and passed sentences of either fines or verbal reprimands. For example, the two lovers locked in the fateful predicament in the crane operator's cabin, mentioned earlier, were found guilty of the misdemeanor of "violating the spirit of socialist behavior."

When I was transferred to the court at Stříbro in 1957, I learned that the tranquility of country life had little beneficial effect on matrimonial harmony. Since adulterers were everywhere, we attempted to generate social pressure in the villages as well.

The meddling of the "masses" in one's private life could easily get out of hand, but at times interference and resultant social ostracism proved to be a healthy recourse. For example, a kolkhoznik from the village of Lom filed a divorce petition. He had, I believe, five children, and was madly in love with a neighbor's wife, the mother of eight. She also came to the court demanding a divorce. I threw them both out and charged the Local People's Committee at Lom with the responsibility of bringing them back to their senses—hardly a proper judicial measure, but an effective one. I did not see the parties again.

In 1963, four years after my leaving the country, a new Family Code was promulgated in Czechoslovakia. The most notable change was the abolition of the concept of guilt, allowing the court to concentrate on the circumstance of the rift and disregard the participants' responsibility for the crisis. This innovation was justified because of similar Soviet and East German practices.

As far as I have been able to determine, the upward trend of the divorce rate in Czechoslovakia still continues. It would of course be foolish to blame all broken marriages on Communism. Let us not forget that thirty years ago in Czechoslovakia, a divorce was viewed as a disgrace, while today it has almost become a sign of social distinction. I would certainly in no way blame the Party for the emancipation of women, notably those in Slovakia, but I do claim that the System has been at least partly guilty for the rise in divorce by transforming the employment of both spouses from choice to economic necessity and by neglecting the housing issue.

1. Reg. C. Ostrava, May 8, 1951, 11 OK 34/51 quoted by "Collection of Decisions of Czechoslovak Courts," No. 7 (1952), pp. 11-12. This reasoning nicely contrasts with the following opinion of the Regional Court at Ústí: "The fact that the wife, with good reason, informed the police about her husband, who had embezzled some property from the national enterprise, could by no means be held against her, and could not constitute a grave reason for a rift in the marriage." (7 OK 93/52, quoted by J. Andrlik, "Commentary to the Code on Family Relations," Prague; Orbis, 1954, p. 117.)

2. In Czech and Slovak languages the suffix "ová" denotes a woman, married or single.

3. Paul Kratochvil, an old friend of mine from the days in Plzeň and at present Lecturer of Modern Chinese at Cambridge University, England, told me that the Chinese knew the answer to this ticklish question. During his stay in Peking in 1958 — the Great Leap Forward Year — he learned about a factory meeting dealing with the complaint submitted by a female worker. The woman accused her husband of excessive sexual activity that impaired her strength to build socialism. The Party called for a meeting where for several hours and in utmost seriousness the acceptable quota of socialist cohabitation was discussed. The comrades arrived at this conclusion: the recommended norm was intercourse three times a week — on Monday, Wednesday, and Saturday, always before midnight, never during the daytime, and never, of course on Sunday. Czechoslovak judges did not enjoy the benefit of similar political guidance.

4. *Alimenty* is a common Czech expression referring both to the alimony paid to a former spouse and to the financial support of the offspring.

5. Upon our request the police later found the elusive husband living in České Budějovice married and the father of four. The Prosecutor, however, did not press charges of bigamy in view of the fact that the May wedding had already proved costly enough: that a Czech's humanitarian assistance to a German girl in 1945 was read by the Czech court as collaboration with the Nazis, a crime for which our Samaritan had spent several years in prison.

21 DISPUTED MINORS

Apart from custody and support claims, the most frequent civil issues involving minors were: petitions from those between sixteen and eighteen years of age requesting judicial consent to marry; actions against delinquent minors, with their eventual placement in state institutions and the lifting of the legal authority of negligent parents; and adoption. The state imposed no court fees in any of these proceedings, and since representation by a counsellor was uncommon, the party's expenses were virtually nil.

Busy as our bench was with such work, the main burden of the task rested with the ÚOM—the Youth Protection Office. This bureau, besides working as the legal representative of minors before the court, had a range of responsibilities akin to those of the children's welfare worker in Western countries—i.e., implementation of court orders, on-the-spot investigations, testimonies accompanied by lengthy reports and, last but not least, the unenviable experience of dealing with all sorts of parental monsters.

The law ordered the civil bench to ask for a written testimony from the Local People's Committee and the minors' respective employers regarding their "moral, civic, political, etc. maturity." As a rule, these affidavits were of little value. If, for example, I requested a statement from the employer of a teenage would-be bride regarding her maturity and sense of responsibility, it was a safe bet to expect the stereotyped answer: "X., national enterprise, states that petitioner Y. has (has not) a positive attitude toward people's democracy and the building socialism in our country. She is (is not) a member of the Czechoslovak Youth Organization and pays (does not pay) her dues on time. Therefore, we urge the petition be granted (denied)." In short, the comrade from the national enterprise failed to answer the question and also failed to notice that the court was not interested in his recommendations. With no better remedy available, the ÚOM, again, had to be dispatched to the field to search for the truth.

Czechoslovakia, in accordance with the Soviet example, lowered the age for the attainment of full legal rights and obligations to eighteen years. A person's eighteenth birthday brought in its wake the right to conclude contracts, to vote (socialist style), or to get married. The exercise of this last right was further modified by the provisions of the Family Code which allowed teenagers —boys or girls—who were at least sixteen years of age to receive marital vows provided they had sought and secured the prior consent of the court. The lawmaker, at this point, could hardly have been less specific. All that was spelled out in the Family Code was that such a permit could only be granted for "important reasons." It was up to the bench to interpret the meaning of "important." The Ministry of Justice and the Supreme Court, however, offered some assistance by advising us to consider as "important reasons" only those circumstances directly relating to the applicant and not to third persons. An interesting rider was added: "Pregnancy *per se* is not a sufficient ground for an affirmative ruling."

Such cases were initiated by would-be brides who, nine times out of ten, were pregnant. This picture did not change with the promulgation of the 1957 Abortion Act. When I asked the petitioners whether they had considered such an operation, they revealed either total ignorance of the new law, or confessed that they had been too perplexed and flustered to act in time.

Sooner or later during the proceedings, the girl would confess that it was only the expected baby that had precipitated her sudden longing for a wedding ring. This may sound rather strange in view of the aforementioned abolition of legal and, supposedly, all other distinctions between children born in and out of wedlock. The stigma of illegitimacy had been tossed into the garbage can containing the vestiges of bourgeois mentality. We were superior to the West; therefore, the Supreme Court ruled that pregnancy was no longer a valid justification for teenage marriage. Such pronouncements were some distance ahead of the reality, though. Admittedly, the fact that one's parents had or had not been joined in holy matrimony was of lesser importance in the Czechoslovakia of the fifties than it had been thirty years before or than it is in the United States today.

Among my colleagues in the Plzeň province I earned a deserved reputation for being insensitive and unresponsive to the pleas of grief-stricken teenagers seeking marriage licenses. But if I chose to interpret the law too literally—i.e., pregnancy alone does not justify marriage—it was not for the sake of punishing the poor girls in order to expose the fallacy of the official political boast. We had not totally disposed of the social stigma. Yet, I did believe and I still do believe that declining to give the blessing to two unfit, immature adolescents was a lesser evil than consenting to a marriage of necessity, in which they might multiply for a while and then approach the court for the second time, seeking a divorce. On more than one occasion, a desperate, worn-out teenage mother of three or more came to me and literally rebuked my predecessor on the bench for failing to have had her thrown out when she had begged for a marriage license. My strict application of the law in these cases was to satisfy my own convictions, not to bring irrevocable disaster to my petitioners. Thus, after the presentation of my ruling, I would inform them of their right to appeal, aware that the higher court would in all probability reverse the verdict.

Whether or not a teenager married then and there with judicial consent or a couple of months later, after there was no longer any need to plead with the state for its gracious approval, was a marginal issue. The power of the court in this instance did not extend beyond temporary harassment.

A far more significant category of civil adjudication affecting minors concerned actions against delinquent children and/or their parents. At this point, the civil bench exercised power approximating the authority of the criminal court. Such proceedings were numerous and hectic—and often resulted in rather alarming findings. The family approached the judges not as applicants but as a defaulting social unit, hauled before the bench under orders initiated by the police, the prosecutor, the Local People's Committee, or "informal channels" (notably, lay assessors)—and after an investigation by the ÚOM.

To repeat: Czechoslovak law considered a juvenile delinquent any person between fifteen and eighteen years of age who, upon commission of a crime, was tried in a regular criminal court, with the benefit of a reduced scale of punishment. According to the Penal Code, however, "A person who has not yet attained fifteen years of age at the time the crime is committed, shall not be held criminally liable." Such a juvenile then came under the jurisdiction of our civil bench, which was empowered to impose a verbal reprimand, "tutelage" by the ÚOM (i.e., periodical controls and reporting to the court), or, as the most severe measure, the placement of the child in a state institution. Similarly, the power of the civil court over the negligent parent ranged from the temporary suspension to the permanent removal of parental authority. A parent, if charged with such felonies as abandoning a child, evasion of financial responsibility, cruelty, endangering the child's moral upbringing, etc., was, of course, tried before the criminal bench. The civil action was usually, though not necessarily, supplementary to the punitive verdict.

After settling in the West I was frequently surprised to find that to many people the most frightful specter of Communism was that of heartless commissars stealing babies from their mothers' breasts and incarcerating them in gargantuan state educational factories, thus turning them into dehumanized robots. Sometimes I almost wished this was so. For Prague, as for Moscow for that matter, the family—a socialist, progressive one—remained the only natural unit, the very center of a child's upbringing. Though Czechoslovakia paid lip service to the late Soviet educator Makarenko (who still ranks as a patron saint of applied Marxist pedagogics) nothing of substance was done by the state to provide for assistance in cases that cried out for an immediate remedy. The Czech Communists failed to recognize the need for emergency placement of an endangered child, not for reasons of ideology but out of inexcusable neglect.

We at the courts suffered the consequences. A child's life in an environment called his "home" could be hell, to put it mildly, but when we ruled for the immediate transfer of the endangered minor into the care of the state, there was no way of enforcing the ruling. Our protests fell on deaf ears, meeting the monotonous response: no space, no money allocated, no competent personnel, no nothing. The few prewar reformatories inherited by the new regime were neglected and their staffs underpaid. The institutions of postwar vintage were in no better condition.

I used to accompany the District Prosecutor on his periodical supervisory trips to such a place located at Trpisty, near Stříbro. It consisted of a dilapidated, filthy baroque mansion from which issued a strong stench of urine. The prosecutor drafted a critical report and sent it to Prague. In vain, of course—low priority; no money. We attempted to tackle the issue from another angle. The Ministry of Justice was informed that an unenforced court decision endangered the respect of the toiling masses for the authority of the state. To this, the Ministry responded laconically that the best way to remedy this "shortcoming" was by refraining from decisions that called for the removal of minors from their home milieu. Any Ivory Tower Bolshevik could be that imaginative, disregarding conveniently the fact that the prime cause of the child's deviant behavior was all too often a defective family.

The cultural heterogeneity of the settlers certainly did not simplify court proceedings. To illustrate this point: A young couple from the Slovakian region of Orava moved to our district, participants in the late-settlers program, and were issued a respectable four-room house in the village boasting the odd name of Holostřevy (literally, "Emptied Intestines"). Disregarding their four rooms, according to a ÚOM report, the parents, with their two toddlers, crowded into only one room, together with a number of assorted domestic animals. The report also stated that the children had apparently never been diapered, and their faces were plastered with feces, their mattresses corroded with urine. I summoned the parents, and the husband in particular proved to be a very unpleasant chap. He was not retarded, but simply rude. First, he denied the charges. After hearing the witnesses, he shifted his ground, accusing us of deliberate discrimination because he was a Slovak, and we on the bench were all Czechs. (Reminiscent of charges sometimes made in court by minorities elsewhere). It is true that the way of life in backward parts of Slovakia, such as Orava, where this man came from, was quite tolerant of hygienic shortcomings. This might explain, but not excuse, the charge. As I told him, "Other countries have other customs, but if you want to live here, you will have to comply. If you will not comply, we shall take your children away from you."

The wounded nationalist was getting very angry. Our conversation continued: He: "All right. Take them away. Take them. I don't mind. But do you know what? I'll tell you. I'll make other kids. See? You'll not lick me."

I: "But we will. We shall also put them in a state institution, and you will pay the upkeep for all the children. And if you don't pay, it'll be deducted from your check until almost nothing is left to you."

He: "How do you think I can work if I don't have any money? I'll be too weak."

I: "Very good. Weak, you say. Weak enough not to be able to make the extra babies you threaten us with."

He: "So take everything away from me. Then I'll die of hunger."

I, with a conciliatory touch: "Now that's a much more reasonable attitude."

And so on. However farcical it sounds, this was the way we conversed.

Our man from Emptied Intestines shared the mistaken but common notion that the removal of a child from parental authority terminated his liability for the baby's material well-being. In fact, every step possible was taken to extract support from the parents. Very often this information made the parents change their minds during the court proceedings, and while at first they were willing to offer up their offspring, when they got the message about continuous financial obligation, their loving paternal instincts were rekindled.

From the freshman year at law school on, it was hammered into our heads that socialist justice was designed to be not so much a *post facto* remedy as a preventive measure of anti-social behavior. Yet with respect to the endangered minors we did not prevent and often could not remedy. By way of illustration, I recall the case of the Silánič family, State Farm laborers—a primitive couple with seven children plus the husband's pregnant mistress, all living in a single room. This was in 1957, and perhaps I should have anticipated what happened two years later, when their children were caught giving practical instructions in sexual intercourse to the other youngsters in the village.

In concluding this account of civil adjudication over delinquent and/or neglected children, I would call state policy on this issue misplaced totalitarianism, in which there was total control of the wrong people for the wrong reasons at the wrong time. Where state control might have been appropriate, it proved to be anything but total.

What about decent foster homes and adoption, the reader might ask. The economic necessity calling for employment of both spouses lessened the desire for children, adopted or natural. Children were viewed not as a pleasure and an enrichment, but a burden, and the fewer of them one had, the better. There were more children available for adoption than volunteers willing to adopt them. Gypsy babies in particular had no chance in allegedly color-blind Czechoslovakia.

Accordingly, the civil court calendar on adoptions was a meager one. In all the years I spent on the bench, I do not think that I presided over more than a dozen such petitions. The provisions of the Family Code regulating adoptions were — if we disregard the indispensable political verbiage of promoting socialist values in the child's upbringing, etc. — rather tolerant. The law did not require the medical examination of the applicants, and in contrast to practices elsewhere, could not have cared less about the color of their eyes.

The adoption of an adult was read as a contradiction in terms: the purpose of finding a new home was to secure this home for the sake of upbringing, and a person of legal age (eighteen) could not qualify. Moreover, the law required a reasonable age difference between the applicant and the child. Compensating for these restrictive rules to some extent was the intelligent provision allowing an unmarried person to become an adoptive parent.

The political edge of these proceedings was considerably blunted by the absence of a conflicting claim. Unlike custody cases, in which the divorced parents were quick to raise the swords of political arguments, vilifications, and denunciations in support of their respective desires, adoption was an essentially uncontested act of a rare tranquility. The Ministry of Justice displayed dissatisfaction with our failure to generate the prerequisite tone of class struggle in the proceedings, and on at least one occasion subjected a judge to savage criticism. The sinner had violated the spirit of socialist justice by granting a petition to a couple who had admitted to a belief in God. The rest of the profession was threatened with serious repercussions should we fail in our vigilance and permit a child to be usurped by "theistic obscurantists." I faced this problem once and ignored comrade Minister with impunity. The Local People's Committee sent me a letter objecting to an adoption on religious grounds. Since the letter arrived at the court unregistered, and there was no one from my staff around whom I did not trust, the message was conveniently lost and nothing more was heard.

The type of adoption petition most likely to appear in court was not to rescue a waif from an orphanage, but to adopt a child that one's wife had born during a previous marriage or out of wedlock. Though I did not turn down a single petition of this kind I felt it my duty to stress the eventual consequences of such a step. First, adoption terminated the financial obligation of the natural father toward the child; second, in case of divorce, the ties between the wife's child and his adoptive father remained unaffected; and, finally, adoption, though easy to obtain, was almost impossible to reverse. These gloomy perspectives deterred a number of individuals contemplating adoption — no doubt merely on the urging of their wives, and without having established any meaningful emotional ties with the children.

The Family Code, in its original 1949 version, required the consent of natural parents (if known) to the adoption of their child. In consequence, the adoptive parents were exposed to eventual blackmail, and the child's image of his identity was at risk. I presided over two cases of this sort: A couple surrendered their child for adoption, and some years later they began to pester the baby's new home, demanding to see their lost darling, and demanding, also, indemnity for their paternal sorrow, accompanied by threats of a civil suit. The distressed foster parents, almost ready to capitulate and pay, nevertheless came to see me to make sure that was what they had to do. My answer was, of course, an emphatic no. Though puzzled by my suggestion that they should not discourage the intruders from filing suit, they calmed down when I gave them my word that they had nothing to worry about. As expected, the indemnity claim was filed, and I summoned the parties. After the opening statements I feigned sympathy with the plaintiffs' entreaties *provided* they would agree to honor promptly the counterclaim of the defendants concerning the costs of rearing the adopted child. And I handed over the bill. Paternal devotion vanished instantly. The plaintiffs withdrew the claim, cleared the premises, and neither I nor the adoptive parents ever heard of the blackmailers again.

The law's insistence that the natural parents consent to the adoption proved a mighty problem in one case which I should like to describe in some detail. Mrs. X., an educated woman in her early fifties, paid me a visit at the Stříbro court and confessed that the cat and mouse game was running thin. Her son, by then seven years old, was not really her son. She did not want to reveal the truth, but neither could she pretend any more. She would tell me all. Several years before, Mrs. X. and her husband had lived in Slovakia, the eastern part of the country. There, Mr. X. had an affair with his secretary, Mrs. Y., whose husband was at the time serving a long prison term for a political crime. When the relationship between Mr. X. and Mrs. Y. resulted in pregnancy, Mr. X. confessed to his wife, adding that it was important that the incarcerated Mr. Y. be kept from the knowledge of his wife's infidelity, since his health was very poor (a heart condition), and the only thing that kept him going was his belief in his wife's affection. Mrs. X. proved to be both magnanimous and imaginative. Having no children of her own, she approached the pregnant Mrs. Y. with the proposal that she claim to be the mother of the child when it was born. Mrs. Y. agreed, and dressed as trimly as her condition would allow, while Mrs. X. padded herself into maternity clothes. Friends of Mrs. X., who was by then of an age when motherhood was rather improbable, congratulated her on her good fortune, and the masquerade remained undetected.

A few days after the child — let us call him minor XY — was born, Mr. and Mrs. X. moved with the baby as far as possible from where they were known, and settled at Stříbro. Years went by. Mr. Y. was paroled and rejoined his wife. According to Mrs. X. — who remained in close correspondence with Mrs. Y. — they led a very happy life. In 1957, the child entered elementary school and the principal insisted, as was his duty, on seeing the birth certificate.

Now, the minor XY, a child of natural parents Mr. X. and Mrs. Y., commonly known by the world as child of Mr. X. and Mrs. X., was, in the eyes of the law, as evidenced by the birth certificate, the child of Mr. Y. and Mrs. Y. Mrs. X., therefore, requested help. An adoption could easily have been arranged, provided — and this brings us back to the beginning of the story — the consent of natural parents had not been required. Alas, Mr. Y., the legal father, had no idea of the child's existence, and such news, Mrs. X. assured me, would kill him; his heart condition had worsened. Even if his consent by some fraudulent means could be obtained, still some damage would remain: on the birth certificate the names of parents Y. would have to be stricken out and those of Mr. and Mrs. X. inserted in their place, thus revealing to the child his true origins. And now, to make Mrs. X.'s life even more miserable, the child had developed a mental defect, and Mr. X. — the true and potentially adoptive father — had died.

I asked Mrs. X. for a day to think the matter over. My suggestion, while causing me to blush as a judge, induced no shame as a human being. "Try to bribe, or steal, or somehow obtain a blank birth certificate form at any office of the birth registry, and fill it out as you please." The flabbergasted Mrs. X. nodded, adding that first she would like to visit the Office of the Prosecutor General in Prague. Perhaps they could suggest something less irregular.

They did not, as Mrs. X. later told me, their advice was identical with mine. Hereby, let me bow before that citadel of totalitarian rigidity in recognition of this instance of flexibility and compassion.

The story ended happily, however, and Mrs. X. did not have to set out along the path of forgery. The Family Code was amended soon afterward, rescinding the requirement of the consent of the negligent natural parents to the adoption and abolishing the need to state the true origin of the child on his birth certificate.

To repeat, the adoption law — except for its meaningless political ballast and the rather ineffectual insistence of the Ministry of Justice that the courts be hostile towards religion-oriented applicants — appears to me a reasonable document, which other countries, still marred by archaic provisions of ethnic and, I would say, anti-ecumenical connotations, could well envy.

22 DISPUTED FATHERHOOD

The complex adoption case of minor XY might well serve as an entry point to the topic of paternity cases. Whenever the court was called upon to pinpoint the child's begetter — unknown, reluctant or protesting — the outcome was highly uncertain. The claim might be settled in a few minutes or could expand into a costly trial dragging on for years. Hardly any other category of civil litigation could provide the judge with more satisfaction with justice well accomplished — or with more doubt about his verdict.

On several occasions I have commented on the so-called principle of material (substantive) truth. This professed cornerstone of socialist justice subordinates form to content and does not allow the facts to be devoured by procedural niceties or courtroom coups. In short, a technicality cannot set a murderer free, as is all too common in the Anglo-Saxon legal tradition. A paternity suit, however, was something of a white crow, owing to the ambivalence concerning the principle of material truth. The Family Code included some legal presumptions which shifted the burden of proof from the accuser to the defendant, to the considerable procedural disadvantage of the latter. Though the judge, by virtue of his role as "a fact-finder rather than an umpire," could mitigate this procedural inequity, his powers in this regard were limited. A successful defense called for more imagination and sophistication than a layman could be expected to display without the assistance of a counsellor. Accordingly, we advised putative fathers to seek legal representation, and if they could not afford a lawyer, to have one assigned to them *ex officio* and free of charge.

The paternity issue was a mongrel of conflicting political pedigrees. The procedural road blocks placed in front of the defendants betrayed a pre-Bolshevik vintage, the authority of the prosecutor to enter into a suit was clearly a Soviet import, and the admissibility of biological hereditary tests oscillated in inverse proportion to the oracular authority of the charlatan biologist Trofim D. Lysenko. In addition, the insistence of the Czechoslovak judiciary on catching elusive fathers contrasted with the strange inertia of Soviet courts in this regard.

The fatherhood disputed before our courts fell into three categories: *uznání otcovství* (admission, acknowledgement of fatherhood), *zjištění otcovství* (ascertainment), and *popření otcovství* (denial, refutation). The first category represented the smooth solution, more an administrative arrangement than a judicial contest. Only when it had failed was the second category — the most complex and frequent of the three — resorted to. While the first and the second related to children born out of wedlock, the last category involved, in most cases, a contest between the spouses.

In the case of a child born out of wedlock, an official of the Local People's Committee, in charge of the birth registry, issued a form to the mother on which she was asked to identify the father. He was then summoned to the registrar, and if he acknowledged his fatherhood, the case was closed and the parents were left to settle matters pertaining to the child's support and upbringing by mutual consent. Only if no agreement could be reached was the issue submitted to the court for decision. It often happened that the man failed to appear before the registrar, or when he did, denied that he was the father; or the mother would not fill out the paternity statement at all. All such cases were referred to the court.

The number of such notices I received at Stříbro averaged five a month. The first step was to summon the mother of the child to my office for an informal interview to find out the circumstances of her mishap, the name and whereabouts of the father and, above all, his willingness to accept responsibility for the adventure. Under the law, the mother was not obliged to divulge his name but, as a rule, a judge neglected to inform her of her right to remain silent and

insisted instead that she tell the whole truth or otherwise. . . This
convenient misinterpretation of the law was motivated both by the
judge's interest in disposing of the pending case in the shortest possible time and by his concern with finding out if the woman was
being intimidated by a partner attempting to insure his anonymity.
Usually, however, a mother was quite eager to identify the man responsible for her trouble. I know of only one mother — the notorious prosecutor of the political show trials, Miss Ludmila Brožová
— who refused to talk.

The girls I questioned at Stříbro fell into a drab pattern of
primitive countryside youth — teenagers, or in their early twenties
— naive rather than promiscuous. Their mishaps concerned casual
acquaintances who failed to honor the promise of marriage — or so
the all-too-familiar story went. Illegitimate motherhood often appeared as a by-product of the building of socialist agriculture. The
long-term so-called "brigades" sponsored by the Czechoslovak
Youth Organization (a copy of the Soviet Komsomol) brought together youths of both sexes under one roof for a prolonged period
of time. They assuaged the boredom and weariness of their rustic
drudgery by cohabiting.

In our district, however, the main source of illegitimacy was
the military garrison of about four thousand soldiers of the Twenty-
Fourth Infantry Regiment located at Stříbro. The anonymity of
the military attire, the widespread use of assumed names and, in
cases of exceptionally devious Don Juans, stolen I.D. cards presented at the request of untrusting love partners brought us many
a headache. I, for my part, had served in the army long enough to
learn that officers were not exactly eager to have the culprits
brought to justice. I well remember the morning when our unit was
assembled so that the commander, accompanied by one pregnant
girl and her furious mother, could confront the company, face to
face, only to find no one since the offender was at the time in protective custody — in the literal sense of the word. The frequent
shifting of the conscripts from detachment to detachment did not
help our court work, either.

Inevitably, many cases had to be closed before reaching the
second step, i.e., the summoning and hearing of the alleged father.
In this connection I would like to mention a story whose outcome
was more a result of luck than ingenuity. In 1958 I questioned a
shy, inarticulate, teenage mother. The history of her trouble was
very simple: The previous summer there in town she had met a

soldier, and they made *al fresco* love a couple of times. Three months later he was discharged, and she had not heard from him since.

"Did he know you had become pregnant?" I asked.

"No."

"Do you know his name and civilian address?"

"Yes."

"Did you write to him at that address and tell him of what had happened to you?"

"No."

"Why did you not write to him?"

"I don't know."

With my monosyllabic visitor gone, I sent a letter to the court in the district of the man's alleged residence, requesting that he be heard on the matter. Soon, however, the fellow judge reported that no one of that name had been registered with the police in the area. The only plausible explanation was that the address given to the girl was false.

I summoned the girl for a second time; perhaps she might tell me something more. She knew nothing. It then occurred to me that it was a practice with many military men before their discharge to have a group photograph taken, surrounding their beaming superior officer, with one copy left in his office for posterity. This was my clue. To get the girl into the post and to secure the cooperation of the military, I called up the commander, Colonel Štětka (an earthy surname which translates as either "Brush" or "Whore"). Štětka and I had sat together on a political committee and knew each other fairly well. Colonel Brush grasped the problem and promptly arranged to have the snapshots of approximately two thousand soldiers, discharged in fall of 1957, gathered for inspection. I furnished the mother with a letter of recommendation and my good wishes.

In less than an hour the researcher was back in my office. The improbable had happened: the first face on the first picture shown to her had been that of her impregnator. The officer had readily supplied the real name and address, and this time my request for a hearing at a distant court bore fruit. The culprit, mesmerized by the perfection of the System, confessed his sin and agreed to pay generously, and the case was closed.

It is my estimate that about fifty per cent of the accused males acknowledged their fatherhood. The recalcitrant alleged fathers had to undergo a contested litigation before a judge and two lay assessors — the trial of "ascertainment of fatherhood." Whenever a disavowal of fatherhood occurred, the court appointed the Youth Protection Office (ÚOM) as the legal representative of the minor to file a suit in the name of the babe in arms as the plaintiff, with his mother figuring either as a co-plaintiff, or, more commonly, as a mere witness.

The claim made short reading:

"To the District Court at................:
The minor plaintiff...........................born on..............................
at.............................. of mother................................. has been
fathered by the defendant.................................. The defendant
maintained intimate relationship with the mother of the minor
plaintiff in the critical period from.................... to...........................
Evidence offered: blood test
                       testimony of the mother of the minor plaintiff
The court is hereby requested to render the judgment:
The defendant........................... is found the father of the minor
plaintiff...................................... born on....................................
of mother................................. and liable to support the minor
plaintiff with the monthly amount of Kčs...............................
retroactively as of...............................

                       Sincerely,
                       (signature illegible)
                       for Youth Protection Office

Simple, it was, and almost unbeatable. The net from which the defendant had to extricate himself was made of stainless steel reinforced by both the law and court practice. In the first place, the Family Code defined a father as any man who cohabitated with the mother of the plaintiff during a period of no less than 180 days and no more than 300 days preceding the birth. Such an assertion aired by the mother of the child established a legal presumption, the burden of any proof to the contrary falling on the shoulders of the accused. To prove the *non-existence* of a fact, the non-occurrence of an act, is, as everybody must agree, a difficult achievement indeed. "Where and how did you, defendant, spend that evening five years ago — the evening of August 23, 1952, to be exact?" "I don't remember." "Ah, that is very suspicious." The defendant lacking photographic memory and an inventory of his whereabouts during his lifetime, accompanied by unshakable evidence, was already almost lost.

To call for a blood test was, as we shall learn later, to back a lame horse. An examination of samples of the blood of the child, his mother and the defendant, and an evaluation on the basis of the criteria known to medical science in Czechoslovakia in the fifties (main groups A, B, AB, O; Rh factors; Mn determinants) furnished imperfect and only negative evidence. The experts could not determine the existence of fatherhood — only its impossibility. The findings they submitted to the court read either "It is impossible for the defendant to be the father of the minor plaintiff," or "The fatherhood of the defendant cannot be ruled out." The chance of being ruled out was about one in ten. In other words, any male had a ninety per cent probability of being unable to rebut an accusation of fatherhood by a woman he had never even met.

On occasions, a defendant, either prior to the blood test or following the failure of the examination to acquit him, would argue that he was not the only one who, during the critical time, had cohabitated with the mother of the child. This claim was ignored by the bench. For example, in the suit of minor N. vs. Mr. P., Miss R.N., the mother of the child, was the prettiest nymphomaniac I have ever met. She testified that she had engaged in sexual intercourse with P., and that she knew P. was the father of the baby. The defendant did not challenge this testimony, though he added that others, too, had slept with Miss R.N. during the period of probable conception. He offered in evidence a list of about fifty alleged cohabitators. Miss R.N. was called to the witness stand and, upon examination of the list, stated that the catalogue of her adventures was accurate, though somewhat incomplete. Notwithstanding this, the witness reiterated that she had no doubts about the defendant's fatherhood. With no legal means of inquiring about this mysterious certainty, the court let it pass. The blood test that followed did not rule out the defendant. Thus Mr. P., whose probability of fatherhood was in this instance about two per cent, lost the case, winning one hundred per cent responsibility for the material support of the child for many years to come.

I hate to appear as some kind of crusader for the protection of helpless males against the wicked fair sex. In the majority of the paternity litigations I presided over, the male defendant lost, and I believe rightly so. There were even instances of retarded and incoherent mothers who won their cases only because of seemingly unrelated pieces of evidence (e.g., a scrap of paper in the mother's possession, identified as the handwriting of the defendant by an

expert in graphology) that I unearthed, venturing beyond —
though not contrary to — the scope of my official duties.

It is not my intention to present a well-balanced record of
cases lost and won, but rather to stress the procedural handicaps
facing the defendants, and the circumstances under which the spirit
of law, but not the spirit of justice, prevailed. Many mothers
pointed their fingers not in the direction of their impregnators but
at men of high incomes. With some accusers, it was the desire for
material gain, with others the wounded pride of a rejected fiancée or
lover, while with still others it was simply malevolence or stupidity.
Also, the cause of truth was not helped by the common knowledge
that the state was reluctant to prosecute "mothers in distress" even
for the most flagrant acts of perjury on the witness stand.

The paternity calendar was also an issue of contention along
generation lines within the judiciary. Regardless of political coloring, most of the young judges felt far less at ease with the rigidity
of the law than did the elders. These older jurists did not accept
the arguments that in the first place an affirmative ruling secured
support, but not an emotional attachment on the part of the unlikely father. In the second place, the material and non-material
damage incurred by the defendant's family usually outweighed the
dubious satisfaction obtained by filling in the fatherhood space in
the child's birth certificate. And we argued that no father was preferable to the wrong father, since such a child would be better taken
care of by the state.

The continental interpretation of judicial powers left us with
a certain procedural initiative which an outsider might have considered incompatible with the canon of judicial impartiality. The
bench was partial, even prejudiced, but the bias was towards truth,
not for or against the litigant. In paternity cases, the judicial initiative was directed towards probing the plausibility of the claim
and the credibility of the crucial witness — the mother of the minor
plaintiff. Occasionally, we succeeded in detecting what we thought
was foul play and acquitted the defendant; rarely was such a verdict
upheld by the Court of Appeals.

During my assignment as an Assistant Judge, I managed to discredit the accuser in two paternity suits. The first case involved a
female non-commissioned officer stationed with an Air Force unit
in Plzeň. She charged a First Lieutenant from the same service
with fathering her child. The defendant, who had recently married, admitted recognizing the witness but emphatically denied

that he had ever been intimate with her. "I would never dream of even asking her for a date," he insisted, and I was quite inclined to believe him. The two people were just too incompatible, and I could not imagine how this handsome and seemingly intelligent man could have been drawn to the very unappealing and rather vulgar witness. The bench, however, did not share my opinion, and after the blood test had not ruled out his fatherhood, his case appeared hopeless.

The chairman of the bench, amused by my idealistic insistence that no effort should be spared to avoid condemning the innocent, consented to an adjournment. "Here, you have the file. Take it home if you wish, and good luck to you, comrade Sherlock Holmes," were his words.

One detail of the evidence determined the outcome of the case. The mother of the child, while testifying about the circumstances that led to her pregnancy, had quoted from her diary. Her statement read something like this: "On June 10, 1952, at 10 p.m., officer X. and I cohabited in Bory Municipal Park in Plzeň. It was a pleasant evening, though it did rain and I had to cover us with my raincoat." At my request, the State Meteorological Service reported that during the first half of June, 1952, not a single drop of rain had fallen in the Plzeň area. At the next court proceedings, the mother of the child repeated her testimony verbatim. When confronted by the evidence of the dry season, she responded with extemporaneous fabrications, contradicting herself more and more until not a shred of credibility was left. The defendant was acquitted.

The second case was similar except for the compatibility of the parties. The couple had at one time been intimate, but the dates each gave for the termination of the relationship differed. The defendant claimed that the affair had ended well over two years before, while the mother of the child insisted it had gone on until the previous February — the time of her conception. "Last February, in the woods, he did it," went the testimony. To dispel my doubts about the likelihood of cohabitation in the open in the coldest month of the year, the witness resorted to persuasive details: "Yes, it was cold with snow everywhere. But it happened. The defendant here drove me to the woods on his motorcycle, make X., license plate Y." This time I obtained unshakable evidence that the motorcycle in question had been inoperative and under repair for a long period well before and after the contested date of the snowbound

February adventure. The case was lost, and the snail-like tempo of the socialist services served a good cause this time.

After my promotion to District Judge in 1956, my endeavours to serve justice in paternity cases were not particularly successful. One of my major defeats was the suit of minor Moravec vs. Hartl. In 1956, when I took over the case, the litigation was well under way, backed by a bulky file of collected evidence. By then the minor was almost of kindergarten age, his mother was serving one of her several prison terms, and the defendant, disgusted with Plzeň, had moved to distant Žďár, married and settled down. Moravcová was an inveterate offender with a record of petty theft, prostitution and vagrancy. When escorted from the state penitentiary to appear before my bench she was a sobbing, pale, pudgy, shapeless woman. The defendant was a skilled manual laborer in the heavy industries, with no criminal record — an inconspicuous and evidently nervous young man.

The court had established that Moravcová and Hartl had become acquainted one autumn in the early fifties, in a cheap bar in the Plzeň suburb of Doudlevce. They were seen leaving the bar together. After a walk of a few minutes, however, Moravcová, dead drunk, fell into the Radbuza river and almost drowned. From this point on the court had been treated to contradictory versions of the story. According to the defendant, after rescuing Moravcová, he recognized this girl as more of a troublemaker than an ideal type for amorous exploits. He was too wet and felt too cold to do anything but leave, quickly and alone, for his room in the housing compound set aside for unmarried male employees of Škoda Industries. The defendant added that he had not met Moravcová since except, of course, at court. He charged her with having accused him of fatherhood only because of his relatively high income and the corresponding prospect of lucrative *alimenty*. Hartl, as he told us, was desperate; the costs of the lengthy trial included not only the fees, travel expenses and lost income, but also the happiness of his marriage.

According to Moravcová, after being fished out of the river, she and her rescuer warmed themselves in his bed, where she also conceived. The witness asserted that she was not a fortune hunter and that her only concern was to secure for her son the father he deserved.

The numerous witnesses had nothing of importance to contribute, with the exception of one man, Špaček. This man, a bachelor in his early forties, testified that Moravcová, prior and during her pregnancy, had lived with him in a one-room-one-bed apartment. Since she was out of work, he provided her with food and shelter. Špaček then hastened to add that he had never sexually approached Moravcová, despite their sleeping together in the same bed and his being neither homosexual nor impotent.

Moravcová, several times questioned by the court on this point, supported Špaček's improbable story.

As expected, the blood test which I ordered did not rule out the defendant as a possible father of the minor plaintiff. The law would have been satisfied if, on the basis of this flimsy evidence, I had handed down an affirmative ruling. I was in no mood to do so, but yet I had to do something.

After some thought, I decided to obtain a detailed plan of the Škoda housing compound and a description and layout of the furniture of the room in which Hartl and Moravcová had allegedly cohabited. Moravcová, recalled to the witness stand, failed to explain how she could have passed the guard at the dormitory unnoticed, and her attempt to describe Hartl's room was a fiasco. However, she insisted that her memory was far from perfect, and that the only thing she was sure of was the date she had met Hartl, fallen into the river and conceived — in that order.

Comparing the date of the claimed conception and the date of the child's birth, it was evident that Moravcová must have delivered "the plaintiff" prematurely. To verify this, I ordered the records of the maternity ward of the state hospital to be submitted to the court. The records revealed that a premature delivery of the minor Moravec was out of the question. Thereupon I appointed Dr. Václav Laně, Professor of Gynecology of Charles University Medical School, to deliver an expert opinion on whether or not the child might have been conceived on the date given by Moravcová. The expert said it was impossible. This was all I needed.

This evidence also altered the focus of the court procedure. So far, we had wrestled with the question of whether Hartl and Moravcová had ever engaged in sexual intercourse. Out of all the morass of fabrications, the only undisputed finding related to the date the two people had met. Now, the expert revealed that by that time Moravcová must have already been pregnant. Since Hartl was on trial not for fornication but for paternity, and since he could not have impregnated the pregnant Moravcová, the issue of the existence or non-existence of their physical contact became irrelevant, and the case was dismissed.

But the Youth Protection Office, representing the minor plaintiff, appealed the verdict, and the Court of Appeals, without much ado, reversed the decision, ruling that "the defendant Hartl had to be considered father of the minor plaintiff Moravec." The higher court arrived at its conclusion after having indicated to the mother of the child that she had better reconsider the date of her meeting with the defendant. This she did, conveniently antedating the encounter with Hartl by one month — a period long enough to render the expert's testimony meaningless. The decision went into force.

Paternity litigations were handicapped by the lack of convincing evidence. The door that might have provided the clue to a correct judgment was never quite open. Behind it lay the hereditary biological tests. Czech worshippers of Lysenko, the sacred cow of Stalinist biological sciences, denounced the tests as unscientific, idealistic, anti-Marxist, Mendelian nonsense. "Not hereditary traits but the molding power of the material environment is what matters, comrades," our determinists told us, and the comrades, including those in the judiciary, had to obey. Yet, during my stay on the bench, the response to the tests varied with the sway of Stalinism. The Ministry of Justice, either in writing or through their representatives in the provinces, passed down short-lived instructions: in the spring the tests were prohibited, in summer prohibited with some exceptions, in the fall still restricted but with more exceptions, and in winter the total ban was imposed once more.

It is not my intention to praise the tests because they were unpopular with the Party. They had their drawbacks. In the first place, they were elaborate and very costly. In the second place, they were not available in the provinces, and the child, his mother and the defendant had to travel to Prague to Professor Bohumil Sekla, the only available expert in the field. Finally Professor Sekla's findings expressed not certainty, but merely probability.

This indication of the probability of fatherhood was the test's main asset. Unlike the blood test, with its routine negative statement "The defendant cannot be ruled out as an eventual father," Professor Sekla submitted to the court a file rich in comparative photographic studies of the participants' physical features (notably, the palms, chin, eyes, ears, nose and forehead). By this means he concluded that the fatherhood of the defendant was probable or improbable by x per cent. Had I been able to order the test in the case of Moravcová, for both the allegedly platonic roommate Špaček and the accused Hartl, the final verdict might have been very different.

On rare occasions the result of the blood test added to the confusion and uncertainty about the child's origin. For example, in a case where twins were the minor plaintiffs, the blood test read as follows: "The defendant cannot be ruled out as a probable father of twin A. but he could not be the father of twin B." All that remained for the court to do was to approach the experts once more to inquire whether medical science considered it possible for a mother to have one set of non-identical twins by two different fathers. Prague University answered that it was not possible.[1] Thus, the defendant who was ruled out as the father of twin B. could not be held to be the father of twin A. either. The case was dismissed.

In another case, the result of the blood examination was truly mysterious: "The defendant cannot be ruled out as the father of child X. However, the mother is definitely not the mother of the child in question." The legal solution in rejecting the claim was very simple: Since the child was not that of the person who claimed to be his mother, the defendant could not be regarded as the father of the child.[2]

Though the law did not oblige the judge to call for the blood test in all litigations, it became the rather thoughtless practice to order this evidence without exception. The tests were not exactly cheap, and as a rule they were paid for by the defendant, who only had a slim chance of recovering the fee from the plaintiff in the none-too-likely event of his winning the case.

I departed from the norm once, in a case filed at my court in the early months of 1959. By then the minor plaintiff was already attending the grade school. His mother, about forty, worked in the Plzeň Hotel Continental as a "maid" — a euphemism for a part-time prostitute. The defendant was single, twenty-three years of age, with a well-paid job at Škoda Industries.

At the first hearing the defendant resolutely denied ever having had any relationship with the mother of the child. He said he had known her casually, since they lived in the same community, Útery. At the time of her conception he had been a boy of fifteen. "This is all nonsense. She wants my money. If I really were the father of the child why did she wait for seven years before charging me?"

Good question. "Why did you wait for seven years?" I asked

the mother. No answer. The witness was neither bright nor easy to understand: her language was an amalgam of Czech, Slovak, and, I guessed, Russian. She also turned out to be a fabulous liar.

Once again I benefitted from the assistance of my lay assessors. A people's judge from Úterý suggested it would be a good idea to call up the court in Prague. "They know her there. You will see," I was told.

Prague forwarded a voluminous file, and indeed I saw. In the early fifties, while the state movie makers had been shooting scenes at Úterý, the mother of the plaintiff had been rendering sterling service to interested males. Her adventure remained not without consequence, and when the child was born, the mother initiated a paternity suit in Prague against one of the cameramen. The case, however, was dismissed, after the mother had failed to identify her alleged impregnator in the court room. Characteristically, the state did not punish her for perjury.

With this fresh information, I had good reason to summon the litigants for a further hearing. The perjurer was called to the witness stand, and we engaged in the following duel:

Q.: "Have you ever before accused another man of being the father of your child?"

A.: "No."

Q.: "Did not you accuse cameraman X. in Prague and then fail to identify him in court?"

A.: "Yes."

Q.: "Why did you lie to this court?"

A.: "I did not lie. I forgot about that business in Prague." The witness then presented her story, reciting with surprising speed and lucidity the circumstances in which she met the present defendant, the number of his house in which they had made love, and so on.

Q.: "What was the number of the building you lived in?"

A.: "I don't remember."

Q.: "Isn't it strange to remember the number of a house you have only visited a few times and not to recall the number of the place where you yourself lived for many years?"

A: "I don't know. What's wrong with remembering what I remember? Is it a crime or something?"

Q.: "It is not. Do you know of anyone who had ever seen you entering the defendant's home, or at least, in whom you might have confided about this affair of yours?"

A.: "Yes, my girl friend. My best friend."

Q.: "Does she live in Úterý?"

A.: "No, she moved back to the Soviet Union. And I don't know her address."

Q.: "What is the name of this best friend of yours?"

A.: "I forgot."

This debilitating discourse continued getting nowhere. I called for a short recess to check the lay assessor's reaction to the possibility of throwing the case out on the spot. They were in favor of the proposal. In the written opinion, I justified the failure of the court to resort to the blood test in the following way: "The claim is based solely on the testimony of the child's mother. This person proved — in Prague as well as at this court — to be an utterly unreliable, worthless witness. There is nothing at all that would indicate an even remote possibility of any relationship between the defendant and the witness. Under these circumstances ordering a blood test would be superfluous. Even if the test did not exculpate the defendant, the court would remain unconvinced about his fatherhood of the minor plaintiff. So ruled." The representative of the Youth Protection Office, startled by this unorthodox decision, launched an immediate appeal. Unfortunately, I had no opportunity to find out the decision of the Court of Appeals, because by the time it appeared, I had succeeded in leaving Czechoslovakia. If experience is any guide, however, I am strongly inclined to believe that my verdict was short-lived.

There was general agreement among civil law judges that financial motives lay behind most of the false accusations of fatherhood. Money was of little or no importance in the third category of paternity suits—the denial (popření) of fatherhood. Here, the litigants were for the part marital partners, and the child concerned was born in wedlock. Such suits could be initiated either by the mother of the child (a not uncommon event) or by the mother's husband.

These cases were fairly frequent, and as a rule lacked the character of a contested issue. The participants often had been living apart for a long period of time, either voluntarily or as a consequence of a spouse's imprisonment. As long as the marriage had not been terminated in the court, the law regarded the husband—though physically absent, sterile or impotent—the father of all the children born to his wife.

In cases of marital triangles resulting in adulterous conception, a denial suit preconditioned the granting of a divorce. The legal actions had to proceed in the following order: first, the denial of fatherhood by the husband; second, acknowledgment of fatherhood by (or ascertainment of) the other man; third, the divorce; and last—hopefully—the marriage of the child's parents.

The husband had to prove beyond the shadow of any doubt that he could not have fathered the child. This requirement notwithstanding, the courts, in view of the litigants' common interest in the outcome of the trial, could proceed swiftly, and, relying on concurrent testimonies, could even omit calling for a blood test.

Occasionally, however, the mother would protest the accusation of extra-marital conception. Then the husband had to fight an almost hopeless battle. In January of 1959, when I sat temporarily at the bench of the Court of Appeals, I witnessed such an exercise in futility. The husband, estranged from his wife for two years and living at the other end of the country, sued for denial. Though it was inconceivable to visualize any residual sympathy between the two very hostile opponents, the husband lost because of one trip he had made to Plzeň to attend the divorce proceeding, during which he had spoken to his wife for a few minutes—alone. "Sufficient time to impregnate," the court decreed, ignoring the record of the wife's energetic sexual life with other men.

Through Prague (the Ministry of Justice) we also received fatherhood claims for children residing abroad. Since cross-national court cooperation is the topic of the last chapter of this book, at this point I shall limit myself to only a few observations. This type of paternity suit was not common; it occurred mainly in areas like Stříbro where prior to 1945 the Germans were the most numerous ethnic element. The skeleton in the closet of our amnesiac consciences once more peered out at us, reminding us of our not-too-illustrious treatment of this minority in the hectic postwar days. Our Czech patriots had not only taken over German property, but also had made formidable use of German women. Thus, for example, a self-appointed captain of the Czech army confiscated the belongings of a German family, whisked the parents into a camp to await expulsion, but kept back their sixteen-year-old daughter in his personal protective custody. Two years later, he kicked her out—when she was just nine months pregnant—as an undesirable alien. The baby was delivered on the train to Germany.

Other expectant mothers were expelled from the country and forgotten, though not all of them, and not forever. By the late fifties, paternity claims began to trickle in, a result of the initiative of the International Youth Protection Office.

The surprise on the part of the defendants can easily be imagined. Affronted by the daring of the capitalist foreigner, and confident that the people's democratic court would not let them down, they badly underestimated the procedural difficulties in store for them. The defendants, instead of pleading mistaken identity or non-involvement with the mother of the child, frequently admitted having had the intimate relationship, arguing that such were the legitimate spoils of former victims of Nazism, and that, in short, a German pregnancy ought not to count. As always, political oratory was substituted for the merit lacking in their case.

The first defendant of this category to appear in my court was a middle-aged manual laborer, who in 1945 had become a prosperous fruit grower in Sudetenland, maintaining a small harem of German girls on his plantation. The man was now outraged. "They were only Germans, and Germans are our enemies. They are in the NATO, and are preparing for a new war. And now you, a socialist judge, want to punish me. I can't believe it." The socialist judge handed down an affirmative ruling. I reminded him that considering the number of his "spoils," he was a rather lucky man to be charged with fathering only one child. This attempt to console him was not appreciated.

Though the *alimenty* was established retroactively for three years in these cases, the financial burden was far from onerous. The reason of this exceptional benevolence toward liable fathers must be attributed to Czechoslovakia's shortage of Western currency. Confidential instructions issued by the Ministry of Justice pertaining to paternity suits in which the defendant was a Czechoslovak resident and the minor plaintiff was living in any non-socialist country ordered us not to assess child support in excess of 50 Kčs per month, i.e., four to six times less than would ordinarily have been the case.

Only once at my court did a defendant willingly acknowledge his fatherhood of a child residing abroad. This exception, stemming from the unusual background of the accused, deserves mentioning. The claim was submitted from West Germany, in the name of a minor plaintiff born in 1957. At first I thought the date was a typing error; after all, we were living behind the Iron Curtain, a most effective prophylactic if ever there was one. To clarify the point, I summoned the defendant for an informal talk. To my considerable surprise, there was nothing wrong with the claim. The defendant was a decent, rather tired middle-aged man who told me the following story—in "Have Gun, Will Travel" style:

"I am a Russian German—a Volga German—born in Russia. When Hitler invaded us in 1941, I was drafted into the Soviet Army. I was soon captured by the advancing Nazis. They ordered that I, as a *Volksdeutsche*, should put on a German uniform and fight against the Russians. Then the Russians captured me, but this time I received the same treatment as any other member of the Wehrmacht. I spent over ten years in Siberian camps. I had no idea where my family was. Not a word for a whole decade. Then Adenauer came to Moscow in 1955 and arranged the release of the *Spaetheimkehrige* ['late home comers']. Thus, I was sent 'home' to Germany, where I had never been in my life."

The fatherland did not impress him. He found the country strange and its people too aloof. "Far less friendly than the Russians are," he assured me. A war widow in Nuremberg became his refuge from loneliness, and the child she bore him was what prompted his appearance in court.

"But what are you doing in Czechoslovakia, of all places?" I could not help asking.

"Because my family lives here. The German Red Cross located them for me. After I obtained their address, I told the woman in Nuremberg that I was leaving, and she understood. Now, finally, I am at home and have some peace."

I had no desire to ask my visitor why his family was living in the Stříbro district. The fact that many Soviet citizens had been running ahead of the advancing Red Army, and that our Western borderlands had been liberated by the Americans seemed to be more than coincidental. This man was yet another example of the humble nobody who is dressed in different uniforms by our twisted age, forced to change nationalities almost as often as his socks.

Political interference in the paternity cases was neither very visible nor very oppressive. The Party was less likely to interfere here than in, say, divorce or custody matters. Out-of-court intimidation of the mother, pressuring her not to reveal the identity of the true father, could not, of course, be ruled out. Once the proceedings were under way, the System seemed to disassociate itself from the sinner. The reluctance to interfere on the mother's behalf was not too difficult to understand: in view of the procedural advantages of the plaintiff, such an effort would have been largely superfluous.

I know, however, of one case that achieved considerable notoriety in informed circles. Both the degree of political interference and the strength of the judges' resistance to it were extraordinary. At the District Court at Rokycany a local potentate and bearer of the high decoration *Řád práce* ("The Banner of Labor") was a defendant in a paternity suit. Against the wishes of the District Secretariat, the court handed down an affirmative ruling that was upheld by the Court of Appeals. The decision went into force. Meanwhile, the political interests from Rokycany had solicited the support of the Supreme Court in Prague. The sympathetic Supreme Court annulled the verdict of the appellate bench and ordered a retrial by the Rokycany court. The judge there complied with the order to re-try but not with the "guidance" to acquit the defendants. The Bolshevik procreator lost once again, and the Court of Appeals, despite mounting Party pressure, upheld again, the verdict. At this point, Václav Škoda, the Minister of Justice —and a former resident of Rokycany—entered into the picture. As I was told by an eyewitness, Škoda personally delivered the file to his old friend Josef Urválek, the Chairman of the Supreme Court, with these words: "Josef, you must find some louse in the stuff and annul it." Accordingly, the Supreme Court, with its invaluable gift for legal legerdemain, interpreted the imaginary cause of "the violation of the spirit of socialist justice" for a second time and ordered a re-retrial.

New trials, new pressures, but still the stubborn judges remained refractory, with the same result both at the district and the appeal level. The Party gave up, and the eighth verdict remained truly final.

Though a woman, married or single, could successfully petition for the interruption of her pregnancy on health, economic and even social grounds, legalized abortion did not significantly reduce the rate of children born out of wedlock.[3.] Correspondingly, paternity suits, which had been expected to vanish from the court calendar, remained. Indeed, in view of the increased tourist traffic and the influx of foreign students to Czechoslovakia, I would not be surprised to learn that instances of cross-national paternity suits were on the rise. In cases of defendants residing abroad, the jurisdiction would naturally not lie with the Czechoslovak court.

1. No lesser authority than Ann Landers enriched my knowledge on this point. In her column (*Sun-Bulletin,* Binghamton, N. Y., April 12, 1965) she referred to Dr. Lugi Gedda, *Twins in Science and History* (1961) reporting the birth of bi-racial twins in 1809 (other case in 1947) who could not possibly been fathered by the same male.

2. Most probably what had happened was a mix up of babies in the maternity ward. The judge who presided over the case found a rather irregular — though under given conditions most humane — solution. Having given him my word to remain silent, I shall not break my pledge.

3. The statistical manual *Statistická ročenka ČSSR* 1966 (Prague: SNTL-SVTL), on pages 82 and 95 reveals the following figures:

	all babies born	out of wedlock
1957 (last year without legalized abortion)	255,711	13,899
1959 (last year of my judgeship)	219,324	10,811
1964 (last year indicated)	243,386	11,944

Other information: in 1965 out of 87,302 applications for the termination of pregnancy, 79,368 (i.e., 90.9%) were granted. The rate of abortions per 100 children born was 45.2.

23 PROPERTY, CONTRACTS, AND TORTS

Except for some marginal references, and for matters relating to agriculture, we have not yet dealt with the "classic" civil law, suits in which the plaintiff seeks a judgment based on a proprietary or contractual right, or on an injurious action caused by a third party. Such legal relations—that of a citizen v. a citizen; a citizen v. the state; and, finally, the state suing itself—are the subject of this chapter.

Outstanding among the axioms of Marxist jurisprudence is the belief that the number of any category of litigations is in inverse proportion to the socio-political health of the society. Thus as the distance between the builders of socialism and their goal diminishes, the cause and occurrence of conflicts requiring settlement in the courts decreases accordingly. But as we have seen in the part of this book dealing with criminal law, this did not seem to be the case.

Compared with the output of prewar Czechoslovak courts, some categories of civil law suits did indeed decline, while some others had vanished altogether. The man in the street had less call to sue his neighbor for a horse if neither of them any longer had one. Capitalists sued each other, and prewar courts rendered thousands of verdicts. Socialist courts do not, because private entrepreneurs, having been expropriated, do not sue.

Furthermore, the volume of litigations had to decline—irrespective of the argumentative mood of the public or of expropriation of private property—because of the restrictions of the courts' jurisdictional powers. If in capitalist Czechoslovakia the courts decided a certain number of libel suits, while the people's democratic judges decided none, this change in itself proves nothing, in view of the fact that this agenda was transferred from the courts to the District People's Committees. Similarly, the state industrial and business enterprises, with few exceptions, do not argue their cases before the court not because of harmonious relations among "the socialist legal persons," but because jurisdiction over such matters is vested with the *Arbitráž*—the panel of arbiters—patterned on the Soviet model.

The new Civil Code of 1950 was a compromise that may be characterized as "semi-capitalist in form, socialist in content." Thus, on the one hand, inalienable property rights and contractual situations, practicable only under a system of a free enterprise, were enumerated, while on the other hand a host of conditioning clauses and exceptions to the rule were introduced, significantly diluting the provisions. The guarantee that "Civil Rights shall be protected by the law," (Section 2 of the Civil Code) was accompanied by the warning that "No one shall be permitted to misuse civil rights to the detriment of the society" (Section 3). A citizen was totally free to acquire property or to conclude a contract *provided* his action did not run afoul of any of the clauses of the Code such as: "the rules of socialist community life;" "fulfillment of the Uniform Economic Plan;" "law;" "common interest;" "important common interest." Nowhere were these instruments of emasculation defined. They could mean anything and could be applied at any time, for whatever good or bad political reason.

One may then paraphrase the law in the following way: "The citizen has the guaranteed right to jump a hundred feet high. This right can only be restricted by the law of gravity." Person A. was free to sell his car to person B., but the state could invalidate the contract and, eventually, incarcerate A. as a speculator. The law allowed for the private ownership of a house. Yet the landlord was not even entitled to sublet his own apartment without the consent of the local administration. Clauses such as "common interest," "rules of socialist community life," etc., hampered legal clarity, encouraged the interference of political interests in judicial process, and were broad enough to accommodate any outside pressures.

Many provisions and legal constructs memorized at law school had to be forgotten on graduation. For example, twenty-three of the Civil Code's thirty-seven chapters were devoted to contracts, among which only a handful of provisions were of practical use. The citizen might request the court to remedy such conflicts as the recovery of a personal loan or, prior to the virtual extinction of independent artisans in the late fifties, restitution or financial compensation for contracted work badly executed or not performed at all. Frequent targets among the ranks of surviving entrepreneurs were tailors, whom irate customers charged with breach of contract, delay in work, or ruining a precious fabric supplied by the plaintiff. The burden of proof rested with the plaintiff, and as long as he was in possession of some relevant evidence, the proceedings were simple, short and no impediment to the judicial production plan.

Experience taught us to beware of actions for division of property between divorced, separated or, simply alienated spouses. Their haggling over trivia, with no supporting evidence for their conflicting claims, threatened us with the specter of a lengthy and complex trial which was likely to outlast a dozen ordinary suits. Accordingly, we spared no effort in counselling such parties to reach *any* settlement except that of a full-blown contested trial.

A major headache of this sort was inflicted upon me by a childless young couple of Czech-Russian origin residing at Kladruby. The litigants were distant cousins married through an arrangement between their families. Neither divorced, nor—when the trial opened—even separated, the husband and the wife, as they freely admitted in court, had decided for no substantive reason to torment each other the judicial way. With harassment rather than victory in mind, each hired a counsellor. Aware that their expenses would exceed the amount of their respective claims, still they plunged into the contest with self-destructive bravado.

According to law, all the property of the spouses was held in common except for valuables brought into or acquired during the marriage that were obtained as a gift or through an inheritance by solely one spouse; or items specifically intended for separate rather than mutual use (e.g., brassieres). The litigants from Kladruby contested everything—effects possessed before the marriage, acquired or consumed later, bought and sold, used individually or in common. Their claims were diligently specified, and included such items as toothbrushes, canned food, rabbits, coal stocks, and—unless I am badly mistaken—even a chamber pot.

Both parties offered innumerable witnesses to testify on their behalf. Although all were relatives by marriage in some way, during the trial every member of the clan took sides in the dispute, as if fighting the battle of their lives, and the sky was the limit so far as perjury was concerned. No matter how often the court might meet, there was never any evidence worthy of the name. How for example, was I supposed to unlock the mystery of the ownership of the rabbits? The rabbits had been a part of the plaintiff's dowry. They had multiplied considerably, some had been consumed by the litigants, some sold, some had been stolen, some had perished, some were simply missing, whereabouts unknown. The animals were fed from supplies furnished in part by the parents of the plaintiff and in part by the parents of the defendant. Question: who gets what, and how much?

The trial consisted of answering over twenty such questions. After several meetings, I became increasingly convinced that the trial was heading towards an impasse. Listening to any further prevaricating witnesses appeared futile, and thus I decided to end the case. Never at ease with accounting, I spent about a week buried in imaginary figures trying to draft what might pass for a just decision. Happily, the Civil Code of Procedure allowed one to substitute intuition for certainty. Section 94 read: "In the case of a claim the basis for which has been established but its exact assessment is either impossible or unduly difficult to reach, the court is empowered to rule according to its own judgment."

Neither party was satisfied with my verdict; they appealed to the higher court, which, in turn, threw out the decision for its failure to be both thorough and convincing and ordered a retrial.[1] In short, even an expropriated, non-affluent citizen could manage to generate property litigations too complex and onerous for the bench.

On occasions, interfamily suits reached heights of bitterness unlikely to rise between strangers, and certainly not commensurate with the value of the contested claims. A quarrel about almost nothing was capable of turning brothers and sisters, children and parents, into savage enemies. Equally, the less illustrious part of human nature was revealed in cases where poverty forced senior citizens to sue their adult, often prosperous, children for support.

As the saying goes, one parent can raise ten children, but ten children cannot take care of one parent.

Everything a citizen of Czechoslovakia might own (laces, shoes, a car and—unlike the case in the Soviet Union—even land) fell under the category of either "personal" (*osobní*) or "private" (*soukromé*) property. The difference in the political appraisal of the two could not have been more momentous. "Personal" ownership was supposed to derive from socialist ownership, was inseparably bound with it, originated from the honest work of the owner, and was designed for socialist enjoyment. The law even attached to this property the adjective "inviolable."

In contrast, "private" property was protected by no one. What was understood as private? Anything could qualify: land, a car, shoes or laces, provided the owner or the object owned could be shown to be tainted by either a capitalist past or of sinister intentions, present or future. As a case in point, a needle could be considered the personal property of a wife patching the trousers of her proletarian husband. The same needle would be the private property of an expropriated tailor who, in his spare time, illicitly fixed a suit for a customer. Or, a purchase of a hundred needles by a worker would be considered personal, while the same purchase made by a former enterpreneur—a person presumably tempted by the evil of speculation—was likely to be labelled private. Red scholasticism allows for a plenitude of elusive angels to dance on the point of a pin. If a house were confiscated, the compensation paid by the state, according to the Ordinance of the Ministry of Finance of April 1, 1964 (No. 73 of 1964 Collection of Laws) would be as follows:

personal property—840 Kčs to 1,930 Kčs per cubic meter;
private property—0.20 Kčs to 0.30 Kčs per cubic meter.

Because of this distinction, promulgated on April Fool's Day, a citizen would receive from four thousand to six thousand times less for his property.

Vagueness in the law is the twin of arbitrariness, and here the lawmaker deliberately failed to deliver any clear-cut criteria of what constituted good or bad property. The concept of the ownership of a house may help to illustrate the point. The reader may remember my lament in the chapter on divorces about the shortage of dwelling space in Czechoslovakia.

Unlike those of the Soviet Union, Czech landlords were not expropriated. They were only made to feel miserable. The owner

of a house that once had earned him an income was no longer entitled to collect rents but remained liable for the costs of the repairs to the property.[2] The landlord, in addition, had no right to
live in his house unless he could prove that the building qualified
as personal (good) property, called a "family house" (*rodinný
domek*), defined as a structure of no more than five rooms or no
more than 120 square meters of living space.

Such a property, typically, consisted of two apartments. The
owner lived with his family in one, the other was occupied by the
tenant. Many such landlords had children who grew up, got married, applied for an apartment, and, getting none, were forced to
live with the parents, to the considerable inconvenience of all concerned. Inevitably, the owner wanted to evict the tenant so that
the young couple might take his place. The tenant, even if willing
to comply, could not move because he would not have anywhere to
go. The landlord turned to the court.

The law empowered him to obtain an eviction decree against
the tenant in favor of occupancy by the owner or his married child.
The proceedings were simple, brief, and largely useless. First, the
court established the fact that the property qualified as a family
house. If it did not, the case was promptly dismissed. Second, the
plaintiff stated his need, or at least his wish, to have the married
child move into the house. The tenant and defendant in the suit
joined or contested the claim—it made no difference which. Then
the court adjourned to ask the People's Committee about the availability of a substitute apartment for the defendant. The local
Soviet sent back the mimeographed message: "As of now, we have
apartments available for no one." Finally, the court, unperturbed,
summoned the litigants and handed down an affirmative ruling that
included a following clause: "According to Section 556 of the Code
of Civil Procedure, the court shall evict the defendant from the
premises only after the plaintiff has forwarded to the court a
declaration issued by the Local People's Committee stating that
supplementary living space has been secured for the defendant."
And so, the landlord had the title, but his children no apartment,
because the People's Committee had no home for the legally evicted
tenant.

These cases proceeded under a canopy of suspended reality.
Reminiscent of senile admirals who conduct naval engagements
with toy ships in a bathtub, we were deciding issues that were
clearly *ultra vires* of the judiciary. Yet the trials had to be held

before the bench of three judges, and when I arranged for a conciliatory settlement between the litigants in the privacy of my office, I was criticized for a highly irregular act.

With a few exceptions, the People's Committees were either incapable of securing new homes for the defendants or unwilling to do so, and by the end of the fifties, there was a backlog of about ten thousand unenforceable vedicts. Again, dialectically speaking, this accumulation of quantity became a new quality. It was the Supreme Court that inaugurated a new line. Prague declared that the situation had gotten out of hand and that the dead verdicts had jeopardized the reverence of the toiling masses for the judiciary. To remedy the situation we were ordered to deny an affirmative judgment to anyone who, at the time of filing the petition, did not produce an affidavit from the People's Committee certifying that a substitute apartment for the tenant had been secured. Such a stipulation wiped out this category of litigation *en bloc*. No landlord could possibly obtain the statements, and had he done so, and had the tenant been willing to move, a court action would have been superfluous. With its characteristically cavalier attitude towards reality, the Communist Party ended up blaming the judges' poor cooperation with the People's Committees for the backlog, not the System's deficiency in housing construction.

A contested inheritance was another type of action between two private parties. The Czechs, however, were more likely to be dissatisfied dwellers than dissatisfied heirs, and a fight over the property of the dear departed rarely ended up in court. Several reasons explain this harmony. For one, Communist expropriation policies did not leave much to be inherited. Also, that part of the Civil Code dealing with inheritances was well drafted and reasonably unambiguous. Had it not been for the clause barring clergymen and monks from acting as witnesses to a testament, the imprint of socialist justice on these provisions would have been hard to detect. Finally, the law did not recognize anything comparable to a Probate Court. It was the State Notary—a legally trained official, not a neighborhood candy store operator—who was in charge of the probate. He drafted the will, summoned the beneficiaries, and presided over the distribution of the estate. The State Notary also determined the degree of inheritance tax. This, however, was rather moderate, especially if the estate qualified as being "good" personal property. An heir, dissatisfied or omitted, could challenge the decision in court. This, happily for the bench, seldom happened. When it did, it was likely to become a costly, complex trial, similar to the case of the spouses quarrelling over their rabbits.

However, the law demanded judicial approval of any probate decision involving heirs who were minors. The role of the court was not to assess and solve conflicting claims, but only to certify that the interest of the child had been duly protected. For judges in urban areas, this was, and remains, a routine engagement, requiring neither time nor acumen. For us in the countryside, however, the matter amounted to a political booby trap likely either to mutilate the child's future or to destroy the career of a judge insufficiently responsive to Party pressure.

I have already touched on this topic in a previous chapter. The socialization of the countryside turned kolkhozy into the preserve of senior citizens. The Party, in its attempt to rejuvenate the farming population, resorted to a variety of devices, and the inheritance law was one of them. Unlike his Soviet counterpart, the Czech farmer owned the land, and by joining a kolkhoz he retained ownership to his property. His title was both purely nominal and onerous. To understand this burden, the old revolutionary slogan "The land belongs to those who till it" has to be rephrased to read "Those who till belong to the land." A farmer who had joined a kolkhoz was doomed to work in the fields, and death was usually his only release. Once this happened, the widow, in order not to jeopardize the future of her children, disclaimed in their name the inheritance—i.e., a lifelong ordeal in the kolkhoz. She had the right to do so, and the law was entirely on her side (Section 517 of the Civil Code). Her statement before the State Notary required the court's approval, but before this could be granted, the judge's arms were swollen from the Party twist. He was told not to approve the claim, but rather to chain the propertied minor heir to the collectivized land. A strange thing: the heir did not fight another heir, but the state. He was allowed to take, but not to leave. Thus we see that grave injustice did not occur only in decisions which sent the innocent to the gallows. A civil judge, too, had ample occasion for sleepless nights.

The Czech citizen could be hurt in a more ordinary way—as an employee, a pedestrian, a victim of an accident, an act of negligence, a felonious assault, etc. The part of the Civil Code on torts allowed the injured party to sue the wrongdoer, be he an individual or—with some qualifications—the State. The basic provision, Section 337, stated "Whoever intentionally or by negligence damages another person by violating an obligation or any other legal duty shall be liable to indemnify him." The obligation for indemnity also arose in cases of "an intentional act against principles of equity." The claimant was entitled to restitution or, if the nature of the damage ruled out such an award, to monetary compensation. In the case of a physical injury, the liability of the wrongdoer extended to include compensation for all medical expenses, (past and future) lost income, pain suffered, and for disfigurement sufficient to handicap the victim's career.

No ruling on punitive damages was possible under Czech law, and the indemnities awarded were anything but excessive. Two other provisions of the Civil Code contributed to the downward trend in the compensation policies: Section 348, concerning contributory negligence, commonplace in all legal systems, and Section 358, somewhat more unusual, especially in the light of its ulterior objective. This rule allowed for a reduction of the indemnity for "reasons worthy of special consideration" and was mainly designed to protect proletarian defendants against possible bourgeois accusers. This interpretation, emanating from Supreme Court, was, however, not too fervently followed by the lower benches. In fact, as we shall see later, it could be used as a device for protecting a working class individual against the State.

The tort adjudication in Czechoslovakia was to my mind preferable to that in the United States. Apparently, I have not been a Yankee long enough to be able to appreciate such practices as blackmailing the rich with charges of simulated injuries, collusion between lawyer and client to split the jackpot, or submitting outrageous claims that settle for a fraction of the amount. I have yet to meet an American lawyer who could convince me of the propriety of the claim of a client who suffered a minor injury, demands a million dollars, and settles for fifty thousand. How can there be any justification for demanding a million dollars on behalf of a person whose expected lifetime earnings are less than half that sum? And why is there such a discrepancy between the claim and the settlement? The two extremes represent an unscrupulous leech and an inept bungler, as I see it, from my Continental viewpoint.

In Czech courts an injured party may sue either an individual or the State or both, as in the following case of minor Bílý versus a truck driver, his employer (a national enterprise), and the state insurance company. The legal representative of the minor plaintiff charged the defendants with negligence resulting in serious injury. One afternoon, Bílý, a boy of six, was sitting on a fence of a bridge. A tractor with a trailer, coming around a sharp curve, entered the bridge so carelessly that it hit the child. Both Bílý's legs were smashed and had to be amputated. The defendants called for dismissal of the claim or, at least, for a ruling of contributory negligence. They argued that the child ought to have known better or ought to have been told by his parents not to sit on a bridge on a busy road and expose himself to danger. At this point, the District Prosecutor, who had entered the suit, threw his support behind the minor plaintiff, stating that the driver's job was to drive and not to mutilate, especially since Bílý had been well off the road. The insurance company rushed in with its conciliation, and a generous settlement was reached.

The interest of the individual over that of the State was probably best upheld in cases of injuries sustained at work. The injured party enjoyed the rare opportunity of support from the labor organization, which here acted in a way worthy of its name and true purpose, providing legal assistance free of charge. In my experience these labor lawyers were always ready to fight in earnest for their client's interests. Though the prosecutor usually took the side of the plaintiff, and the Party stayed neutral, we were rather unhappy with these litigations because of their complexity. In addition to the medical experts, specialists in a variety of fields of engineering, safety officials, and a host of other witnesses had to be heard. Plans of factories, equipment and procedures had to be studied, and at times the court was called upon to make an on-site inspection of the scene of the accident.

Presiding over these trials, I was amazed to learn of the antiquated working conditions in industrially advanced Czechoslovakia. For example, in the steel foundry at Červený Hrádek, the casting of iron from huge suspended boilers was coordinated by hand signals. In the steamy, noisy environment, with poor visibility, the workers communicated by holding out fingers to indicate the number of the boiler to be cast. On one occasion, a laborer confused the Roman V with the Arabic 2, with the result that he was buried in an avalanche of molten iron. Thanks to an impressive job by the physicians, the patient, after total skin transplants and prolonged hospitalization, survived and sued. Both the prosecutor and the court subjected the management to very unfriendly questioning.

We reasoned that once we had socialism—the pride and only hope of mankind—we should at least occasionally try to prove it. As a rule, a fatal accident or a near-fatality was needed to provoke some partial improvement in the safety standards.

The citizen felt fairly uninhibited in making the State the defendant in a civil suit, and the totalitarian State for its part did not seem to object to such a move, provided certain conditions were met. In the first place, the claim could not constitute a challenge to the ideology, supremacy or political practices of the Party. In short, the "System" itself could never seem to be on trial. Instead, claims had to center on the remedy of a situation, mainly on an economic nature, and had to be devoid of broader implications.

Let us assume that person A. sued national enterprise B. for damages caused by the management's negligence. The claim was confined to comrades C. and D., who noticed the construction defect in the factory building only after the roof had collapsed on the head of A. The latter, having suffered concussion, demanded some indemnity. A. did not suggest that there was a defect in the concept of nationalization of industry, nor did he criticize the Party for having appointed idiots to positions of responsibility. Because A. was a faithful proletarian, the Party did not interpret his claim as a challenge to the political sacrosanctum, but viewed it as a legitimate contribution to the perennial struggle against "shortcomings." The Party also did not suspect the plaintiff of attempting to pilfer socialist property in a sophisticated way. Both sides knew only too well that straightforward theft from the State's riches was faster, widely practiced, and not all that risky.

The socio-political evaluation of the plaintiff determined to a large extent whether the motive behind the claim was regarded as bona fide. Class enemies—and this was the second restrictive condition—were not granted the benefit of the doubt. A suit launched by former beneficiaries of a deposed unjust order—by the *býval*í *lidé* ("former people") as they were called at times[3]—would be seen as a daring, provocative gesture aimed against the very foundations of all the Party stood for. Accordingly, a bourgeois plaintiff was a rarity, and a bourgeois winner was a collector's item.

Finally, the Civil Code furnished the State with ultimate insurance against litigations that could hit below the belt. It stipulated that a special law was to regulate the conditions under which a person could sue the State for injuries sustained through "incorrect procedures in official business," leaving it up to the wrongdoer to interpret the meaning of the phrase. The Civil Code went into force in January, 1951. By June, 1959, when I left the country, no "special laws" had yet been enacted. In other words, the King could do no wrong, and the subject was given the right to redress—but no law through which this right might be expressed and secured.

The Party often lamented that too many people saw the State only as a *dojná kráva* ("a cow to be milked"). The complaint was well founded, for the majority of the populace asked what the country could do for them and not vice versa. The procedural rights of "the toiling masses," much as they contrasted with the lot of the disadvantaged bourgeois litigants, did not mean that the State would decline to put up a fight in court. Political loyalty was not enough to secure a plaintiff's victory. If his claim was doubtful he headed not towards a dismissal from job or the Party, but towards the dismissal of his case.

One such anemic claim was filed by a certain female physician against the KÚNZ (Regional Institute of National Health). She charged her employer with negligent maintenance of the footpaths within the hospital compound, which had resulted in her breaking her leg. The accident had occurred in winter, when she had slipped and fallen on the icy path. The defendant called for dismissal, contending that for one thing, the plaintiff had avoided the cleared pathway, using a short cut through the snow at her own risk. Secondly, she could have had no official business in that direction. The litigants requested that the court inspect the place of the accident, and the motion was granted. The judges, having reached the spot in late spring, found, of course, no slippery road, though they found enough to exculpate the defendant and dismiss the claim.

The second case was of more interest from a legal point of view, as it attempted to translate the repeated violation of a rule into a legitimate usage that in turn would obligate a third party to respect that usage, and, in the event of non-compliance, would render him liable for any resultant injury.

A young, pretty girl, an aspiring ski champion, used to commute by train from the Plzeň suburb of Chrást to the city. She, in common with many others, did not board the train at the rather distant station, but at a curve around which the train moved at a reduced speed. One day, attempting a jump she had been making for years, she slipped and fell under the wheels. Despite losing both legs, the victim survived the accident, combating the handicap with admirable persistence—I could not believe my eyes when I saw her with artificial limbs riding a bicycle—and married. Her father-in-law, a respected judge at the Court of Appeals, drafted a claim against the ČSD (State Railways System). The elaborate though not too persuasive reasoning centered on the argument that the well-established and widely-practiced boarding of the train while it was in motion obligated the train operator to exercise extreme caution at this critical place. It was charged that his failure to do so rendered him and his employer liable for the damage. The counsel for the defense expressed sympathy for the suffering of the victim but demanded the claim be dismissed. Multiple violations of a rule did not invalidate the rule. The plaintiff in time withdrew the claim.

To repeat, neither the doctor with the broken leg nor the girl with no legs was accused or suspected of plotting to seek illegitimate profit at the expense of the State.

As I pointed out earlier, the law entitled the prosecutor to enter into *any* civil case. Once he decided to appear as "the third litigant" it was entirely up to him whether to take sides in the dispute, whether to offer evidence, to appeal the verdict, or remain inactive. The prosecutors were instructed when to intervene, but not how. Prague demanded action, but the responsibility for its implementation rested with the prosecutor in his role as "the guardian of socialist justice." These broad powers, if properly executed, ruled out indiscriminate support for the socialist litigant. The guardian's concern extended beyond the confines of the pending civil contest; he was supposed to detect in its background possible violations of the criminal law or irregularities indicating a more fundamental social malady. Many judges viewed the prosecutor's rôle as that of a watchdog over the bench. While this suspicion was not without basis in the case of the prewar-trained judicial personnel, colleagues of my generation did not quite share the fear. In our experience, the intruders rushed neither the private litigant nor the bench in the direction of a victory for the State. To the contrary, they often spoke up for the citizen; the weight of their office softened the rigid state corporation into a more compromising mood.

The procedural practices of socialist litigants varied widely. Some fought hard, while others could not care less. Some would appeal any verdict short of total victory, while others would indicate to the court that any decision would do. "Comrade judge," they often pleaded in my chambers, "all we need is a verdict. If we lose the better for us. Then at least we can write off the claim and won't have to bother about collecting the award." While some enterprises were represented by competent, knowledgeable and alert counsellors, others were handled by employees with negligible legal training—or none.

With the exception of ministerial and similar offices, the socialist legal persons employed lawyers noted for professional mediocrity and/or an objectionable political past. The career of a "corporate lawyer" held little attraction, since both the material and non-material rewards were slim. True, the judiciary was not overpaid, but at least our office carried some prestige and allowed for engagement in interesting matters. No lawyer would hurry to seek employment with a national enterprise, in which he would be subjected to the whims of semi-literate executives and be given boring, routine work. Accountants rather than jurists, bureaucrats rather than professionals, without the right of independent thinking, they often complained to us about their lot.

If dumb lawyers were a nuisance, smart ones, too, proved to be a mixed blessing. Some behaved in the courtroom like misplaced lions. In search of an outlet for their numerous frustrations, they tended to resort to a tornado of eloquent arguments, and where we expected a sober pragmatic approach toward a reasonable settlement, we witnessed a degree of passion which had been out of date for at least two decades. On occasions, my colleagues and I discussed this strange phenomenon, reaching agreement on at least one point: the *ex-advokáti*, by employing political rhetoric, intended to beat the System they detested at its own game, with every litigation won a means of harvesting eventual bonuses from the employer and, above all, improving their tarnished political images. This effort deserved sympathy as long as one did not have to preside over such a spectacle. Take, for example, Mr. Křepinský, the last anti-Communist Mayor of Plzeň, who, during the Communist coup in February, 1948, had jumped on the bandwagon of the new masters. There was nothing he would not do for the Party. Křepinský served ardently and well, but in time the Party expelled him from its ranks, regardless of his efforts. He ended up as an attorney with the State Construction Material Supply Administration, and in this capacity he represented the firm in a number of suits. Most of the claims were addressed against kolkhozy which had ordered, received, but not paid for materials. It was as simple as that; the kolkhozy had no money, and one would have expected that a reasonable settlement could be worked out. Not with Křepinský, who would overpower the court with his insincere Bolshevik bombast, quotations from Marx, and irrelevant battle cries invoking world revolution. When Křepinský was subsequently arrested and sentenced for an alleged political crime, I sighed with relief.

From the point of view of the bench, the highest marks for professional competence and willingness to reach conciliatory settlements went to the attorneys for the Ministry of Defense. Litigations involving the military, though limited in scope, were not infrequent. The Ministry sued discharged veterans for damages resulting from traffic accidents. Military personnel, unlike civilians, were not covered by insurance, and this could lead to great hardship. If, for example, a driver obeyed a superior officer's order—and he had to obey—to exceed the safe speed limit, and the car went out of control, only the driver was held liable for the damage. The military postponed action until the discharge of the driver, who was then sued for a sum well beyond his means. The spokesmen for the Ministry shared the distaste of the bench for any harsh measures and they were very willing to entertain our suggestions on means of alleviating the defendant's burden. Rulings of contributory negligence, with extraordinary reductions in the award, and payment in modest installments, were commonplace.

The most significant category of civil actions between a citizen and the State were the contests relating to socialist property, with the State cast in the role of accuser. Earlier I stated that the most popular felonious behavior in Czechoslovakia was that of pilfering public riches. This trend was also reflected in civil adjudication, concerning mainly managers of state retail stores and services. As a rule, if the criminal court found the defendant guilty of having stolen a ton of nails valued at 500 Kčs, the verdict included a clause stating that the culprit had to repay the injured party in full. In cases of managers accused of having caused damage through intent or negligence, the complexity of the claim dissuaded the court from ruling upon the award. Instead, the enterprise was advised to seek the remedy in a civil suit.

These litigations were called *manko* ("deficit") cases, and since this term is short and easy to pronounce I will continue to use it. Managers charged with *manko* could be those found guilty of pilferage by the criminal court, or those acquitted at such a trial, or those

not indicted at all. Even in the absence of a verdict by a criminal
court, the procedural position of the defendant was a rather difficult
one because of his liability for the entrusted goods. According to
this concept, the manager, by signing "the statement of material
liability" became responsible for *manko* — all losses, deficits and
damages — unless he could prove that he was free of any blame for
the injurious result. As in paternity suits, the burden of proof lay
with the defendant, and the victim of a *manko* charge had to do
battle against enormous odds.

All the enterprise had to do in order to win a *manko* case was
to produce threefold evidence: the statement of liability signed by
the defendant; an inventory of all the items entrusted to the manager; and the inventory of goods remaining at the time the manager
was relieved from his duties. These documents had to be signed by
both parties. The difference in financial evaluation between the
first inventory and the last constituted the *manko*.

It hardly does credit to the socialist economy to reveal that
about fifty per cent of all claims were dismissed by the courts, while
the awards made in the rest of the cases were rather meager. A
complete victory for the plaintiff was an event worth talking about.
With so little expected from the plaintiff, he could not manage even
this, as we shall see in a typical example of the state-owned Hotel
E. v. former manager K. Demanding an impressive indemnity, the
counsel for the enterprise produced a statement of liability signed
by the defendant, and the required inventories. The defendant
called for the dismissal of the case, pleading innocence. With the
appointment of an expert in accounting to evaluate the evidence,
the proceedings were adjourned.

The expert then testified that on the basis of the available
evidence the amount of *manko*, if any, could not be ascertained.
Nothing could be figured out. When K. had taken over the hotel,
the inventory had not been signed, and it could not be held as an
indication of anything. For example, the itemized column of stored
goods did not specify whether the figures referred to bottles, kilos,
boxes, bundles, etc. The case was dismissed under heavy protests
by the plaintiff, complaining about the court's carefree unconcern
with the preservation of our socialist fortunes.

The losers were knocking on the wrong door, and both the
judge and the prosecutor were not slow in telling them so in court.
"You had so little to prove in order to win, yet even this was beyond

your capacity. Your incompetence and indolence is the best insurance for the dishonest."

The slap-dash housekeeping practices of the socialist enterprises neutralized their procedural advantages against a defendant who had little if any chance to produce evidence to support his innocence.

There was no doubt in our minds that several successful defendants were guilty of mismanagement and even of outright theft of state funds. The Party criticized us for this lenience. Our response was that acquitting the guilty was a lesser evil than sentencing the innocent. Since this argument sounded too liberal to the apparatchiki's ears, we added that defeat for the plaintiff was a healthy lesson and an inducement toward the improvement of its economic practices. Once we hitched our wagon to the star of "combatting shortcomings," the Party ceased mumbling.

The shortest route to defeat in a *manko* case was reserved for enterprises that employed minors (i.e., persons of less than eighteen years of age) as managers, provided the signed statement of liability for any losses did not carry the parents' written consent. Such claims, irrespective of their merits, were summarily dismissed.

Unless the court found the inventory deficient, or unless the manager was a minor who held the job without paternal approval, all defendants — whether honest, incompetent or crooked — fought an uphill battle in attempting to exculpate themselves. We on the bench could not help but feel sorry for many of them, aware that pity was a poor substitute for the justice we could not deliver.

Let us assume that you are a manager in a state grocery store that employs three salesgirls. You did not select them, and you do not trust them. Everything points to the conclusion that they are stealing — both cash and goods. Yet, unless you catch the unauthorized hand in the cash register or detect a marinated herring in the pilferer's purse, suspicion remains your sole company on the road to grave trouble. All you can do is to call up the personnel office and demand the dismissal of your employees. The enterprise will not comply. For one thing, you will be told, no replacement is available, and, second, you are chasing phantom evils. The girls are honest, since they come from proletarian families and always pay their dues to the Czech Komsomol on time. A year later, an inventory reveals a huge deficit and you, as the only liable person, are tried in the court. With nothing to prove your innocence, you are the loser.

The manager had to foot the bill not only for goods stolen by employees but also for those pilfered by customers and filched by delivery men. Take the following case: A truck arrived, unloaded supplies, and the impatient driver, complaining about his difficulty in meeting his "production plan," maneuvered the manager into signing the receipt before he had a chance to check the delivery. With the truck gone, the manager belatedly discovered that instead of 100 kilos of salt he had received only 80 kilos, and that what he signed for as sugar was in fact flour. He had ordered 100 kilos of carrots and had received instead cauliflower, which neither he nor his customers wanted. He hurried to call up the central office. Nobody listened. "Comrade, never sign a receipt unless you check all the items carefully," he was told. The comrade knew better. He was at the mercy of the trucker; to antagonize him might lead to even more costly problems. Here were the cauliflowers. The manager demanded their transfer to another store where selling the vegetables would be an easier proposition. The driver (hostile or not) did not turn up for a week. The supply meanwhile had gone rotten and could not be written off. The manager was liable for the loss.

Most of the defendants in *manko* cases before my court were housewives who had signed a contract of liability with the cooperative *Jednota* ("Unity"), a chain of grocery and hardware stores in West Bohemia's countryside. It seldom happened that the woman was made aware of the scope of the responsibility she had taken on. The employer promised anything: training courses, assistance from the cooperative's accountants, reconstruction of the premises and the like. Not a word was kept. The semi-literate housewife-manager became an easy prey for unscrupulous truckers and a nuisance to the enterprise whenever she complained and demanded remedial action. In one case, for example, *Jednota* was told about rats which were devouring the supplies in a village store. When the manager had signed the contract, *Jednota* had promised to send an exterminator, masons, and even an architect. Nothing had been done. The case came to trial — a *manko* case, to be sure — and the plaintiff, without blushing, demanded that the defendant also foot the bill for the rats' feast.

Happily for the defendants and our consciences, two provisions of the Civil Code — Section 348 on contributory negligence and Section 358 on further reduction of the award for reasons worthy of special considerations — were found applicable to the *manko* rulings. Whenever some fault with the plaintiff could be ascertained — and this was almost always — the award was slashed to reasonable proportions or even dissolved.

The greater the number of items on the shelves, the more tortuous was the path towards the truth. The biggest grocery stores — resembling a sort of an antediluvian supermarket — and restaurants were the least negotiable commercial labyrinths. Simplicity, however, was no insurance that a litigation against a mischievous hot dog vendor would not turn into a date with the supernatural. In one of the first *manko* cases I presided over, the national enterprise *Kniha* ("Book") was suing an elderly couple in charge of a shop specializing in political literature. Because of their merchandise, the employees had led a quiet, undisturbed life, until the day arrived when the controlling organs discovered that hundreds of copies of writings by Marx, Engels, Lenin — Stalin was already out — and some minor prophets were missing. The attorney for *Kniha* filed a suit for an enormous amount of money. I summoned the litigants for the first hearing and this is what the defendants told me:

"Comrade judge, your honor, we are no thieves. Even if we were thieves, we are no idiots. What possible good would it do to us to steal books written by the Classics? Do you know of anyone who would steal this merchandise and be intelligent and imaginative enough to make any profit out of it? We don't."

Neither did I. I aired the issue, asking both the representative for the plaintiff and the prosecutor, who happened to be present, whether they could think of an eventuality whereby the Classics could be a source of material enrichment. They could not.

The proceedings were adjourned, and I did not know what to do next. Inactivity appeared to be the best solution, so I shelved the case for further mellowing. Had I proceeded in the matter, I might well have arrived at the absurd conclusion that the defendants were guilty. The delay paid off. After a few weeks, the plaintiff informed me that the claim was based on an accounting error and was being withdrawn, with apologies to both the court and the defendants.

In *manko* cases we had a fair chance of adequately serving the cause of justice, provided that the roots of the claim could be identified and the claim itself reduced to manageable proportions. Let me illustrate this point with an example which, though more reminiscent of Rabelais than of Bolshevism, threatened the person concerned with prolonged incarceration in a state penitentiary. The cause of it all was beer. The Czechs are beer-drinking people, and my hometown, Plzeň (Pilsen), produces the one and only Pilsener, unsurpassed by any of its imitators. The imitators might be pleased to learn of the following mishap.

One summer, during the peak harvest season, the imbibers in one village developed an inconvenient handicap — a galloping diarrhea so disastrous that the suffering kolkhozniki had to stay home from the fields, endangering the fulfillment of the production plan. The secret police smelled foul play and traced it to the manager of a state-owned inn in the village. The alleged mastermind behind this devious act of sabotage was a frightened, aging housewife, capable of nothing, certainly not of paralyzing socialist agriculture. The criminal court acquitted her. Though saved from jail, she was not safe from financial liability. Her employer filed a suit for damages, as a number of unconsumed barrels containing the debilitating liquid remained in her cellar. The defendant did not deny the undeniable — that her beer acted as a laxative — but argued that she by no means had caused the regrettable malady of her fellow citizens and the further losses in unsold merchandise. She had been selling and storing beer with equal care for many years, and nothing had ever gone wrong before. The argument in the court was reduced to the issue of her care and storage of the beer.

I appointed a renowned expert in brewing techniques to prepare an expert opinion. The elaborate treatise he submitted contained information about the durability and perishability of the product, a detailed picture of the equipment in the defendant's cellar, its temperature, humidity, etc. His conclusion was that nothing indicated the defendant's malice or negligence. The court was happy to believe the expert. Though the statement of liability did not seem to exculpate the defendant, I decided to interpret her "material responsibility" very restrictively and dismissed the case. The verdict was not challenged in the higher court.

Manko disputes are likely to remain the most significant category of civil actions that involve both the accusing State and the accused citizen. The State cannot help entrusting considerable wealth to the care of private persons, with the risk that they may turn out to be wicked, negligent, or simply luckless custodians.

So far we have dealt with cases between private parties, and between the State and the individual. Conflicts between socialist legal persons is the remaining—and in a sense the least important—topic left in this chapter. Save for some exceptions, the legal disputes between the components of the national economy, originating from or relating to the fulfillment of the production plan were not in our jurisdiction. If, for example, a steel mill sold a defective product to a tractor manufacturer, and the tractors fell apart upon delivery, the latter socialist legal person would turn to an *Arbitráž* seeking an indemnity. Proceedings before the arbiters were informal, almost casual. To the clink of coffee cups and under a cloud of cigarette smoke, a national enterprise could win or lose a million in a matter of minutes.

The first reaction of a civil judge to a suit filed by a socialist legal person against a fellow national enterprise was to search for a cause—or a pretext—to declare the absence of the court's jurisdiction and to forward the case to the *Arbitráž*. If the claim could be tied to the state economic plan, we were off the hook.

The jurisdiction of the court was always necessary if at least one of the litigants was a "Uniform Agricultural Cooperative"—in short, a kolkhoz. The Party rightly assumed that a kolkhoz was a frail, emerging entity, administered by individuals of low sophistication who needed more protection than they could find at the assembly line of the arbiters' speedy decision-making. I presided over dozens of such cases and, to my dismay, no apparatchik ever dropped by to discover for himself that the harmonious relations between the urban and rural toiling masses existed mainly in books. If the industrial producer supplied merchandise as ordered by the kolkhoz and the latter did not pay, the plaintiff could not care less about the customer's insolvency. When the kolkhoz—in a way spoiled by the state subsidies and generous writing off of debts in the early fifties—asked that a debt be forgotten, the plaintiff would only laugh. After all, collection of the payment determined the financial standing of the enterprise, and the bonuses for the management.

Had the apparatchiki been present during the litigation between the plaintiff ČSAO ("Cars Repairs Enterprise") and the defending kolkhoz at Otročín, they might have shed tears—or had someone arrested. The parties were no strangers to each other. On the contrary, the ČSAO enterprise had performed the role of a "patron" (sponsor; big brother) to the villagers, supplying—free of charge—manpower in the fields whenever needed. The system of "patronage" over the kolkhozy was a practice common throughout the country, designed to assist the ailing agriculture. At Otročín, however, the relations between the helpers and the helped, for undisclosed reasons, had turned sour, and ended in court. The plaintiff demanded compensation for gasoline spent in transporting employees from Plzeň to Otročín—a payment which the kolkhoz flatly refused. According to the defendants' version, the patrons came to the village not to work but to earn political merits, to devour good country food, and to fornicate in the adjacent woods. The plaintiff explained that, though the patrons' morale at work was not exemplary, they still deserved praise in view of the fact that the food offered was not edible and the shelter reserved for the ČSAO personnel was suitable for pigs, or perhaps for the kolkhozniki, but certainly not for the city comrades. The litigants continued this exchange of uncomplimentary remarks. Expecting that fists would soon supplement the invective, I hurriedly called for a recess, awarded the plaintiff one half of the claim, and was quite relieved when the practitioners of patronage were out of sight.

Next day I happened to run into Vojtěch Horák, the First District Secretary of the Party. To ward off questions about my work, I brought up the case from Otročín and asked him for a "Marxist analysis" of my disconcerting experience. The apparatchik relapsed into meditation from which he emerged with the following oracular evaluation: "It's a simple matter, comrade. Difficulties of growth." Thus enlightened, I departed with thanks.

The courts also retained jurisdiction provided the dispute related to transportation and international commerce. The occurrence of such claims was rather sporadic. In one rather interesting case over which I presided, the plaintiff was Import Enterprise; the Railways and the Insurance Company were co-defendants, and the issue was a damage claim wreathed in mystery. The plaintiff had purchased in Hungary a cargo of excellent and rather expensive salami. The shipment was transported by train and duly insured. The freight car was sealed, the seals checked and re-checked at both the Hungarian and Czechoslovak border. When the cargo reached its ultimate destination at Plzeň, the seals unbroken, yet the freight car was empty. There was no indication of violent entry —but also no salami. The importer demanded compensation for his loss, only to run into opposition from both the railways and the insurance officials. Their argument was based on the legal presumption that undamaged seals constituted a sufficient evidence of the proper care on their part, thus absolving them from all liability for the loss. The importer remained dissatisfied, and the dispute landed in court.

First, I tried to determine what might have happened to the cargo. Second, I tried—again, without success—to reconcile the parties. Then, I had to adjudicate. The conflict was a fundamental one—between the legalistic approach and the search for material truth. I chose horse sense over formalistic niceties, and decided the case in favor of the plaintiff, employing approximately this reasoning: "The plaintiff entrusted the defendant with the shipment of the salami and insured the cargo—not for the sake of transporting untouched seals, but salami. He received no salami. He is interested in nothing else, and so is the court."

I am as hesitant to speculate about future trends in civil litigations in Czechoslovakia as I am about the fate of the vanished salami. Implementation of the "New Economic Model," directed toward the resurrection of the profit motive, the gradual withering away of the fictitious distinction between the private (bad) and personal (good) property, the sincerity of the Party in coping with the housing problem, improvement in managerial know-how in retail businesses and services, these and many other factors are likely to play determining roles in what the Czech civil judge faces in days to come.

1. I was quite incensed with the appellate decision. Given the circumstances of the case, it was beyond my comprehension how I could have ruled better or more convincingly. I hurried to Plzeň to hear more from the higher bench. As expected, the colleagues' response was that of good humored conciliation, along the old lines "Don't be mad, you are young, try once again." Instead of the retrial, I used undoubtedly malicious tactics. First, I shelved the case (contrary to all that socialist competition stood for) for about two months and summoned the litigants, their lawyers, and a host of witnesses for the day following the scheduled return from my vacation spent in East Germany. The stay in East Germany was only a pretext for attempting to confuse the two German states and reach the West. Should the plan not work, I reasoned, I would be disappointed enough by my return so that my mood could hardly be further aggravated by the litigants in question. Should I, however, managed to get to West Berlin—which is what happened—my colleagues, in addition to being embarrassed by my defection, would have to send an emergency substitute to Stříbro from the higher court to wrestle with the retrial they themselves had asked for.

2. These reasons help to explain the state's reluctance to take over the title to such real estate. Several landlords approached me to draft a request begging the state to accept the building as a donation, free of charge. Sometimes we succeeded, sometimes we did not.

3. In the late fifties the term *bývalí lidé* was dropped. The Party explained that the label "former people" was not quite accurate and confused the less educated practitioners of class warfare who tended to interpret it in a starkly literal way.

24 JUDICIAL MINIATURES

A variety of what I have termed "judicial miniatures" were entered in the records under the heading of non-contested cases. Though numerous, this calendar attracted only our marginal attention; besides being uncontested, these cases counted little toward our fulfillment of the production plan. Any court lucky enough to have a competent senior clerk available relegated the bulk of this routine work to him.

The clerk was usually entrusted with claims calling for the payment of debts up to a certain (modest) amount. The court, instead of summoning the parties, forwarded a copy of the claim to the defendant, enclosing instructions on how he could challenge the charge and notifying him that should he fail to do so within two weeks, the claim took on the same force of law as any other verdict. If the defendant's protest reached the court in time, the case became a contested litigation of the type referred to in the preceding chapter. This method of recovering bad debts had considerable merit. It saved court time and costs and was usually effective in securing for the creditor a speedy settlement of his claim.

The calendar relating to land registry, however, deserves no such praise. The land-register was of respectable age—it had existed since the end of the thirteenth century. Its purpose, as in other countries, was to provide for legal certainty: to give evidence of title to real estate. When they took power, the Communists had to choose between following the Soviet example and abolishing the land-register altogether, or leaving operative this venerable testament. The Party decided to compromise: neither to abolish it nor to retain it intact—but to emasculate the register of its legally binding effects. An entry in the register after the promulgation of the 1950 Civil Code did not confer any material rights, but was solely of a declaratory nature. This meant that though a person might be the owner of immovable property, this right was not incorporated in the books, while on the other hand, the registered owner might not be the owner any longer.

Notwithstanding this, applications for extracts from the land-register did not stop arriving at court. This was particularly odd in the Sudetenland, where the books were in a state of chaos—or to use the Marxist parlance, "they did not adequately reflect the material reality." When, after 1945, the German farmer was expelled from the country, his property was taken over by one settler, then another, and so on, until it was transferred to the tutelage of a kolkhoz, which eventually fell apart. If the ex-kolkhoznik wanted to move into a city and managed to find (a very unlikely prospect, indeed) a successor to his property, the successor would come to court "to ascertain the legal reality" from the land-register, only to find that the last entry listed as owner one Wolfgang Amadeus Sauerbraten, a Teuton remembered by no one. At the request of the neophyte kolkhoznik, his fictitious property rights would be entered into the books, he would beam with satisfaction, and I would be left wondering why.

Less voluminous, though of more practical importance than the land-registry matters, were proceedings concerning the legal declaration of death. According to the Civil Code, a missing person could be declared legally dead if at least five years had passed since the end of the year in which his whereabouts had last been known. The time limit of five years was reduced to one year in the case of a person missing in connection with an especially dangerous event.

Departing from this life unobserved and unseconded by the State was an unlikely eventuality in a totalitarian system which meticulously recorded all the whereabouts of its citizenry. Moreover, Czechoslovakia is a landlocked country, free of hurricanes, earthquakes, avalanches or similar disasters. The Czech re-emigrants who left the U.S.S.R. after 1945 and settled in Sudeten-land were the only such petitioners at my court. Incredible as it may seem, these people arrived in Czechoslovakia with almost no documents: no birth certificates, no marriage certificates, no proof of death of their family members. They had nothing. The stauncher Communists within the judiciary rushed to exculpate the Soviet bureaucracy, and the state of Soviet civilization in general, blaming instead the ravages of the last war, though it is unlikely that the Germans had destroyed population records in areas they had never set foot in. Several times I approached the Soviet authorities—via the Ministry of Justice in Prague—requesting a transcript from their registries. Either I received no answer, or the Russians responded with the standardized sentence: "Owing to the damages caused by the Fascist invaders we are unable to com-ply with your request." With or without supporting documents, the family status of the re-emigrants was gradually settled.

Another type of marginal judicial engagement concerned mentally defective citizens. Ruling on detainment and insanity was a purely formal affair, the outcome of which depended on the recommendation of experts—two psychiatrists in each case. The mental institution had to report within forty-eight hours any case of a person confined against his will and had to obtain the court's approval of his further detainment. Judicial consent was valid for only one year, after which re-application had to be made.

Quite often I had to decide whether or not to take away the legal responsibility of some person who, though mentally defective, was harmless according to medical opinion, and thus free to go his own way. A declaration of legal insanity did not terminate the court's intervention into the life of the person concerned. Had he, for example, a savings account, the bank would not allow him to withdraw any funds without the specific consent of the court.

In this capacity I met some truly peculiar characters. Perhaps the most notorious in Plzeň was a senior citizen and a self-appointed nobleman who claimed his name was Count Schoenborn. His age was a mystery. According to sober calculations he must have been between a hundred and fifty and two hundred years old. My grandmother told me that when she was a little girl, at the turn of the century, she remembered the Count as reputedly the oldest man in town. Stalinism or no Stalinism, the Count adhered to the rococo style of dress, sporting a large artificial rose in his lapel and the only known male pigtail in Czechoslovakia, neatly tied with a ribbon. Totally deaf, he hated Social Democrats, seemingly unaware that a different political party ran the State. When Mr. Pacanda, the attendant in the Anatomy Institute of the Medical School and an avid amateur movie maker, contemplated the creation of an opus entitled "Mozart in Plzeň," the Count was the undisputed choice for the leading role.

The Count is irrelevant. The privilege of a mental case—or of an eccentric posing as a mental case—to wear a pigtail with impunity is relevant. Just as the survivors of a nuclear holocaust might well envy the dead, the sane subjects of totalitarianism often envied the insane. Who else but Madam Marie Klírová could afford to offend the Prosecutor General, Jan Bartuška, to his face? Mrs. Klírová was a certified lunatic living at Kladruby in the Stříbro district. She paid me a visit at least once a week. Each time I went into hiding. Whenever she managed to apprehend me, she treated me either as her main enemy or as her son. When I placed her minor daughter, a part-time prostitute, in an institution, the mother told me I was a neo-colonialist. At other times, she showed concern for my well-being, advising me, for example, that since I was a bachelor, I should dye my bed sheets pitch black as she had done, thus disposing of the need for laundry service.

Whatever Mrs. Klírová said or did to me, I excused, because of her encounter with the Prosecutor General. Jan Bartuška was accompanying a group of prominent jurists from fraternal countries on their way to Marienbad, and passing through Stříbro, he hit on the unfortunate idea of showing the visitors a "typical people's court." Through sheer coincidence, neither the prosecutor nor one of the two judges happened to be in the building at the time, and Dr. Kostial, the State Notary and the only jurist around, panicked and locked himself in his office.

When the dignitaries entered the premises, they encountered only a handful of clerical employees, stupified with horror, and one more person who did not seem to mind the commotion. This was Mrs. Klírová, on one of her periodical visits. Jan Bartuška, an enormously conceited, pompous ass, could not hide his embarrassment before his guests. The deserted court hardly fulfilled the expectations of what the efficient Czechoslovak judicial machinery was supposed to be like. By way of compensating for this setback, the Prosecutor General decided to introduce the only member of the toiling masses available—Mrs. Klírová. The witnesses reconstructed the dialogues as follows:

"Comrades, this, as you can see, is a proletarian, hard-working woman."

"What kind of nonsense are you talking, Mister?"

"Pardon me! I am Bartuška."

"And I am Klírová."

"I am Prosecutor General Bartuška."

"And I couldn't care less."

"Citizen [no comrade this time] this is inexcusable."

"Look here, prosecutor or whoever you are. Do you really expect me because of whatever you are to smear my underwear [censored translation] in awe?"

Slavic languages having a great deal in common, the distinguished guests understood the exchange and could not hide their amusement. The governmental party left, and from that time on, as long as I was on the bench in Stříbro, Bartuška did not set foot in this place of his disgrace. Only Klírová and those like her could expect to live up to their constitutional right of free speech.

On occasions, the judge had to officiate away from the court. If another court requested that I interview a litigant or witness living in my district, I had to comply. Not every addressee, however, responded to the summons. In such an event I ordered a police escort for the reluctant visitor, unless he was too old or sick, in which case I visited him.

The "E Calendar"—the so-called *exekuce*—was another area of judicial responsibility requiring field trips. A debtor who failed to honor the judgment was liable to have his funds attached or movable property seized and sold at public auction with the proceeds turned over to the creditor. Though the majority of debtors were impoverished and devoid of anything worthy of seizure, the senior court clerk in charge of the *exekuce* had to undertake a visit to their homes to search for valuables. This exasperating duty was further aggravated by the inadequate public transportation on which the clerk was dependent. The backlog of cases at our court ran into the hundreds.

It occurred to me that I might profit from this crisis. I had just sold my twenty-year-old Fiat Topolino (for the princely sum of about $2,300 at the official exchange rate) and had applied for permission to buy an automobile of a lesser vintage. In some countries one purchased a car; in ours one applied to purchase one, and obtained it only if one had previously deposited 20,000 Kčs in a frozen bank account, had obtained an application backed by one's

employer and trade union, and had the patience to wait for at least
five years. I was not patient; I attempted to circumvent the procedure, aiming at a privilege reserved for members of the New
Class far above my ranking.

Each cabinet minister had at his disposal a handful of "purchase licenses" to be distributed to the most meritorious comrades.
I approached the Chairman of the Regional Court, Adam Pittner,
and presented him with an exaggerated account of our difficulties
at the court in clearing the backlog of the *exekuce*, of hearing incapacitated witnesses, and of settling the issues of bankrupt kolkhozy. Pittner concluded that I had a good case, intervened with
the Minister of Justice and, finally, I became the owner of a brand
new Fiat 600 and the target of universal envy and hatred.

That car delivered the court clerk and me to many otherwise
inaccessible places. I would never have believed that in the midst
of Europe so much filth, inertia and poverty could exist. To leave
the main highway was to leave the twentieth century. Similar material and spiritual squalor I have seen only in the most backward
corners of the Balkans—and later in New York City.

One's friends and acquaintances, their friends and acquaintances and, at times, total strangers approached the judge requesting out-of-court legal advice. Assistance, if rendered, guaranteed
nothing. When I served in the army I met a boy, Josef V., who in
1952 had been expelled from Prague University, where he had been
a student in a branch comparable to that of Institute of Tech-
nology. Prague, the city of Franz Kafka, presented Josef V. with
an ordeal reminiscent of Josef K. An anonymous letter accused
the student of having uttered a disrespectful remark about
Vyshinsky, the former Prosecutor General and by then the Foreign
Minister of the Soviet Union. The accused protested, arguing,
inter alia, that he had never heard of Vyshinsky and, consequently,
could not have insulted him, except by daring not to know of the
existence of this illustrious Bolshevik. This defense was dismissed
as irrelevant. I liked Josef V. and promised to help him after I
returned to the court. The resumption of my judicial activities coincided with the denunciation of Vyshinsky as a murderer and
"pirate of socialist justice"—in short, a villain *par excellence*. To
be disrespectful of a villain is not so bad after all. Accordingly, I
wrote a letter—using the court's stationery—to the University,
inquiring about Josef V.'s dismissal and about the possibility of
re-admission by the school. Surprisingly, the comrades in Prague

deigned to reply: "Re the expulsion of Josef V. in 1952 from the University. It has been established that the comrades who were in charge of the case are not with us any more, and their present whereabouts are not known to us. Similarly, the files, including that of Josef V. have been moved in the recent reorganization, and we have no power to trace them. In view of these circumstances we see no justification for reviewing the case as you had suggested. With comradely greeting, Labor be Honored, X.Y."

That was it. Josef V. lost because he allegedly criticized when he was not supposed to criticize a person whom everybody else criticized. Even had he not criticized, he had been ignorant of the existence of the criticized. With the accusers and the file gone, there was no way of re-opening the case.

Czechoslovakia was not quite the favorite retreat of aliens, and the majority of foreign-born residents—ranging from re-emigrants of Czech descent to Greek children kidnapped during the Communist involvement in the Greek civil war—acquired, in little time, Czechoslovak citizenship. An alien before our bench and proceedings that required communication with a foreign court were events worth talking about.

The rules concerning the recognition of foreign laws and court decisions followed the generally accepted principles of private international law and made no explicit distinction between capitalist and socialist states. The application of a double standard, of course, was not ruled out. For example, the Supreme Court was empowered to declare binding only such decisions of a foreign court "the enforcement of which would not imperil public order and the principles of propriety"—a vague clause that could mean anything.

During my stay on the bench the Polish courts were the only ones with which we were permitted to communicate directly. If a party or a witness crucial to a case pending before my court lived in Poland, I dispatched a request (in Czech) that the person be heard at his local court. As a rule, the Polish colleague acted promptly, and in no more than a month the reply (in Polish) appeared on my desk. When the Poles asked for a similar favor we did our best to be equally cooperative.

Contacts with the rest of the world were not so simple. All communication had to be channeled through Department L/III of the Ministry of Justice, which also provided the translation of the outgoing and incoming messages. Though the Prague bureau-

crats were no champions of efficiency, the prime blame for delay
had to be attributed to the addressees. The Ministry on occasions
even intervened on our behalf with the dormant judiciary abroad.
This assistance, however, was often ineffectual, as may be illustrated in the case of minor Slovák (a surname, not ethnic identification), who was suing his Bulgarian father for support.

When I took over the case in January, 1957, the claim had
already been pending for six years. My predecessor on the bench
had attempted, several times, to reach the Bulgarian court in the
district of Kazanlik. Kazanlik did not respond. I repeated the
request twice, again with no success. Thereafter, my patience
dissipated, I sent a lengthy report to the Ministry in Prague, complaining that Slovák was already attending grade school, still without a cent of support from his father, and adding that since we
claimed we were a family of socialist brethren, something should
be done before the minor plaintiff died of old age. Roughly a year
later, the Ministry replied. They informed me that they had forwarded the complaint to the Czech Ministry of Foreign Affairs,
which had instructed the Ambassador to Sofia to register an official
protest with the Bulgarian government. What the Bulgarian
government did was anybody's guess. At any rate, at the time of
my leaving the country, nothing had been heard from the court
at Kazanlik.

Of all the European Communist countries, the East Germans
appeared the most competent, the Poles the speediest, and the
Russians the sloppiest. When one wrote to a court in the Soviet
Union, one either obtained no results or a handwritten statement
scrawled on paper negligently torn off a pad, of a quality which we
would hesitate to use in the toilet. The inadequacy in both form
and substance of messages received from our Soviet mentors was
politically so embarrassing that it called for comment in whispers
only.

In contrast, the capitalist courts were both cooperative and
efficient. Once, a colleague of mine simultaneously requested the
hearing of two witnesses—one in Rumania and the other in
Argentina. Bets were placed on which court would be the first to
reply. I backed the Argentinians and won.

The deficient system of communications among the judiciaries
of Eastern Europe was a symptom of a fundamental political fact.
The West, in my opinion, did not quite realize that the satellite
countries sheltering behind the Iron Curtain were separated from

each other by equally effective barriers. In the first post-war decade—and, to a lesser degree, until the end of the fifties—the individual people's democracies were structured and operated as self-contained entities, with little cross-national communication. A Czech citizen, in whatever direction he wandered, ran into watch-towers and barbed wire, whether on the West German, Austrian, East German, Polish, Hungarian or Soviet borders. Had I a grand-mother living in Georgia, U.S.A., and another in Georgia, U.S.S.R., my application to visit either would have been turned down. I could not buy the *New York Times* in Prague; nor could I buy the Polish *Po prostu*. Fellow masterbuilders of the classless world talked to us on the newsreels, but not on the streets.[1·] Conducted tours for the privileged helped little to further understanding. The fraternal delegations that were whisked through our country were neither representative nor communicative. Stalin took care to pre-empt the danger of an even psychologically integrated Eastern Europe that might one day counterbalance and eventually chal-lenge Soviet authority and power. When Dimitrov of Bulgaria and Marshall Tito of Yugoslavia toyed with the idea of a Danubian Federation, the Kremlin stopped them very fast. The people's democracies molded their social, economic, and political existence according to the Soviet blueprint—whether in terms of nationali-zation, emphasis on heavy industry, collectivization, kulaks, or the class struggle. That the results were not dissimilar has to be traced to the rigidity of each country's acceptance of the model, not to a hands-across-the-border merging of political acumen by the dis-ciples of sovietization. A course in historical inevitability was simultaneously taught in several class rooms, with only one student in each.

In the sphere of law, the People's Democracies adopted all the Soviets had to offer—notably, the legal doctrine and the pattern of judicial organization. The Prosecutor General in Budapest be-came "the guardian of socialist legality" with powers very similar to those of his counterpart in Prague or the other fraternal capitals. This distinguished Hungarian comrade would pop up in Prague, heading a governmental discussion on "the exchange of experiences with the building of socialism." It would not, however, occur to the participants that a Czech district prosecutor might meet with a Hungarian prosecutor to tackle the problems of socialist legality at a level other than that of stratospheric meditations. I would certainly have been interested in meeting the Hungarian civil judge from Hödmezövasarhely, if for no other reason than that the name of the town is so bewitchingly unpronounceable. My chances were about as remote as the prospect of embracing an adjudicator from New Caledonia. I have not met a single judge from a country that was building socialism, and I have known of no Czech colleagues who ever did. Our law schools had no exchange program to bring in students or visiting lecturers.

The public chuckled when, on rare occasions, some Soviet tourists appeared in Prague in their ill-fitting suits, the pudgy, shapeless matrons dressed in attire strongly reminiscent of the Great Depression years. "So, these are the wonderful Soviet people," commented the smug natives. The alleged or actual primitivism of the Russians was the favorite topic for uncomplimentary jokes.

Initially, the University, and later the Ministry of Justice, kept us well clear of the Soviet jurists. They did not come to our courts and we did not visit theirs. Exceptions to this rule could end in embarrassment. For example, a Deputy Prosecutor General of the U.S.S.R. arrived to deliver a lecture to our prosecutors. The audience was, according to what I was told later, somewhat taken aback by what they heard. "Imagine, how they punish! That guy told us that a drunkard in Moscow can get three years—only for being drunk. There was another case. A girl, only eighteen, was caught stealing in the factory. An insignificant amount and the result was eight years!" Even the most loyal comrades shook their heads in disbelief.

The myth should not be tested. Prudent gods do not grant audiences; exposure may infect the worshipper with doubt about their deity. It was demanded that we venerate the Soviets from a distance, safe for their splendor, safe for our illusions.

Our attitude toward cases involving foreign courts was mixed. On the one hand, we welcomed any relief from the parochial monotony of our daily calendar. After some fifty identical claims filed by Machine Tractor Station, a claim submitted by a Mexican court was a refreshing experience. On the other hand, we were socialist judges, mindful of the production quotas, and a dilatory foreign court was likely to hamper our monthly turnover.

Another negative feature of westbound cross-national litigations was the likelihood of their political coloring. Thus, had I awarded the expatriate Mrs. S. the custody of the child she had left behind—which I did not—such a ruling would have developed into a considerable personal hazard on my part. No politically mature judge could afford to ignore the guidance of the Supreme Court that forbade "the exposure of minors to the uncertainties of the capitalist way of life." My colleague Václav Fotr once committed—by mistake more than anything else, I would think—this political oversight. He entrusted a child to the custody of a father, resident in Addis Ababa, Ethiopia, "pending the issuance of the passport and exit visa by the Ministry of Foreign Affairs." The higher court swiftly dismissed the decision, and the Minister of Justice almost did the same to Judge Fotr.

My experience with interstate cooperation in criminal matters is scant and with respect to Western countries is nil. The apprehension, mentioned earlier, of some Gypsy murderers in the Polish port city of Gdansk, and their extradition to Czechoslovakia, was exceptional. Few suspects and fugitives from justice were brought back to Czechoslovakia from Balkan countries.[2.]

We Czechs were most active in dealings with the East Germans. For one thing, they had been catching Nazi war criminals for us well up into the fifties, and second, our own citizens were occasionally discovered *en route* illegally to West Berlin and West Germany via the DDR. The procedure for extraditing would-be escapees was smooth and uncomplicated. Thus, for instance, in 1959 two Czech mine technicians on a visit to the international fair in Leipzig left the guided tour and boarded a train for Berlin. To elude the patrol at the city limits, they went straight to the police, where they explained their desire to see the socialist part of the capital. The commander listened and was so impressed that he offered them a chauffeur-driven car. The travelling pair beamed with satisfaction at having outwitted the Teutonic totalitarian machinery, until they recognized that the car was heading towards the Czech border, where the police van was already waiting.

I heard this story while putting the final touches to the preparations for my own departure from the country. Rather than ask the police for a lift, I thought of the idea of establishing a kind of socialist brotherhood between the court in Plzeň and one in East Germany, and since I spoke German rather well I considered myself the right kind of person to be sent to East Germany. I proceeded to work out the necessary arrangements. The head of the Regional Court in Plzeň decided that this idea of mine should be encouraged. The brotherhood project was one of five alibis I had ready in case I was caught. I was not caught. I never saw the

German fellow judges, and I rather suspect that the wickedness of my abandoning the judicial bench tarred the project of socialist fraternity with ill repute for some time afterwards.

1. A few young people from fraternal countries did appear. They came and went. First, the Yugoslav apprentices in the Škoda Industries were ordered to leave after the expulsion of Tito from the Kominform in 1948. The first foreign students were Bulgarians with scholarships at the medical schools. However, after experiencing their reluctance to return home after graduation—an attitude not dissimilar from that of Afro-Asian students at Western universities—the Bulgarian government cut off this one-way foreign exchange program. (The smuggling of the young Bulgarians continued, owing to the black market in fake marriage certificates in Prague). In the fifties Koreans began to arrive. After my departure from the country, Prague became only second to Moscow in luring Afro-Asian students to the East.

2. Once, I was told, the Soviets returned to us not a criminal but a confused bureaucrat of the Youth Organization. He had fled to the Soviet Union requesting political asylum. According to his statement there was not enough socialism in Czechoslovakia to suit his taste. The dissatisfied Bolshevik ended in a Czech asylum of a different sort.

FINAL NOTE

The reader may have noticed that "the fortunate generation," born at the right time to be chosen for the exercise of responsibilities reserved by other countries for men of more experience and wisdom, was not so fortunate after all. Our elevation to the judicial bench by the accident of political circumstances provided us with power that was neither tenured nor immune from outside interference. The role of permanent impersonator was demanding; the rules of the game for survival complex.

Yet, to many among the juvenile elite the taste of fickle power was gratifying enough to enable them to exculpate themselves from responsibility for the misdeeds committed through their association —often involuntary—with the System. In short, the awareness that I might be able to arrange for the arrest of my mother-in-law neutralized my uneasy feelings about the liquidation of the kulaks. The judges rationalized in a variety of ways. To some the blame lay with the System and its laws—not with those implementing them. As one colleague, a secretly practicing Catholic, confided to me, "It is not we who are immoral but the laws we administer. Look at it this way and pangs of conscience will disappear." Some judges found an excuse in their concern for the welfare of their families. I once participated in a political seminar sponsored by

300

the Ministry of Justice. Each evening I used to obliterate the day's load of indoctrination with wine in a village tavern with a young army colonel, a judge in a military court. The talk inevitably turned to our respective judicial roles. "What's your line, comrade?" I asked, only to be told his line was "the first chapter"—the standard euphemism denoting political crimes. Rather surprised by the association of this mild-mannered person with the macabre tribunal, I wanted to know more.

"Have you ever passed a death sentence?"

"Yes, of course. Why do you ask?"

I asked because I wanted to know how it felt to condemn someone to death and attend his hanging.

"Well, the first time you tremble a bit. But you get used to it."

The inquisitive Ulč wanted to know still more. "How many people have you sent to the gallows, comrade?"

The gentle comrade was becoming irritated. "What kind of a silly question is that? Man, do you think I can remember? Ten, twenty, or probably more. What's the difference?"

After we had left the tavern the colonel went on to imply that he rather disliked "Communism" adding quite casually that he expected every reasonable person to understand his position. Married, and with two children, he had no choice but to continue hanging.

The handful of the genuine believers in the System among us were, in a way, the luckiest. As one female prosecutor put it, "Communism has proved its historical justification. It has committed so many follies, and even crimes, and yet, it survives. What could assure us more of the righteousness of our cause?" Though none too original, if one recalls the apologetics during the less illustrious periods of Christianity, such reasoning apparently proved effective enough in furnishing peace of mind to the initiated.

I was neither a believer, a father, an advocate of the theory of the law's sole guilt, nor intoxicated by the exercise of temporary power. On the other hand, I was not a particularly distressed individual. In a "soft" district and able to call on a generous supply of luck, I played the game rather well and an occasional victory over the System—be that only one child saved from the servitude of a kolkhoz—pleased me considerably. What I feared most was the day when the Party would force me to cause harm. That day arrived in spring of 1959.

The greatest dilemma of my entire judicial career arose out of a simple eviction decree. In 1953, following the less than popular monetary reform, the Party exiled a number of urban residents of bourgeois extraction into the countryside. Among the victims was a certain Mr. Bíba, an architect from Prague. He and his family of three were ordered to move and were assigned a shack in the village of Úterý in the Stříbro district. Over the course of the years, however, the family rebuilt the place into a passable home. But in early 1959, the daughter of one of the local officials got married, and the loving father began to shop for an apartment for the newlyweds. Since nothing was available in the village, the potentate decided to create a vacancy by writing an eviction decree for the Bíba family, assigning them to an abandoned stable totally devoid of facilities—*sans* window, *sans* stove, *sans* everything. One of the Bíba children was a polio victim who had undergone treatment at state expense in the nation's best hospitals. Now he was to live in a stable.

The eviction decree was based on the new Housing Law, which allowed a tenant to appeal a decision to the District Court. The architect appealed. Before I had a chance to settle the case, I received a phone call from Vojtěch Horák, the First Secretary of the Party District Committee. This apparatchik, who, although interested in adultery, had otherwise left me in peace, this time had something else in mind. "Comrade Ulč, pick up the Bíba file and be in my office in five minutes." The independent judge made it in four.

"What can I do for you, comrade Horák?"

"Well, comrade. First, tell me what you think about this Bíba stuff."

"Comrade Horák, the stuff, as you say, is very simple. No problem at all. The eviction order is idiotic, illegal, and I'll throw it out as soon as possible and the Bíbas can stay where they are."

"I am glad, very glad indeed that I called you on time," Horák said warmly. "You see, I've just received a call from Prague. Comrade Hlína from the Central Committee called. Well, you know him. I introduced you to him the last time he was here. So he wants and orders you to confirm the eviction, and I am held co-responsible to see that you go along." There was no point in arguing with Horak. Comrade Hlína from the Central Committee was a very powerful man. I left the Secretariat with vague assurance, having no idea what I should do next.

To comply or not to comply? Neither alternative appealed to me. To disobey the Party would be tantamount to challenging its supremacy, and, in any case, a courageous verdict would not remain final. The Supreme Court was standing in the wings, ready to nullify any act of defiance by declaring it "contrary to the spirit of socialist legality." Moreover, I might end—as was the case with some of my more principled ex-colleagues—in mines digging uranium ore for the greater glory of Soviet nuclear might. Nevertheless, I resented the idea of being a prostitute. The golden rule for the hesitant is to decide nothing. My luck held out. This affair coincided with my unorthodox abdication from the bench. I pigeonholed the case of Bíba until I managed to leave for the West.

Cheap, happy ending. But I have never laid claim to heroism or aspired to sainthood. The former I do not appreciate, the latter I distrust. I fail to feel embarrassed for not having engaged in a hopeless battle—a pure, defiant, admirable loser whose best hope amounts to an encapsulated obituary in the Western press with his name inevitably misspelled. I am equally insensitive to reprimands voiced at a safe distance by those who in all likelihood would close their windows rather than be bothered by the screams of victims being strangled on their doorsteps. Willingness to sacrifice self implies idealism and trust in human nature. The quantity of malice I experienced for so long renders me a poor choice for grabbing the trumpet of the Salvation Army and converting mankind.

To be an instrument in "the historically justified pursuit of injustice," is in bad taste in many ways. In the summer of 1957 I participated in a state-sponsored vacation for two weeks on the Rumanian shores of the Black Sea. On the train I became acquainted with a secret police officer, Libor Kraft. When we were passing through Budapest—it was less than a year after the Hungarian revolution of 1956—Libor, pointing to a lamp post, remarked: "See those lamp posts? We might have been hanging there. Yes, you and I." *We* might have been hanging! I disliked hanging, in particular if I were on the receiving end of the rope, and above all were I to expire in the company of the thugs our Gestapo employed. A further reason for my departure.

I have often been asked whether my defection brought on retaliation against the innocent. The Party was too confused and embarrassed by my sudden disappearance to be vindictive. Their puzzlement displayed a sort of crude bread-and-butter realism, devoid of ideological wrapping. "He must have gone mad," they reasoned, "to forfeit his whole career, and, above all, to leave behind a new automobile." Yes, a car, the Fiat 600—the zenith of socialist happiness purchased through the gracious assistance of the Ministry of Justice—was the cardinal riddle, not soul-searching into why the prep school for the earthly paradise could graduate infidels. Why had the wine turned sour? The negligent winemaker, the harsh climate? No such thought. The Fiat was the issue. Some of my former lay assessors, however, completely refused to believe in the aberration of their comrade chairman and insisted that he had either drowned or been kidnapped or perhaps both.

The Party was embarrassed to the point of preferring silent inactivity in the hope the incident would soon be forgotten, rather than undertaking punitive measures against my friends or relatives (none of whom knew about my migratory plans, anyway). Actually, my action enhanced, by default, the market value of the prewar-trained colleagues. During the last week of my stay in Czechoslovakia the judges' annual examination in advanced Marxism-Leninism was scheduled in our province. Aware that this was perhaps my last appearance in the role of a permanent impersonator, I was determined to leave the stage with a virtuoso performance. I passed the examination with flying colors, and the supervisor, Madam Michlová, the Deputy Minister of Justice, was so impressed that she issued a statement praising me as a comrade worthy of emulation by other judges. The statement coincided with my disappearance. Malicious colleagues were elated, and anyone of the old school had good cause to raise the issue—and many did—with the apparatchiki, complaining about the latters' misplaced favoritism. "He was trusted. He defected. We are not trusted. We are staying," they were reported to have said.

I rather resent being called, as I have been on occasions, "the red judge who defected." I am neither "red" nor a "defector," insofar I can understand the meaning of the latter. If defection implies a negation of a previous voluntarily accepted identity, then I do not qualify. I dissociated myself from a judiciary that I was *made* to belong to, and I could not have betrayed a cause I had not chosen as my own, any more than I could be charged with deserting a wife whom I had never married. The System precipitated me into a vulgar embrace, and I knew of no better release than the one I chose.

Recently, at the Surrogate Court in New York City, I met a

junior diplomat attached to the Czech Embassy in Washington. He was a law school classmate of mine and more than a casual acquaintance. We both testified in a complex probate case involving assets in my country and beneficiaries in his country. During the recess we had a talk in private. The diplomat even offered me a stick of chewing gum. When I told him my reasons for having left the bench he countered by stressing the maladies within the American judicial system. The wickedness of both sides, he continued, cancelled each other out, thus diminishing my switch into a futile action.

Admittedly, the capitalist variant leaves much to be desired. Equality before the law that has not freed itself from the Orwellian gloss is suspect. Justice for the rich alone is bad justice. Justice that allows the tentacles of procedure to strangle substance; that pretends not to see the slice the counsellors' greed is taking out of the award, does not appeal to me either. True, this is a country notorious for her criminality and her fondness for acquitting the criminals. True, this is the country that failed to honor her slain President by at least bringing his assassin to trial—the country that even failed to reach a final verdict over the assassin of the alleged assassin, over a period of time which exceeded the entire span of the victim's presidency. Slow justice, in my opinion, is also bad justice. In fact, we did not have to go that far. The Czech diplomat and I had left a court room in which the judge passed the time reading a newspaper while the attorneys haggled over irrelevancies. To deny the possibility of political patronage within the ponderous edifice of the New York Surrogate Court might cause the walls to crack under the impact of such a flattering inexactitude. Still, the diplomat completely missed my point. This country provides me with the freedom of non-involvement. Nobody forces me to sit on the bench, and that is my victory and my solace.

Shortly after my departure, Czechoslovakia experienced one of her numerous reorganizations; the district of Stříbro was abolished, and the courthouse was turned into a museum. A few months later the Party declared that the era of People's Democracy had come to an end, that as of 1960 the monumental historical change had arrived—socialism had been achieved. The millenium demanded new laws, and in a short time the new Codes—not too dissimilar from those of the people's democracy—went into effect. With the advent of paradise, the national economy took a sharp turn for the worse, reaching its nadir in 1963. To compensate for the tightened belt, the Party finally inaugurated the long overdue program of de-Stalinization and the restoration of socialist legality. All crimes imaginable were attributed to the regrettable period of the cult of personality, some of the victims were rehabilitated (also *post mortem*), and the thunder of breast-beating officialdom spread throughout the land.

I followed this development rather closely. It reminded me of a dialogue between two deaf men. One source denounced class discrimination as obsolete and immoral, while another source passed a new law authorizing further discrimination against the children of bourgeois pedigree. Identification of the sins was not accompanied by identification of the sinners. The Party admitted that the judges had committed legal murders. The Party also permitted the murderers to remain judges. I had the opportunity to see the 1965 directory of Czechoslovak judicial personnel. The same Stalinists held the same seats. The same Stalinists vilify Stalinism and try to prove that socialist legality is not a contradiction in terms, that a deformation of socialist legality is not tautological nonsense.

Totalitarianism maimed the soul of the nation. Moths of envy, jealousy and egotism have eaten away the national moral fabric. The malaise will certainly not be cured by the miracle of our exile politicians arriving in Prague on splendid white horses. Only political somnambulists can offer liberation from one's own shadow.

Though mindful of the stones reserved for false prophets, I still would dare to close on a note of long-range optimism. The passage of time is the hereditary disease of totalitarianism. A committed revolutionary eventually gets tired. Almost two decades of required dedication to the cause leave the disciple with strained vocal cords and sore feet. Invocation of a dream that refuses to bear tangible results ends in fatigue. "A hundred times nothing killed a donkey," as our venerated, purged, incarcerated and rehabilitated Professor of Marxism Václav Vlk used to say, commenting on the basic laws of dialectics. It is unrealistic to expect an orgasm to last for twenty years. Determination turns into improvisation, zeal into hypocrisy, and the Marxist Writ becomes as impractical and misplaced a source of inspiration as a Gideon Bible in a brothel.

I would like to offer a test of the vitality of the totalitarian

Behemoth. Back in Czechoslovakia I saw a movie—a British comedy. At one point, an elderly Englishman is accosted by the police, and he protests with the words, "What have you got against me? I am a good citizen. I pay my taxes." The Czech audience roared with laughter. My former fellow-countrymen thought this the best joke in the movie in view of their experience with the Party's standards of proper citizenship: the criteria of dedication, enthusiasm, relentless mobilization of spare energy, with no right to stand aside and with no chance of lasting appreciation for any sacrifice. Should this movie be released again some day, and the audience not react with derision to the indignant taxpayer's protest, the clinical death of totalitarianism could thereby be certified.

If nothing else, the traumatic year of 1968 provided for such a change. Whatever the outcome of imposed "normalization," the nation, after having experimented for eight months with freedom and political decency, will not be the same.

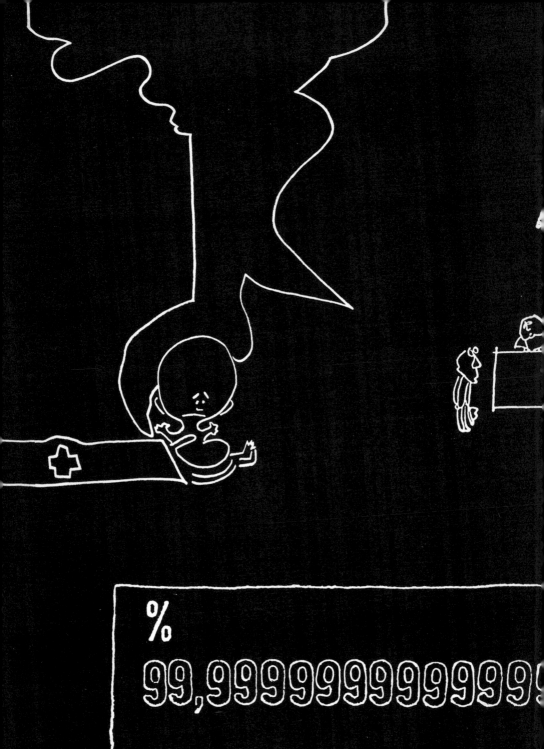